Boccaccio's Fabliaux

UNIVERSITY PRESS OF FLORIDA

Florida A&M University, Tallahassee
Florida Atlantic University, Boca Raton
Florida Gulf Coast University, Ft. Myers
Florida International University, Miami
Florida State University, Tallahassee
New College of Florida, Sarasota
University of Central Florida, Orlando
University of Florida, Gainesville
University of North Florida, Jacksonville
University of South Florida, Tampa
University of West Florida, Pensacola

Boccaccio's Fabliaux

Medieval Short Stories
and the Function of Reversal

Katherine A. Brown

UNIVERSITY PRESS OF FLORIDA
Gainesville/Tallahassee/Tampa/Boca Raton
Pensacola/Orlando/Miami/Jacksonville/Ft. Myers/Sarasota

Copyright 2014 by Katherine A. Brown
All rights reserved

The production of this book was made possible in part by support from the Skidmore College Faculty Development Committee.

Published in the United States of America

First cloth printing, 2014
First paperback printing, 2020

25 24 23 22 21 20   6 5 4 3 2 1

Library of Congress Cataloging-in-Publication Data
Brown, Katherine Adams, 1978–
Boccaccio's fabliaux : medieval short stories and the function of reversal / Katherine A. Brown.
pages cm
Includes bibliographical references and index.
ISBN 978-0-8130-4917-5 (cloth : alk. paper)
ISBN 978-0-8130-6827-5 (pbk.)
1. Fabliaux—History and criticism. 2. Boccaccio, Giovanni, 1313–1375. Decamerone.
3. Boccaccio, Giovanni, 1313–1375—Criticism and interpretation. 4. Poetry—
Early works to 1800. I. Title.
PQ207.B76 2014
853'.1—dc23   2013029225

The University Press of Florida is the scholarly publishing agency for the State University System of Florida, comprising Florida A&M University, Florida Atlantic University, Florida Gulf Coast University, Florida International University, Florida State University, New College of Florida, University of Central Florida, University of Florida, University of North Florida, University of South Florida, and University of West Florida.

University Press of Florida
2046 NE Waldo Road
Suite 2100
Gainesville, FL 32609
http://upress.ufl.edu

CONTENTS

Acknowledgments vii

Introduction 1

1. Fabliaux Reversals and *La Grue* 10

2. The Fabliaux in Context: BNF fr. 2173 46

3. Medieval Story Collections and Framing Devices 84

4. Boccaccio's Fabliaux: Transmission and Transformation of the Fabliaux to the *Decameron* 125

Conclusion 163

Appendix 169

Notes 173

Bibliography 205

Index 221

ACKNOWLEDGMENTS

I wish to express my profound gratitude to everyone who has helped me in the course of writing this book. First of all, I would like to thank the late Karl D. Uitti for introducing me to the fabliaux. This book would not have been possible without his guidance. I am especially grateful to Simone Marchesi for his tireless help and feedback, as well as his generosity, kindness, and patience with me. I would also like to extend my sincerest thanks to Sarah Kay, whose support has been invaluable and whose comments have helped me to shape this book beyond what I had imagined possible.

This study has also benefited immensely from the input and help of those who read various parts at various stages and offered their insights, especially François Rigolot, Lionel Gossman, and Léon-François Hoffmann. I would also like to thank the editors and reviewers for their work in producing this book. Additionally, I am grateful for the support and resources of the manuscript division of the Bibliothèque Nationale de France, the Skidmore College Faculty Development Committee, and my colleagues, especially Grace Burton.

Finally, I would like to express my deepest gratitude to my friends for their help, especially Thomas Boeve, Lawrence Kritzman, Joyce Lowrie, Ève Morisi, Brian Reilly, and, of course, to my family.

Introduction

Modernorum quidam . . . conati insuper fermento mendatii meram ac simplicem ipsam corrumpere ueritatem et ueritatis pallio mendatium obumbrare. . . . ad tantam eciam stulticiam deuenerunt, ut quibusdam monstruosarum fabularum laruis repertis diuersas partes sibique repugnantes coniungere niterentur. . . . Horum tamen omnium studia diuersa magnam utilitatem sequentibus attulerunt, quia, . . . quid eligendum quidue respuendum foret, posterorum iudicio reliquerunt.

[Some contemporary (writers), have attempted to corrupt the pure and simple truth with a lie and to hide their lie behind a cloak of truth. They have gone to such lengths of stupidity as to attempt, having invented malevolent spirits of monstrous tales, to join together different items contradictory to each other. . . . But the various efforts of all these (writers) has granted one great favor to those following them, that . . . they have left it to the judgment of those following them what is to be favored and what is to be rejected.]

DOLOPATHOS

Medieval short stories took many forms from the middle of the twelfth century until the end of the fourteenth century. During this period, oral tradition passed to written record and short stories were transcribed, translated, and preserved in various collections. The Old French fabliaux constitute one popular form of short narrative. Known for their humor and ostensible frivolity, the fabliaux left a significant mark on subsequent short stories. Two features of the genre stand out: fabliaux often figure in collections of stories, and they lend themselves to reworkings.

In the middle of the fourteenth century, Giovanni Boccaccio codified medieval short fiction in his collection of one hundred *novelle* called the *Decameron* (1349–51). The *Decameron* would be imitated for centuries, in large part because of the ways in which it transformed the medieval short story and story collections. One of the innovations of the novella was that it brought together different types of narrative material under a new, uniform genre. Many of the tales in Boccaccio's masterpiece resemble Old French fabliaux, yet the influence of the fabliaux on the *Decameron* has been underrated. Most comparisons of the fabliaux to the *Decameron* are limited to the thematic similarities observed in select stories.[1] In this study I argue that the influence of the fabliaux on the *Decameron* surpasses the thematic to reach the structure of the work. Similarly, the manuscripts that preserve the fabliaux have been noted for their resemblance to the *Decameron*,[2] but only in general terms. No previous study has shown specifically how Boccaccio adapted the so-called fabliaux anthologies, since the Eastern story collections are privileged as sources for the *cornice*, the frame narrative that unites Boccaccio's hundred tales.[3] The present analysis offers an account of the contributions of the codices that preserve the fabliaux to the structure of the *Decameron*, and specifically to the order of the *novelle*. Moreover, it outlines the ways in which the fabliaux function and interact with other genres in their manuscript contexts, which heralded the creation of the novella. This study proposes to explain the reason the fabliaux, more than any other type of medieval short fiction in Old French, influenced the *Decameron*. A critical trait of the fabliaux distinguishes them from other types of contemporaneous short stories, operates in the anthologies in which they were preserved, and was adapted by Boccaccio at all levels of his *Decameron*: reversal.

Reversal in the fabliaux brings together linguistic and thematic opposites, such as truth and lies or life and death, and interchanges them in order to show that these opposites offer equally valid positions from which the stories can be interpreted. Reversal also allows the fabliaux to adapt to a variety of contemporaneous genres, often through parody, while still maintaining their fundamental character and humor. While some scholars have noted thematic and structural reversals in the fabliaux,[4] none has undertaken a systematic analysis of this mechanism or has identified reversal as a defining feature of either the fabliau or the Boccaccian novella. This study combines a literary-historical approach with elements of formalism to define reversal using the terms of medieval rhetoric and logic. Although the use of reversal in this study at times complements Michael Riffaterre's definition of inversion—one of the mechanisms by which the idiolect of the texts transforms the sociolect to produce meaning[5]—the current use of reversal is concerned with more traditional notions of literary influence and sources, as it also encompasses rhetoric, thematics, and structure in the stories and their collections.

As a key feature of the fabliaux, reversal functions in several ways. Fundamentally, reversal emphasizes any binary system at work in the fabliaux tradition. A binary system should be understood as the opposition of "logical minimal pairs," such as black and white, male and female, alive and dead.[6] The issue of opposites permeates much fiction in the late twelfth and the thirteenth centuries. The epigraph to this introduction, from the late twelfth-century Latin story collection *Dolopathos*, points to this preoccupation with opposites, suggesting that the value of opposites is that they force the audience to judge and interpret texts.

One likely source for the prevalence of contradictions in medieval literature is the rise of dialectic in the twelfth century. A "species" of logic, as John of Salisbury referred to it, dialectic is a method of inquiry that explores opposing sides of an argument in search of truth.[7] Peter Abelard's twelfth-century work *Sic et non* is a model of dialectic. *Sic et non* is composed of a series of contradictory writings from the Church fathers. It offers no resolution to the oppositions it lays out but rather outlines methods of inquiry and the way to a resolution. Abelard's primary directives include exploring the greater context of *sententia* and considering the multiple meanings of words that will allow the learned reader to judge them reasonably.[8] Beginning in the twelfth century, interpretive acts drew more and more from dialectic. As formal logic in the medieval world sought to respond to questions involving seemingly irreconcilable opposites, the application of dialectic expanded in the late twelfth century to include literature.

In vernacular writing, the poetry of the troubadours highlights what Sarah Kay has called the "paradox of antitheses" at the base of dialectic.[9] Similarly, Chrétien de Troyes' romances often furnish instances of the interplay between literature and formal logic: Yvain and Gauvain's battle at the end of the *Chevalier au lion* poses a logical dilemma when the narrator explains that the two men both love and hate each other at the same time, whereas Fenice is both dead and alive near the end of *Cligès*, and Lancelot is both the exalted hero and debased lover of the Queen in the *Chevalier de la Charrette*.[10] These contradictions, or logical minimal pairs—love and hate, life and death, exalted and debased—are the foundation of the dialectical method of inquiry.

As dialectical *quaestiones* and argumentation influenced courtly literature and lyric poetry, they were also prevalent in such popular literature as the fabliaux. In his *Logic and Humour in the Fabliaux*, Roy J. Pearcy has argued that the false inferences and logical fallacies inherent in fabliaux narratives are based on oppositions of truth and falsehood.[11] While this may not be true of all fabliaux, many critics have observed that the fabliaux often deal with tricks and the creation of falsehoods.[12] These tricks are dependent on logical fallacies and the inability of characters to determine what is true from false, right from wrong. The audience, especially later readers who transformed these stories, is akin to the characters within them, who must interpret the narrative world and judge the good from the bad.

The oppositions in vernacular texts point to one of the dangers of dialectic, namely that the immoderate use of dialectic, if not tempered by the other liberal arts, becomes sterile because it only "resolves questions relative to itself."[13] As John of Salisbury explains, truth is at the center of logic, but dialectic, a "species" of logic, "establishes opinion, not truth."[14] In this way, the oppositional pairs in the fabliaux deal effectively with the limits of dialectical inquiry and of language itself. They do not establish truth but rather lead to opinion and judgment. It would be convenient to claim that the fabliaux systematically critique dialectic, but the heterogeneity of the fabliaux suggests that each text posits its own relationship to logic. The resolutions of contradictions and conflicts in the fabliaux are not focused on the truth, whether absolute or relative to the text, as much as they reveal an open-ended interpretation. The dupe in the fabliaux does not need to learn that he has been tricked, unless he retaliates and becomes the trickster himself. "Good" and "bad" characters and actions in the fabliaux are relative categories, not absolutes. For this reason, the trickster is lauded and the dupe mocked. Applying moral terms to these texts counteracts the logic of the narratives and runs the risk of limiting interpretations to the strictly didactic and reducing the fabliaux to negative *exempla*.[15] Reversal specifically calls attention to this open, nondidactic interpretation of texts because it equates, or at least gives equal weight to, both parts of an opposition.

The focus on truth and lies in so many fabliaux highlights the interpretive poles of these stories. Reversals in the fabliaux ultimately ask the audience to judge the tales. Consequently, reversals and calls for judgment in the fabliaux expose interpretive choices to the audience. Whereas reversals play on oppositional pairs, open judgments reveal multiple possibilities.

The reversals that characterize the fabliaux play a crucial role in challenging moralistic and didactic interpretive practices in reading manuscripts. For the most part, these manuscripts may be considered anthologies, meaning that they are collections of texts with principles of organization.[16] This study will maintain that the majority of codices preserving fabliaux are in fact anthologies and not miscellanies. Using Theo Stemmler's definition, an anthology is a "careful collection [of works] selected as representative specimens of various genres."[17] Because they display a clear order of texts, usually along thematic lines, anthologies differ from both miscellanies, which are somewhat arbitrary collections of works without any unifying or structuring principles, and compilations, which are collections of a single generic type, such as *exempla*. In anthologies, the fabliaux, rather than serving as negative *exempla*, model opposing interpretations and values.

The manuscripts in which the fabliaux are preserved reveal the inherent fluidity of the genre. In the larger anthologies, fabliaux interact with a wide variety of texts. These interactions are both intertextual in a structuralist sense, because they draw on other works, and intratextual because they connect to works preserved within the same frame narrative or collection.[18] Within these anthologies, the fabliaux represent the *élément perturbateur* of the whole, whose ultimate message is the polyvalent nature of narrative itself.

As a collection, the *Decameron* is composed of different narrative layers that generate a complex system of internal oppositions and theoretical contradictions. These tensions are evident in the reversals that permeate all levels of the text: in narratives where plots systematically undo themselves; in reversals of Fortune in many *novelle*; in the association of pairs of *novelle* that convey opposite messages; and often in authorial shifts of focus from one narrative level to another. Reversals operate to achieve the symmetry and balance that characterize the *Decameron*, as they also suggest a choice of interpretation. This study proposes that the essence of the Old French fabliaux resides in their use of reversals and that Boccaccio adapted this technique for the *Decameron*. By using the reversals inherent in the fabliaux, Boccaccio brought together opposite types of narratives, particularly the fabliaux and *exempla*, in a framed narrative to create a new form: the novella. Boccaccio used the fabliaux in part to promote the openness of literary interpretation and the enjoyment of literature on its own terms. But he also developed the techniques of reversal characteristic of the fabliaux in order to question the relationship between literature and the individual, to create "an absolute space where the real and the imagined, the inner and the outer, are systematically confused."[19]

The novella would endure through the sixteenth century as the dominant form of medieval and Renaissance short narrative. As the Boccaccian novella constitutes an amalgamation of different types of short stories previously considered discrete genres, it owes much of its content to these anterior forms. In particular, the fabliaux furnish a model for Boccaccio that accounts for the prevalence of themes involving sexuality and trickery. In addition to thematic material, the fabliaux also provide the models for the structural reversals observed in many of the *novelle*, as well as the pairing of opposite tales. As the first writer to adapt fabliaux into another vernacular, Boccaccio recognized and extracted from them their logic of reversal and their attention to different interpretive possibilities for his *Decameron*. The use of reversal in the fabliaux is not a reduction of the genre to a formula, but rather a significant means by which many fabliaux not only distinguish themselves from other short narrative forms but also were understood by later writers, and especially Boccaccio. For Boccaccio, this use of reversal and the interpretive possibilities it generates upend certainty, revealing that order and perfection are myths that can only exist in tales and in the imagination of the audience.[20]

While the novella was a new form, the idea of a frame narrative has its origins in Middle Eastern collections that predate the fabliaux. Moreover, there were many other types of contemporary vernacular story collections, such as compilations of miracle stories, *lais*, fables, and *exempla* that offer generic uniformity, to which Boccaccio had access and that seem more pertinent to the organization of his tales than anthologies with fabliaux. The variety of story collections and compilations in the Middle Ages suggests a number of questions: Would a frame incongruent with the stories alter the interpretation of the stories or provide another meaning for the work as a whole? Would replacing the moral tales with other types of stories, whose lessons are either less overtly moralizing or not moralizing at all, change the nature of the frame? If the frame disappeared and no longer justified the stories, would the stories still be considered an organized collection? What justifies these stories? How do medieval stories and collections relate contemporary concerns of interpretation and the reconciliation of opposites? In sum, what is the relationship between the short narrative form in a collection of any type and the larger context in which it appears? The Old French fabliaux respond to these questions.

In the manuscripts that preserve them, and in their reinvention in Boccaccio's *Decameron*, the fabliaux shape the medieval short narrative form and its relation to the collection in the broadest sense. The fabliaux push the limits of literary value from the strictly moral toward the explicitly hermeneutic. A double comparison, first of the fabliaux with works preserved in the same manuscripts, and second with analogues in the *Decameron*, will isolate the salient features of the fabliaux and illuminate their influence on medieval fiction. Boccaccio's reception and transformation of this tradition unlocks a view of the fabliaux that complements and adds to what can be gleaned about them from their manuscript transmission. This process of reading in reverse from the *Decameron* to the fabliaux brings into focus features of the fabliaux that would otherwise remain veiled, but that are nonetheless essential to understanding them and their impact.

To this end, the first chapter of the present study defines the nature of these reversals in relation to dialectic and establishes three distinct types of reversal in the fabliaux: rhetorical, narrative or sociogenic, and structural reversal, here called inversion. Examples of each type demonstrate that reversal is one characteristic of the genre and that it serves to open the fabliaux to interpretation. The first type of reversal, illustrated by chiasmus, is in some respects the most variable. The deployment of chiasmus in the fabliaux is central to notions of inversion and exchange. As chiasmus in the fabliaux reinforces other reversals in the texts, it is a valid point of departure for an inquiry into textual and structural inversions. *Le Fablel de la Grue* is taken as a model text because it incorporates all three types of reversal. An analysis of this archetypal fabliau exemplifies how the fabliaux in general can combine different genres, such as *exempla* and *lais*, through reversal. A study of the manuscript contexts of *La Grue* shows the ways in which this fabliau interacts with contemporary texts and that each manuscript has its own characteristics.

The second chapter examines the fabliaux in the contexts in which they were produced and in relation to the works they influenced. It explores the rhetorical and structural distinctions between fabliaux and other types of narratives within a single manuscript, BNF fr. 2173, in order to show the specificity of the fabliaux and their role in shaping the interpretation of anthologies. In particular, the relationships of fabliaux to fables reveal the generic specificity of the fabliau form as well as the interwoven structure of the system of genres in medieval literature. Rhetorical reversal in the fabliaux of MS BNF fr. 2173 serves to undermine the genre's ostensible didactic aims, whereas similar techniques in fables reinforce the didacticism of that genre. By examining fabliaux alongside contemporary short fiction within a single codex, it becomes possible to see how the fabliaux distinguish themselves from these works, and how and why they were reused and transformed by Boccaccio.

The third chapter investigates intermediary compilations between the anthologies of fabliaux and the *Decameron* in order to show the relationships between the stories and frames that Boccaccio inherited. The principles of organization for codices containing fabliaux reflect wide-ranging preoccupations with genre and structure in the thirteenth and fourteenth centuries that are relevant to a number of story collections composed in the interval between the fabliaux's prime and the completion of the *Decameron*. This chapter argues that Eastern frame narrative collections such as the *Seven Sages of Rome* were being combined with Western stories in medieval manuscripts before Boccaccio wrote the *Decameron*. The anthologies of fabliaux were often repositories of other short narrative collections such as vernacular versions of the *Seven Sages of Rome* and the *Disciplina Clericalis*. More than other types of Western story collections, the codices containing fabliaux can be seen as prefiguring the combination of different narrative traditions in the *Decameron*. These collections and the anthologies of fabliaux anticipate the polyvalent structure of the *Decameron*, while also reinforcing the vital role of the fabliaux in anthologies. The levels of organization in the *Decameron* reflect Boccaccio's combining of the Eastern frame narrative with the Old French manuscript tradition, which also offers a structural archetype for the organization of the *novelle* and the arrangement of the ten days of storytelling. In the *Decameron*, the *novelle* that are most similar to fabliaux are placed strategically in the work's structural symmetry: Days III, VII, and VIII, which are highly symmetrical and clearly structured, draw the most on fabliaux. The *novelle* derived from fabliaux also interact across the different days of narration, creating an intratextual dialogue that is written into the discussions of the *brigata*. This role of the fabliaux in intratextuality results from the reversals that permeate their rhetoric, narratives, and structure. The symmetry, structure, and intratextuality of the *Decameron* are deliberately articulated with fabliaux material in order to associate the consciously artificial *beffe* with contrived structural perfection. Thus, the reinforcement of order in the *Decameron* is concomitant with the social reversals that the fabliaux material represents, undermining both.

Chapter 4 shows how Boccaccio's manipulation of fabliaux and other narratives results in the creation of a new genre. Boccaccio combines fabliaux plot devices with other types of works, without compromising essential characteristics of the fabliaux. The ways in which Boccaccio recasts narrative material, both structurally and rhetorically, draw on the reversals that characterize the fabliaux. This final chapter examines, through close readings, the different ways in which Boccaccio transposes the reversals inherent in the fabliaux tradition in order to combine different narratives and diverse registers of language that draw on a variety of genres. This chapter also suggests that Boccaccio's transformations offer a new model of intergeneric comparisons that ultimately exposes the fluidity of boundaries and order. The first texts, *La Nonete* and novella IX:2, show that Boccaccio used reversal both within individual narratives as well as among different narratives, since novella I:4 is a gendered reversal of novella IX:2, in order to underscore the openness of interpretation. The second example shows that novella III:10 is a combination through reversals of opposite genres: fabliaux and hagiographic texts. This combination of diverse genres shows their innate analogies. The final example shows that Boccaccio used one fabliau, *Le Vilain de Bailleul*, in two different novellas, III:8 and IX:3, revealing that stories can be endlessly adapted as well as interpreted. In this way, the *Decameron* continues the tradition of fabliaux reversals and sheds light on their capacity to reinforce contraries as a means to necessitate multiple readings, contributing to a nondidactic literature informed by and responding to formal logic, a paradigm shift in the understanding of literature. In "join[ing] opposites together" through inversion, the fabliaux demonstrate the need for judgment outside of a moralistic context, and thus contribute to the shift in vernacular fiction from a didactic- to a hermeneutic-based literary system.

Finally, reversal is shown as a key concept by which to analyze these stories and collections because it explains how the fabliaux can both adapt to other forms, as they do in the *Decameron*, and still maintain their essential "fabliauxness." Similarly, the Boccaccian novella often repeats the reversing mechanisms of the fabliaux, at the rhetorical level, at the thematic level, and finally at the structural level, while maintaining its perceived coherence. Through the *Decameron*, didacticism and Eastern literary traditions are subsumed into Western framing techniques to reveal a new focus on texts whose meaning is open-ended. By appropriating the generic fluidity and reversals characteristic of the fabliaux, Boccaccio creates a genre based less on theme and more on structure and rhetoric. This ability to manipulate other genres, which the fabliaux share with *exempla*, indicates that the fabliaux are a crucial component of the medieval short story, one that opposes the traditional didacticism of *exempla* in favor of literature for its own sake.

1

Fabliaux Reversals and *La Grue*

> Exhibeas te in rege philosophum et in philosopho regem, regiam philosophie disciplina temperans maiestatem commendansque philosophiam regie maiesti.
>
> [Show yourself to be a philosopher king and a king philosopher. Temper your kingly majesty with the training of philosophy, and entrust philosophy to the care of your kingly majesty.]
>
> DOLOPATHOS

Reversal is one of the key features of the fabliaux that Boccaccio borrowed and reproduced in the *Decameron*. This chapter will explore the ways in which reversal functions in the fabliaux, first by defining the types of reversal through examples, and second by illustrating how these reversals distinguish the fabliaux from other contemporary short stories.

Encompassing diverse readings of the fabliaux, reversal has three discrete senses in this study. The rhetorical figure of chiasmus is the basis of the first type of reversal. Chiasmus is defined as a grammatical, semantic, or phonetic construction whose parallel parts ABAB are inverted to form the pattern ABBA.[1] Although the term chiasmus is modern, the concept was familiar in the Middle Ages through rhetorical manuals and other models of writing learned in the *studia generalia*. Heinrich Lausberg categorizes chiasmus as a type of *commutatio*, which "consists in the opposition of an idea and its converse by means of the repetition of the two word stems, with reciprocal exchange of the syntactic function of both stems in the repetition."[2] In the section on figures of diction in the rhetorical manual *Rhetorica ad Herennium*, attributed to Cicero, the definition of *commutatio* also implies antithesis or contradiction among the parts transposed.[3] The antithesis applies to the entire statement, not necessarily to the relationship of the transposed words. An example in the *Rhetorica ad Herennium*, "Esse oportet ut vivas, non vivere ut edas" [You must eat to live, not live to eat], clearly shows that living and eating are not themselves in opposition, but rather that two relationships between eating and living are opposed.[4] The transposed words do not necessarily retain the same form; thus "vivere" and "vivas" can be equivalent and represent the same word and the same idea, albeit in different forms. Similarly, Johannes de Alta Silva makes frequent use of chiasmus in *Dolopathos*, as shown in the citation presented as the epigraph to this chapter.[5] In this instance, Johannes brings together the roles of king and philosopher in order to offer advice on ruling to prince Lucinius, future king of Sicily. These examples of chiasmus correspond to a pattern that pervades Old French narrative more generally, and the fabliaux specifically, where it reinforces narrative reversals.

The other two types of reversal in the fabliaux borrow from the rhetorical model of inversion to transform the narrative. The second type comprises reversals of narrative material. Such reversals transform traditional literary and social expectations into their opposites, whether in the form of parody or burlesque of other genres, or by reversing expectations of gender, power and authority, social standing, or other social and literary parameters. In this type of reversal, the fabliau is created by the manipulation—often as parody—of various generic forms. Thus, parody in the fabliaux may result from inverting the expected norms of the target text or genre. This second type of reversal accounts for reversals observed in sociogenic studies of the fabliaux, whether of gender roles or class. For example, cross-dressing or "courtly" *vilains* constitute two types of narrative reversals. The use in the fabliaux of proverbs that do not fit the narrative in their traditional sense, unless the application of the proverb is inverted and reinterpreted to suit the story, also falls into this category of reversal. By utilizing ill-fitting proverbs, the fabliaux point to the ambiguity of their own interpretation. This ironic use of reversal will appear frequently in the *Decameron* within single *novelle*.

Finally, the third type of reversal common to the fabliaux consists of inversion, or a reversal of structure. Although inversion is most familiar in the theme of the trickster who is tricked, it applies to any narrative act that is accomplished and then undone, overturned, or otherwise reversed in a way that maintains structural symmetry. Inversion may be emphasized by rhetorical and narrative reversals, but is not dependent on them. The examples below will show that these three types of reversal are essential to an understanding of the fabliaux and that they also characterize the fabliaux material in the *Decameron*.

The following investigation of the ways in which reversal functions in the fabliaux will culminate in an extensive analysis of *Le Fablel de la Grue*. An extraordinary example, *La Grue* serves as a model text because it illustrates and synthesizes all three types of reversal and highlights the genre's interpretive openness. The three types of reversal identified in the fabliaux relate logically oppositional pairs to narrative structure and the rhetorical figure chiasmus. The relationship established between the three species of reversal suggests that the form of the texts is in harmony with their content. Reversals of logic, reversals of language, and reversals of narrative structure all function to reveal the fabliaux's handling of opposites. In some instances, reversals integrate generically diverse material into a single form; at other times they serve as a commentary on the interpretation of literature. These two functions of reversal are not mutually exclusive, but they do indicate a different focus in a text. The following examples of chiasmus, the first type of reversal, reveal the application of this device and its relation to narrative in some fabliaux that are representative of the kind Boccaccio employed.

Type 1: Chiasmus

The fabliau *Les Perdrix* (4.3–21) illustrates the comic and metatextual functions of chiasmus. As this fabliau exists in only one manuscript (MS A),[6] there are no scribal variants to introduce different interpretations of this text. In the story, a peasant catches two partridges and asks his *gourmande* wife to prepare them for a dinner with the priest. After the peasant leaves to find the priest, the wife begins to nibble at one of the cooked birds until she has consumed it all. Fearing what her husband will say, she decides to invent a story that a cat ate the bird while her back was turned. As her husband tarries, the wife begins to eat the second bird, finishing it before her husband returns home. When the peasant arrives home and asks about the birds, the wife claims the cat ate them both, but quickly changes her story when she sees her husband's anger, instead claiming that she covered the partridges to keep them warm. She then asks her husband to go sharpen his knife in preparation for cutting the birds. Meanwhile, at the arrival of the priest,—who is apparently the wife's *amant* because he embraces her—the wife tells him to flee because her husband is angry and is sharpening his knife in order to emasculate him. The priest runs off in fear; in the interim, the wife tells her husband that the priest stole the partridges. The peasant, brandishing the knife, sets off after the priest, who has locked himself inside his home. The final lesson warns the audience to beware of woman's deceit.

The terms of the primary chiasmus in this story are connected to the beginning of the tale where the narrator explains: "Por ce que *fabliaus* dire sueil, / En lieu de *fable* dire vueil / Une aventure qui est vraie," (1–3, emphasis added) [Because I am used to telling fabliaux, instead of a fable I want to tell an adventure/story that is true]. Here the narrator contrasts "fabliaus" and "fable"—used nearly synonymously to mean false story—with the truth (*aventure qui est vraie*). Although the narrator declares the veracity of his own tale, the repetition of "fable/fabliaus" emphasizes false discourse and calls into question the very fiction of this *aventure*.[7] The mixture of true and false stories in this short introduction also highlights the essence of the tale, a wife who invents stories. In this way, the beginning of the story informs the audience that the *aventure* concerns a fiction, one that will be understood as truth. One message of the story is the value of storytelling itself; it frees the wife from trouble.

The ending of the fabliau explains the interlocking of truth and fiction through a three-part chiasmus, where the subject is womankind:

A, B, C   Mençonge *fet devenir* **voir**
//C, B, A   Et **voir** *fet devenir* Mençonge. (152–53, emphasis added)

[(woman) makes lies become the truth and makes the truth become lies.]

The convention for describing a chiasmus is to label the terms in alphabetical order, A, B, C, etc., and to distinguish them by font style (in order: underline, italics, bold, and then combinations of these). There is no limit to the number of terms in a chiasmus, although the majority of examples identified do not go beyond three. The symbol // designates the pivot or midpoint of the chiasmus where the meaning shifts and after which the mirrored terms begin. The mirrored forms C, B, A denote the same form as the A, B, C terms, whereas the prime terms (A', B', C') indicate another form of the same word, or else a different word with the same meaning. The word mençonge represents the A term of this chiasmus, *fet devenir* is the B term, **voir** is the C term; the // represents the pivot, which in this case is the word "et" that links and equates the two phrases. In this fabliau, the wife creates stories in order to extricate herself from trouble; one story she tells her husband and another to the priest, both of whom take her at her word. The woman's stories become the content (*matiere*) of the narrator's "aventure qui est vraie," such that he creates a "true fiction" by making the wife's lies the truth of his own story. In this way, the woman's lies have become truth, and the truth is nothing but a lie since it is a story. The chiasmus that equates truth and lies exposes the role of language in fabricating lies and literary truth; it illustrates the reversal of truth and lies in the narrative. These opposites brought together reflect the same questions announced in the preface to *Dolopathos* and show the type of chiasmus not subject to scribal variation that is found in the fabliaux more generally.

The reversal at the end of the story expressed as a chiasmus evolves from the first twenty-six lines of the fabliau, where the use of paronomasia—which P.

Kunstmann defines as words that sound alike but that differ in meaning[8]—no less than five times, plays on the idea of turning and consequently of reversals:

> En l'**atorner** mist mout sa cure. . . .
> A Le feu a fet, la haste **atorne**.
> B Et li vilains tantost **s'en torne**. . . .
> // (La dame) s'en pinça une peleüre,
>   Quar mout ama la lecheüre. . . .
> B' Tantost arriere **s'en retorne**,
> A Et le remanant tel **atorne**
>   Mal du morsel qui remainsist! (6, 9–10, 15–16, 25–27, emphasis added)

[He was very careful in preparing it (his catch). . . . She started the fire and prepared the spit. And the peasant leaves right away. . . . (The woman) plucked at some of the skin, for she really liked gluttony. . . . Right away she returns to the house, and arranges the leftovers such that there is nothing left!]

These emphasized words, mostly rhymed, link the idea of preparation (*atorner*) with departure (**s'en torner**, and **retorner**), as if to suggest that the wife is preparing to turn a story to trick her husband. The rhymes in lines 9–26 form a chiasmus based on the repetition of the word "atorne" and the *adnominatio*—different forms of words that are etymologically related—"torne/retorne"; the pivot of the chiasmus explains the woman's fault, her gluttony, which is the first turn in the narrative and the reason she needs to invent a story. Moreover, the notion of turning is itself central to reversals, as the Latin VERSUS, from which the words "reversal" and "inversion" are derived, means "a turning point." The word *lecheüre* denotes both gluttony and lechery, or rather lustfulness; its placement in the middle of the chiasmus implies that the narrative turns on more than one meaning. The wife is doubly guilty, of eating the birds and of consorting with the priest; either or both reasons may explain her inventing the stories. Moreover, her trick involves the partridges becoming the priest's genitals, another substitution of food for sex.[9] Like both men in the tale, the audience must judge the truth from the lies. In this way, the rhetoric of the fabliau underscores the central issue of the text that turning language can lead lies to seem like the truth, and truth to be like lies. This notion reflects the art of narrative itself because false stories may illustrate truth. Ultimately, the truth that the birds are gone, regardless of the real reason for their disappearance, cannot be undone, but the wife's stories have hidden this truth from both her husband and the priest.

Le Chevalier qui fist parler les cons (3.45–173) furnishes another example of a chiasmus in a fabliau that reinforces the narrative. The story is of an impoverished knight and his squire who are trying to go to a tournament in order to earn some money. When the squire steals some fine garments from three ladies, the knight generously returns them. The three women, who are in fact fairies, offer the knight three gifts for his honesty: the first gift is that the knight will be well received wherever he goes; the second, from which the title of the fabliau is derived, is that he may make *cons* speak; and the third gift is to make the *cul* speak if the *con* should fail. The second part of the story involves a wager with a countess over his ability to make her *con* speak, which the knight eventually wins. Of the seven manuscripts that preserve this fabliau in whole or in part, only MS M uses a chiasmus in the introduction to support the narrative. In manuscript M, the narrator announces:

A	<u>Aventures e enseignement</u>
B, C	*Fount* **solas** molt sovent
// C, B', A'	E **solas** *fet* <u>releggement</u>
	Ce dit Gwaryn q[ui] ne ment. (1–4, emphasis added)

[Adventures/stories and teaching very often act as entertainment and entertainment acts as relief. So says Gwaryn who does not lie.]

This chiasmus equates the A terms "<u>Aventures e enseignement</u>" with "<u>releggement</u>," which are themselves connected to "**solas**," a word that also connotes sexual pleasure, in order to show that the purpose of stories and teaching in general, and of this fabliau in particular, is to serve as entertainment and (sexual) relief for the audience. Strikingly similar to Johannes's critique and defense of "bad writers" in the introduction to *Dolopathos*, the narrator promotes the audience's relief as the final good of storytelling, subtly linking this activity to sex. Indeed, like the audience, the knight of the fabliau receives entertainment and <u>releggement</u> after doing a good deed for three fairies, since his gifts bring him both amusement and money, but there is only the hint of sexual pleasure to come. The introductions to five of the other manuscript versions of this text emphasize the same relationship between telling stories and bringing comfort, but these are further connected to earning money. MS M, on the other hand, focuses on the benefit of storytelling for the audience who receives "solas." Unlike the other versions, the chiasmus in MS M illustrates the purpose of the story as it recalls the issue of truth, since Gwaryn (also sometimes spelled Garin or Guerin) claims he does not lie. The redactor of MS M deliberately uses a chiasmus to strengthen this message through the syntactic structure.

The fabliau *Jouglet* (2.185–214) provides another example of a chiasmus unchanged by scribal variants. Although *Jouglet* is one of the most scatological fabliaux, the story presents the theme of the trickster tricked. Jouglet the *jongleur*, who initially tricked Robin into not relieving himself prior to his wedding night, receives his comeuppance in the form of excrement thanks to Robin and his new bride. The final proverb in both manuscript versions of this text is presented as a chiasmus:

> A, B, C Teus cuide **cunchier** *autrui*
> C', B', A' *Qui* tout avant **cunchie** lui. (MS A, 445–46, emphasis added)

[He who believes he deceives another is first deceived.]¹⁰

or

> A, B, C Tel cuide **conchier** *autrui*
> C', B', A' *Qui* assez miez **conchie** lui. (MS Y, 419–20, emphasis added)

[He who believes he deceives another, is deceived much more.]

Both versions of the proverb preserve the same terms of the chiasmus that illustrate the theme of the trickster tricked. The terms A and A' have the relationship of subject and direct object respectively, which is reversed for the terms C and C', showing that, through the art of deception, the trickster is also a victim, and the victim can become the trickster. The B terms of the chiasmus have a double meaning, for "conchier" may mean both to deceive and to cover in excrement. Although "conchier" has a double meaning, both meanings reinforce the theme of the trickster tricked, since covering objects in excrement is the method of revenge in the tale. Unlike *Les Perdrix* where the ambiguity of the word "lecheüre" advanced more than one interpretation of the wife's behavior, in this example the double-valence of "conchier" gives rise to a literal—the physical covering in excrement—and a figurative interpretation of the proverb and by extension of the entire fabliau. The chiasmus expresses the reversal of fortune depicted in the fabliau, and in this case the proverb corresponds to the structure of the tale, reinforcing the theme. The three preceding examples of chiasmus in the fabliaux show that this device strategically reinforces narrative and thematic reversals in a text by calling attention to a work's structure through related syntactic structures. Moreover, like *Dolopathos*, these fabliaux call attention to the value of fiction through chiasmus.

Type 2: Narrative Reversal

The second type of reversal, generally understood as narrative reversal, is based on oppositional pairs. These are external to the text and are defined by logic, even though such logically opposite pairs as male and female (or husband and wife), young and old, alive and dead are based on a physical reality. In most fabliaux, the logical relation of opposition is distorted through language and false inferences, such that a woman may be understood as a man or a living man may be understood to be dead, as the examples below will illustrate. As the fabliaux are more concerned with humor, trickery, and winning an argument than with truth, the texts frequently exploit reversals of logic and the triumph of false logic. The practices of reversal in the fabliaux consequently respond to contemporary questions and methods of logic in a humorous and at times mocking way.[11]

Narrative reversal may be divided into three subtypes. The first subtype is of the sociogenic order and includes any reversal of hierarchy, class, gender, or age. *Frere Denise* (6.1–23), which will be discussed more in chapter 4, provides an example of a sociogenic reversal because it involves cross-dressing when a young lady pretends to be a monk. The castrated mother-in-law of the *Dame escoillee* (9.1–125) serves as another example of gender reversal, this time from the outside in, since the overbearing woman is said to have testicles which need to be removed. *Bérengier au lonc cul* (4.245–77) depicts a noblewoman who dresses as a knight in order to trick her low-born husband, and thus exemplifies a reversal of both gender and class. *Le Chevalier qui fist sa fame confesse* (4.227–43), which has an analogue in *Decameron* VII:5, inverts layman and cleric when a husband dresses up as a priest to hear his wife's confession. In *L'Evesque qui beneï le con* (6.193–205) a priest, with the help of his *drue*, tricks the bishop to whom he is responsible, whereas in *La Nonete* (10.33–47), a nun catches her superior with a priest. *L'Evesque qui beneï le con* and *La Nonete* represent hierarchical reversals, which will be repeated in *Decameron* I:4 and IX:2 respectively.[12] Both *Le Vilain qui conquist paradis par plait* (5.1–38) and *St. Pierre et le jongleur* (1.127–59) exhibit reversals of social hierarchy when a deceased character, who is neither a cleric nor a nobleman, tricks his superior with logical argumentation in order to find his way into heaven.[13] In *Le Vilain de Farbu* (6.111–23) a son proves to be wiser than his father. There are reversals of life and death in *Le Vilain de Bailleul* (5.223–49) and *Le Chevalier qui recovra l'amor de sa dame* (7.239–53) because characters either believe they are dead or pretend to be as part of a trick. Finally, whether or not it is a fabliau, *Trubert* (10.143–262) contains possibly every type of sociogenic reversal imaginable, but all these reversals serve the protagonist's tricks. Any tale where a wife (inferior) tricks her husband (superior), and so reverses the logic of the medieval marriage relation, may also be considered a reversal of domestic order or hierarchy. Thus, the fabliaux exhibit tricks through and because of sociogenic reversals, which consist of false inferences and reversals of logical minimal pairs. In the *Decameron*, similar reversals of gender as well as domestic and monastic hierarchy play a significant role and will be discussed in chapter 4.

Parody is one of the forms taken by sociogenic reversals in the fabliaux. Parody often reverses features of the texts it imitates along sociogenic lines. *Bérengier au lonc cul* parodies epic literature. Roy J. Pearcy has argued one reversal in that parody is the replacement of the "cort nez" [short nose] of the chivalric-epic Guillaume with the "lonc cul" [long bottom] of the fabliau's Bérengier.[14] The mock battle scene in *Bérengier* also inverts courtly narrative in order to parody it, especially because the climactic episode in which the cowardly husband is subjected to delivering a *baiser honteux* [shameful kiss] to his chevalier-wife constitutes a reversal of both a feudal kiss of loyalty and a courtly kiss. The reversal of the kiss allows for the conjoining of an epic scene with a courtly one. In *La Damoisele qui ne pooit oïr parler de foutre* (4.57–89), the young couple's extended metaphor to describe their sexual parts inverts the typical romance conquest scenes it parodies through several substitutions, most notably in all but the MS D version, by replacing the knight's "destrier" [battle steed] with a "poulain" [colt] as a metaphor for the vulgar *vit*.[15] Extended metaphors such as this, or "making a girl into a bird" in *La Pucele qui voloit voler* (6.155–70), are usually substitutes for the sexual act in the fabliaux and do not in themselves denote reversal, but rather are the tools of narrative and structural reversals; they need not necessarily be parodies. In an analysis of fabliaux love triangles in the manner of Per Nykrog, the substitution in many tales of a priest or a cleric for a courtly lover constitutes a parodic reversal, just as transferring courtly language to characters of a lower social milieu is a reversal of literary if not social norms.[16] While such parodic reversals highlight the humor of the fabliaux, they also reinforce the structural reversals in these texts. In this way, reversals can transform and combine topoi, particularly those of romance and chivalric-epic literature, in the fabliaux.

The use of ill-fitting proverbs constitutes the third subtype of narrative reversal. Although some proverbs in the fabliaux give appropriate summaries of the tales to which they are appended, examples where tales do not illustrate the proverbs affixed to them are common. As several critics have noted, the moralizing proverbs at the end of some fabliaux stand in sharp contrast to the tales to which they ostensibly apply.[17] This type of contrast establishes a reversal between story and moral or practical lesson that calls for interpretation. Simon Gaunt has argued that *Le Vallet aus douze fames* (4.131–50) demonstrates the opposite of one of the proverbs at the end.[18] In this fabliau, a young valet boasts that one wife will not be enough to satisfy him and that he will need ten or twelve. His father convinces him to start with one wife for a year. The bride-to-be has heard about the young man's boasting and decides to exhaust him in their first year of marriage to the point where he does not want any more wives. The MS C version of the tale finishes with three proverbs:

> Cist fableaus dit au definer
> Qui croit sa fame plus que lui
> Sovent aura duel et anui.
> Por ce ne doit nul aastir
> De chose qu'il ne puet fornir.
> Por ce est droiz qui mal porchace
> Qu'a la fiee mau li face. (154–60)

[This fabliau teaches at the end that a man who believes his wife more than himself will often have pain and suffering. For this reason no man should promise something he cannot deliver. Thus it is right that he should reap what he sows.][19]

As Gaunt has remarked, the last two proverbs in the series suit the narrative, for the valet should not have bragged if he could not satisfy even one wife. For this reason, the valet does deserve what he gets, a sexually demanding wife. Although MSS A and E do not contain final proverbs, the lesson in MS I treats the same theme of boasting as the second proverb in the MS C version of the text. The first proverb in MS C quoted above, however, does not correspond to the narrative. Gaunt argues that the text reveals the opposite of this proverb since "the man suffers because his own words are taken too seriously. Male boasting is satirized in this text . . . rather than women's language or femininity as the first moral suggests."[20] Since, as Gaunt notes, the first lesson in one manuscript of this fabliau does not help to explain the text, but in fact presents the opposite interpretation, the effect is arguably intentionally ironic. Whether the scribe is accidentally or intentionally responsible for the ironic proverb or whether it was a lesson of the so-called original text cannot be known. As many fabliaux contain such ironic proverbs, they are more likely a feature of the genre rather than a series of errors. For this reason, it is likely that the proverb is intentionally ironic. More than irony, however, this reversal of the messages of text and lesson, which is also common to many fabliaux, suggests that this fabliau is not intended to be didactic. Instead of communicating a clear message, the texts point to the need for interpretation. The disparity between text and proverb parodies didactic literature and prefigures one use of didactic texts in the *Decameron*.

Even in tales where the proverbs do harmonize with the narrative, the proverbs often have multiple applications, as in *Celui qui bota la pierre* (6.125–44), which will be discussed in chapter 2. *Frere Denise* begins with a proverb that exploits the theme of appearances not aligning with reality. The initial proverb, "Li abiz ne fait pas l'ermite" (1) [the habit does not make the monk], is found in both versions and seemingly refers to Denise, a young lady who leaves home, dresses as a monk, and is "taught to pray" by brother Simon. The proverb, however, also applies to Simon who is not as saintly as his garments would suggest. As Gaunt points out, even Denise may not be as virtuous as she appears, for she seems willing to join Simon in sexual activity.[21] Though the tale illustrates the proverb, the proverb is subject to multiple applications to the tale. Thus, while the inconsistency between certain tales and the proverbs appended to them exemplifies a kind of narrative reversal that requires the audience to reinterpret the text, there are also fabliaux with suitable proverbs that may be variously applied. The ironic proverbs constitute a type of reversal, either because the proverbs invert the message of the narrative, or because they require different interpretations of the narrative.[22] Whether ironic or appropriate, the proverbs applied to fabliaux force the audience to interpret the stories.

Type 3: Inversion

The final type of reversal in the fabliaux involves structure and is crucial to the role of fabliaux material in the *Decameron*. Structural reversal, or rather inversion in the fabliaux, displays a reversal of previously established narrative order—whether of events, characters, or descriptions—during the story's climax. Thus, oppositional pairs of actions such as leaving and arriving (returning), or giving and receiving, do not in themselves constitute inversion. They do so only when they constitute key parts of a narrative reversal.[23] Inversions are often circular in the fabliaux, restoring the appearance of the initial situation of the text, which often belies a fundamental transformation.

The fabliau *Les Quatre souhais St. Martin* (4.189–216) provides an example of inversion.[24] As it is structural, the reversal in this fabliau applies to all manuscript versions of the tale. A Norman peasant, who shows a particular devotion to St. Martin, receives a reward of four wishes one day from the saint. The peasant hurries home to tell his wife, who then cajoles him into giving her one of the wishes. The wishes themselves form a chiastic structure that restores the initial order of the tale. The wife's wish, which is the first of the four wishes, "que vous soiez chargiez de vis" (MS A, 95) [that you may be covered in members], effectively disfigures her husband. Through the first wish, the couple have gone from an ordinary pair (**A**), to a pair with an abnormal, member-laden husband (**B**). In revenge, the husband wishes that his wife have as many *cons* as he has *vits*. Thus, the second wish leads to a situation where both husband and wife have an excess of sexual parts (**B + C**). In an attempt to restore normalcy, the husband then wishes "qu'ele n'ait con ne il n'ait vit" (MS A, 172) [that she not have a *con* nor he have a member], a wish that results in an opposite abnormality since neither one has any sexual organ (**−C −B**). The wife initially articulates the final wish, "qu'aiez .i. vit et ie .i. con" (MS A, 180) [that you have a/one member and I a/one *con*], which the husband then performs. The final wish restores the original situation (**A**) and reveals the inversion of the text.

> A = ordinary couple, everything in its place
> B = extra-endowed husband, corresponds to wish 1
> C = extra-endowed wife, corresponds to wish 2
> −C = wife without parts, corresponds to wish 3
> −B = husband without parts, corresponds to wish 3
> A = restoration of ordinary couple, corresponds to wish 4

In all manuscript versions, the third wish clearly puts the wife first, "qu'ele n'ait con ne il n'ait vit." The order of the wishes inverts the text, following a chiastic structure that is based on oppositional pairs **C,−C** and **B,−B**, where **B** and **C** are complementary. The chiastic structure of the wishes is not strictly necessary for the narrative, since the couple could have undone the first two wishes had the husband properly worded the third wish. In effect, there is no good narrative reason for four wishes, since one of the wishes could have been made superfluous. In fact, earlier analogues of this tale usually present only three wishes, for which the last restores the initial situation. The number of wishes varies from one to six in versions where two people each get three wishes, but the structure is never chiastic as in the fabliau. The versions of this tale in the Eastern tradition of the Seven Sages give only three wishes. This tale is not found in the Western Seven Sages tradition. The majority of analogues focus on the stupidity of women or else the exemplarity of the man who wishes for salvation. The fabliau does not make use of either the misogynist message or the exemplary intent of these other versions. The fabliau presents the only text in this tradition with four wishes.[25]

The arrangement and wording of the wishes in the fabliau suggests that inversion, the practice of doing and undoing actions (and wishes), is central to the structure of the text, and to its emphasis on opposed pairs. The essential opposition in the tale between husband and wife remains unresolved. Although the **A** terms of this structure indicate that the couple are the same after all the wishes as they were at the beginning of the story, the final restoration is merely physical. As Gaunt has stated, the couple have paid a price for their foolishness: "we are in fact left with the troubling knowledge that the return to the *status quo* entails loss and lack: of the four wishes, of the wealth they might have brought, of the abundance of genitals, of the pleasure these might have afforded. Normality is now patently unsatisfactory."[26] In this way, the tale leaves open the opposition between reality and fantasy, with the implication that the four wishes could have transformed reality. Yet, the wishes, like the fabliau, are the stuff of fantasy, not of reality; only in a wish or in a story could these events be true.

Even though the ordering of the wishes is closed because they bring the couple full circle to their original physical state, the effect of the wishes in a chiastic structure opens marvelous, even magical possibilities for the narrative. On the other hand, the lesson could also return to reality and to the idea that the couple should appreciate life and each other as they are. Whether the status quo is unsatisfactory or should not be taken for granted is not spelled out by the text. While the inverted structure in this fabliau reflects narrative symmetry, it also calls attention to interpretive openness. This structure displays the fabliau's ability to resolve questions relative to itself, as it also provokes the audience to seek truth in an external source and judge the characters. The resolution on the physical level corresponds to the resolution of the language, but the couple and the narrative have otherwise been transformed.[27]

Other fabliaux that exhibit inversion resemble *novelle* in the *Decameron*. For example, *Gombert et les deus clers* (4.279–301) and its analogue *Le Meunier et les deus clers* (7.271–305), sources for *Decameron* IX:6, deploy chiastic structures in order to achieve the bed-swapping trick central to all three tales.[28] Another fabliau, *Le Prestre qui abevete* (8.299–309), which was used by Boccaccio in *Decameron* VII:9, is an example of inversion, since it concerns twin scenes that replace two characters and two actions. In this fabliau, a priest goes to his mistress's house and finds the door closed. Through a hole in the door, the priest sees the woman and her husband eating dinner. When the priest exclaims that they are having sex, the husband denies it and says they are merely eating. The priest then offers to change places with the husband so that he may see for himself if the priest is telling the truth. Once inside, the priest and the woman proceed to have sex, and the husband is told that they are eating. The husband is thus tricked into thinking that his eyes deceive him, just as the priest had said.

The narrative is composed of the same scene repeated twice: a man peeks through a hole in the door at a couple who are either eating or having sex. In the first instance, the man is the priest and the couple are eating, in the second instance, the man is the husband and the couple inside are having sex. The tale involves the substitution of two characters (the priest for the husband) and of two actions (having sex for eating). The husband is tricked because he accepts the substitution of one action for another. Furthermore, each action corresponds to the opposite name, so that when the couple is actually eating, they are said by the priest to be having sex, and when the priest and the wife are having sex, the priest claims they are eating. The priest's explanatory language first renames and then substitutes the actions of having sex and eating, and thus inverts the two scenes that make up the trick so that they are mirror images of each other. Once again, lies have become the truth, and truth lies.

The middle of the story reinforces the inverted structure through a chiasmus involving locking and unlocking the door to the house. Shortly after the midpoint of the text, the priest convinces the husband to change places with him:

>   "Bien me volés ore avuler.
>   O moi venés cha fors ester
>   Et je m'en irai la seoir:
>   Lors porrés bien appercevoir
>   Se j'ai voir dit u j'ai menti."
>   Li vilains tantost sus sali:
> A, B A l'<u>uis</u> vint, si le **desfrema**,
> //   Et li prestre dedens entra,
> B', A Si **frema** l'<u>uis</u> a le keville. (43–51, emphasis added)

["You really want to make me believe an illusion now. Come outside with me and I'll go sit down there. Then you will realize if I told the truth or lied." The peasant immediately got up, went to the door and unlocked it. And the priest entered (the house) and locked the door with the key.]

The chiasmus in this passage highlights the door as the turning point of the exchange, since it serves as the literal and figurative threshold between inside and outside, as well as between the mirrored scenes. The B terms of the chiasmus are opposite actions, unlocking ("desfrema") and locking ("frema"), which are equated in this chiasmus as moments of transition. The pivot of the chiasmus, line 50, "*Et li prestre dedens entra*" [And the priest entered (the house)], draws attention to the trickster, who is the agent of reversal. The pivot also represents the decisive moment of the trick, for the priest could neither have had sex with the wife nor convinced the husband of his deception without entering the house. This chiasmus is preceded by the priest's invitation to the husband to see if what he said was true ("Se j'ai voir dit u j'ai menti"). In this way, the priest's words, not his actions, are linked to lies, but will be understood by the husband as truth, whereas his actions will be perceived as a deception, a lie. The chiasmus emphasizes the inversion of *Le Prestre qui abevete* in order to underscore the interpretive differences between (physical) truth and (verbal) mendacity. The priest's lies triumph over his actions precisely because the husband fails to recognize what he sees and instead relies on what he hears. The husband's idiocy is revealed through his failure of interpretation, his failure to attribute the correct meaning to visual signs and instead bestow the power of reality and truth on language alone. Through this trick, the fabliau suggests that language and stories can distort the truth and deceive the audience if they are interpreted literally. By refusing to understand the priest's words as anything other than literal truth, the husband is shown to be a fool. For the audience to avoid this fate, they must carefully interpret the story, for which they are rewarded with the joke.

Le Fablel de la Grue as a Model Fabliau

The fabliau entitled *Cele qui fu foutue et desfoutue* (4.151–87) exemplifies the poetic and comic potential of inversion. Although not an analogue of a specific novella in the *Decameron*, it shares many features with *Decameron* III:10, which will be discussed in chapter 4, and with Boccaccio's work more generally. This fabliau also embodies all types of reversal and announces Boccaccio's use of the fabliaux in three ways. First, *Cele qui fu foutue et desfoutue*, henceforth known as *La Grue*, provides an example of the theme that Boccaccio also develops of sexual innocence lost or exploited in a humorous way. Second, *La Grue* deploys all three types of reversal, as does Boccaccio, in order to support both the humor and the nonmoralizing intentions of the text. Finally, this fabliau uses reversal to bring together and synthesize diverse sources, just as Boccaccio combines different types of narrative throughout the *Decameron*.

La Grue is preserved in six codices: MSS A, B, D, E, F, i. The last of these is an Anglo-Norman version entitled *Le Héron*, which does not have a single line in common with the continental version represented by the other manuscripts.[29] The confusion between "crane" and "heron" may be a result of the physical similarity of the two birds. The symbolic meaning of each bird, although different, bears little significance on the interpretation of the tale. The *grue* [crane] was renowned in the Middle Ages for its vigilance, while the *héron* was considered a pacific, non-rapacious bird.[30] In either case, the symbolism of the bird is ironic for the fabliau. As van den Boogaard has noted, there is little difference structurally between the versions. For this reason, the following discussion of *La Grue* accounts for all versions of the text, but for practical purposes refers to van den Boogaard and Noomen's critical edition unless otherwise noted.

La Grue relates the tale of a nobleman who locks up his daughter in a tower with a nursemaid in order to keep her away from men (or talk of *druerie* in MS i). One day the nursemaid exits the tower, leaving the door open. At this time the girl is looking out the window where a young man passes by holding a bird. The girl calls to him and asks to buy the bird, and the young man is only too willing to sell it. When the girl asks what she can give him for the animal, he replies that she should give him a "foutre" (or a *croistre* in MS i). Even though the girl declares that she is not sure she has one of these, she soon invites the young man up to her room in the tower to look for one, which he finds under her dress. Once the two make the exchange of a *foutre* for a *grue* (or a *croistre* for a *héron*), the young man goes on his way, leaving the bird behind. When the nurse returns and learns what has happened, she is so distraught that she faints (or reprimands the girl in MS i). As soon as she is revived, however, the nurse decides to cook the bird. After preparing the crane, the nursemaid again leaves the tower in order to fetch another item for the cooked bird, leaving the door open once again. The girl goes back to the window, sees the young man, and tells him that her nursemaid was very angry and that they need to undo their exchange. The young man hurries up to the girl so that she may return the bird and be "desfoutre" (*descroitre*). When the nursemaid returns, she is once more distraught to find the bird missing and to hear the girl's explanation of the transaction. In the final lesson in MSS A, B, D, E, the nursemaid, blaming herself, informs the audience that "la male garde pest lo leu" (160) [the bad shepherd feeds the wolf].[31]

The fabliau consists of two exchanges of a bird for sex that are supposedly reversals of each other. In MS B, the introduction to *La Grue* highlights the theme of exchange when the narrator states that "la matiere oï retrere / A Vercelai devant les changes" (4–5) [I heard the subject matter told at Vézelay in front of the money changing tables]. In this way, the narrator announces the theme that is realized in both the content and the structure of the tale; the specific reference to "les changes" serves a literary function.[32] Furthermore, these two lines link the idea of exchange with narration, suggesting not only that the fabliau to follow involves transactions, but also that storytelling itself is a type of exchange between writer/performer and public.

As a whole, the narrative exploits, or rather exaggerates, reversal as a function of exchange. Indeed, reversals involve substitutions of one word, action, or idea for another. The two inverted transactions in *La Grue* form a chiastic structure. The work presents two nearly identical chiastic structures consisting of two opposing motions; (A) the nurse leaves, (B) the young man enters, (//) the pivot involves the exchange of the *grue* for a *foutre*, (B') the young man leaves, and finally (A') the nurse returns. The terms A and A' are opposite motions, just as the two B terms are opposed. In addition, the syntax in each case is inverted to form a chiasmus, such that the word order of A and A' is chiastic, as is that of B and B'. This structure equates opposite actions. The pattern is repeated twice in the story and consequently presents a mirror image:

A   [La norice] <u>s'en corut</u>[33] *cele*/A lor ostel ... l'uis de la tor overt laissa. ... La pucele ert a la fenestre (30–32, 38)
B   li vaslez fu assez cortois:/<u>En la tor</u> *monta* demenois (69–70)
//   la damoisele a enbraciee. ... "Drois est," fet il, "que je vos doingne:/Ma grue soit vostre tot quite" (77, 88–89)[34]
B'   si *s'en issi* <u>de la tor fors</u> (93)
A'   Et *la norice* i <u>entra</u> lors. (94)

[(The nursemaid) ran to their house ... and left the door of the tower open. ... The girl was at the window. The young man was very kind: He climbed to the top of the tower immediately ... he embraced the girl. "It's only right," he said "that I give it to you: My crane is all yours." He left the tower and then the nursemaid entered.]

Following this exchange presented in a chiastic structure, the girl reveals what has happened to her nursemaid, who reacts rather dramatically by fainting (98–117). The undoing or reversal of the transaction in the second half of the narrative mirrors the first chiastic structure:

A1   Puis [la norice] <u>se reva querre</u> un cotel. ... Et la meschine est revenue/A la fenestre regarder (124, 126–27)
B1   [Li vaslés] Lors *monte sus* (139)
//   Si li remet[35] lou foutre el ventre. ... Mes la grue pas n'i laissa (141 and 144)
B1'   Ainz *l'en a avec soi portee* (145)
A1'   Et la norice <u>est retornee</u> (146)[36]

[Then she (the nursemaid) went to look for a knife. ... And the young girl went back to look out the window. The young man then climbed up to the tower. He returned the screw to her stomach, but he did not leave the crane there, rather he took it with him. And the nursemaid returned.]

The opposite motions of the nurse's leaving and the young man's entering the tower are brought together and equated as the main parts of the inversion. The young man could not enter or exit the tower unnoticed without the nurse's doing the opposite action. The pivot of each segment is the trade of the bird for the sexual act. The text establishes a parallel between the two words *grue* and *foutre*, which represent two appetites. Since a chiasmus can bring together and even equate two actions or ideas, this structural chiasmus not only illustrates the physical transactions of the tale, it also serves as a metaphor for exchange, one that is reinforced by the structure. The difference between the first and second chiastic structures is the reversal of the exchange; in the first instance, the girl receives the *grue* for a *foutre*, whereas in the second she returns the *grue* and is *desfoutue*.

Of course, there is no difference in the action of *foutre* and *desfoutre*, just as there is no difference in the structure surrounding these pivotal actions. The difference is strictly a play on the word and idea of *foutre*, which has become currency for the *grue*. The word "desfoutre" is an invention of the narrative. Although this neologism observes the rules of word formation as the opposite of "foutre," it lacks meaning and substance except in relation to "foutre." Much of the comic appeal of this text is derived from the separation of the word and the physical thing it represents, such that a *foutre* can come to equal a *grue*, and a *desfoutre* may exist. The girl's subtle distinction between *foutre* and *desfoutre* is humorous because it is not useful and signifies nothing.

Whether or not the girl literally does not know the meaning of the word *foutre*, however, is almost irrelevant because she certainly seems aware of the action implied. Her inability to understand the literal meaning of the word is a device that facilitates the linguistic and physical equivalence of a bird for sex. It would be difficult to argue that the girl is completely ignorant of what she is doing, that she is taken advantage of, because the first time she speaks to the young man she admits her awareness of an interdiction: "Si je n'en fusse mescreüe / Je l'achetasse ja de toi" (48–49) [If I weren't worried about how it looked, I would buy it from you].[37] The second time it is impossible to argue that the girl remains ignorant of the meaning of the word, for she has experienced it, and she initiates the second encounter by inviting the young man up to undo their exchange.

The two irrevocable transformations in the tale are the girl's being *dépucelée* and the bird's being plucked and cooked. These transformations alter the substance of each transaction without altering the structure in which the exchanges are presented. The inversion facilitates the notion of exchange, specifically the semantic substitution of *grue* for *foutre*. As the exchanges involve a substantial transformation of the girl and the bird, the inversions in which each exchange is shown are fundamentally different. Money is not the equivalent of a bird any more than a *foutre* is. Therefore, these substitutions of language, like money, are based on arbitrary criteria, but they call attention to reality. *La Grue* points out the arbitrary nature of language as it reinforces physical realities that are more than a matter of signs. Whether the girl says *foutre* or *desfoutre*, the action is the same and is irreversible. The structure of the exchanges undermines this physical reality because it presents the two transactions as the same. The chiastic structure of each exchange is the same because the language in which it is presented remains the same. Thus, language is mutable, arbitrary, and requires interpretation. It remains for the audience to interpret the meaning of *desfoutre* as a synonym of *foutre*. It also remains for the audience to determine how innocent the girl is.

Yet it is the very arbitrariness of language that allows it to transform and to be transformed. A bird can be the equivalent of the sexual act through (narrative) language alone. The discrepancy between the inversion where the exchanges are equivalent, and the underlying reality where they are not, highlights the interpretability of language and of narrative more broadly. Since narrative is fabricated, it may be open to interpretation, whereas cooking a bird and having sex are physical, unalterable states of being. For this reason, *La Grue* reinforces the notion that literary language is mendacious by its nature, and that it is not reality. Even though it is false, literary language has the capacity to transform the appearance of reality.

The final proverb of the fabliau, "la male garde pest lo leu," is also open to various applications. If the "male garde" represents the nursemaid, the "leu" seemingly corresponds to the young man, but certainly the second half of the story (if not the first as well) contradicts this assertion because the *demoiselle* herself initiates the encounter. In both instances it is the girl who first addresses the young man and invites him into the tower precisely when the nursemaid is away. It is also curious that the daughter of a castellan could not identify the bird in the first place, since she asks the young man about it ("quel oisel est ce que tu tiens," 43). She is arguably aware of violating an interdiction ("se je n'en fusse mescrëue," 48), especially the second time when she obviously feigns naïveté.[38] It must not necessarily be understood literally when the girl is described as "sote et nice" (74). This girl's naïveté may be as questionable as the girl-monk's in *Frere Denise*. In both cases, the characters' words and actions may be interpreted as contradicting the narrator's initial presentation of the characters.

When the girl asks the young man to return, she says: "venez, si fetes *pes* a moi!" (137, emphasis added). The word "pes" is echoed in the final proverb in the word "pest," a homophone suggesting that the girl could be the *leu*, for she is certainly satisfied with and "fed" by the nurse's absences that resulted in the exchanges.[39] In this interpretation, the final lesson responds to the demands of the narrative, even though it twists the application of the proverb so that the ostensible victim has become the aggressor. The MSS F and i versions of the text suggest that the nursemaid, and not the girl, is the victim both because she lost the opportunity to eat the bird that she cooked and because she allowed the girl in her charge to be *dépucelée*. In this way, the final proverb could also apply ironically to the nursemaid. This proverb, like so many others in the fabliaux, does not demand a literal understanding, but is rather subject to different applications that respond to alternate interpretations of the story.

As this examination of *La Grue* has shown, reversal brings together opposite ideas, especially the relationship between reality and fiction, in order to highlight the value of open interpretation. More generally, reversal in the fabliaux presents the conflation of truth and lies as a means to avoid didactic claims and moral imperatives.

The Tower Motif

Since *La Grue* builds on themes common to courtly literature, the following section will suggest how the reversals in this text differ from other texts with similar themes and motifs. In particular, this section will show that *La Grue* uses reversal to combine different narrative traditions. The premise of *La Grue*, the daughter's imprisonment in a tower, employs a thematic motif common to a variety of literary genres in the Middle Ages. Marie de France's late twelfth-century *lais* "Yonec" and "Guigemar"[40] portray familiar courtly examples of this motif, whereas Chrétien de Troyes' romances, especially *Le Chevalier de la Charrette*, exploit the tower motif to different ends.[41] While the women in the *lais* are locked up by their jealous, older husbands (in a tower in "Yonec" and a *donjon* in "Guigemar"), the girl in the fabliau is locked in the tower by her father, and both Queen Guinevere and later Lancelot are imprisoned by Méléagant in *Le Chevalier de la Charrette*. The theme of imprisonment in a tower represents forced sexual restraint—jealous husbands lock up their wives to keep them from other men, Méléagant imprisons the Queen out of jealousy and later Lancelot in order to keep him from the tournament where the Queen will be. In *La Grue* the father's motives are explicitly stated: "li chastelains n'avoit cure / Qu'en la veïst se petit non, / Ne que a li parlast nus hom" (16–18) [the castellan did not want anyone to see her when she was small, nor that any man speak to her.][42] In all but *Le Chevalier de la Charrette*, the tower becomes the locus of transgression, where young couples consummate their relationships in spite of the space's implied purpose of sexual restriction. Even in Chrétien's *Cligès*, the tower where Fenice and Cligés hide after she pretends to die constitutes the location of their love's consummation. In this respect, *La Grue* maintains the tradition of the tower as prison and *locus amœnus* prevalent in courtly literature.[43]

In the Eastern-inspired traditions of the *Seven Sages of Rome*, its derivative *Dolopathos*, and *Barlaam et Josaphat*, the tower represents a locus of exile or confinement for the young prince. In these collections, isolation purportedly safeguards the prince against bad influences, but serves ultimately as the space of learning. In *Barlaam et Josaphat*, the prince remains confined, ostensibly to prevent him from learning about Christianity, but ironically he converts through interaction with his teacher in this confinement. Similarly in the *Seven Sages of Rome* and *Dolopathos*, the prince is removed from his father and stepmother for an education, one that also keeps him innocent of women. In these works, a father imprisons and isolates his son in an effort to educate the prince and preserve his innocence, but eventually these situations lead to the son's intellectual and moral refinement, which surpasses his father's. At the end of both *Dolopathos* and *Barlaam et Josaphat*, the son outshines the example of his father by converting to Christianity.

The fabliau *La Grue* brings together the Eastern and Western traditions of innocence, education, and sexual repression through the use of reversal. A comparison of "Yonec" and of the Eastern collections with *La Grue* reveals the specific nature of the fabliau's deployment of the tower motif through reversal. In "Yonec" a beautiful, young, married woman is locked in a tower because her husband is afraid of being made a cuckold; "pur sa beauté l'a mult amee /. . . . Dedenz sa tur l'a enserree" (24, 31) [he loved her very much for her beauty . . . he locked her in his tower]. The justification for locking the girl in a tower in *La Grue* is similar, for the father "tant l'avoit chiere et tant l'aimoit / Que en une tor l'enfermoit" (19–20) [he held her so dear and loved her so much that he shut her up in a tower]. Love—whether of a husband for his wife or a father for his daughter—acts as the pretext for locking a woman in a tower in this literary motif and is common to both the fabliau and the *lai*. What is not common to each, however, is the reaction of the women. The lady in "Yonec" laments her situation to the point that her sadness causes her to lose her beauty. There is no mention of the girl's reaction to imprisonment in *La Grue*, but her actions betray her passive acceptance. In this respect the daughter resembles the prince of the Eastern tradition more than the wife of the *lai*. In both "Yonec" and *La Grue*, the women are guarded by an older woman: in

La Grue, it is the girl's nursemaid, whereas in "Yonec" it is the old, widowed sister of her jealous husband. Similar to the role of the prince's tutor(s) in the Eastern stories, the nursemaid in *La Grue* is in some way responsible for the girl's education and protection.

Only in the Western tradition are the wards left alone in the tower. One day while temporarily alone, the woman in "Yonec" wishes for a knight to find her. Soon after, a bird flies into the tower and transforms into a beautiful knight who offers his love to the lady. Keeping the secret from her guard and her husband, the woman calls the marvelous bird-man, known as Muldumarec, to visit her whenever she is left alone and the two engage in acts of love. The scene of sexual transgression in *La Grue* reverses many of the details in its counterpart scene in "Yonec." The *lai* is a scene of adultery, the fabliau one of innocence lost; the characters in the *lai* are fully mature while those in the fabliau are adolescent; the woman in the *lai* is not only married but presumably slightly older than the *pucele* in the fabliau, and their men are a knight and a valet respectively; the vocabulary of the *lai* concerns love, that of the fabliau is strictly carnal. Nevertheless, both relationships commence with the appearance of a bird (a hawk in "Yonec" and a crane in *La Grue*). Both birds are transformed, since the hawk in "Yonec" becomes a man, and the man in turn morphs into the figure of the woman he loves in order to prove to her his faith and love. In the fabliau, the *grue* is literally altered when the nurse cooks it, and is linguistically transformed into a *foutre*, since the two are rendered equivalent through their exchange at the midpoints of the text's double chiastic structure. Similarly, both women are changed by their encounters: the lady in "Yonec" becomes beautiful once more, while the girl in the fabliau has lost her virginity.

The departure of the female guard that precipitates the scene of transgression in each text also involves a reversal in the fabliau. While the narrator in "Yonec" points to the door of the tower being locked when the old woman leaves ("et aprés lui fermer les hus," 60), in *La Grue* the door is open ("l'uis de la tor overt laissa," 32). This reversal of the closed door eliminates the need in the fabliau for the marvelous aspect that is essential to "Yonec" and that is one of the characteristic features of Marie de France's *lais*.[44] Moreover, the closed door symbolizes both protection and intimacy, if not secrecy, in the *lai*, whereas the open door in the fabliau emphasizes the guard's laziness and the nonintimate, nonsecretive nature of the young couple's encounters. It is, however, the structure that most distinguishes the fabliau from the *lai*. The basic structure of the first meeting between the young man and the girl in the fabliau is:

A: old woman exits tower, leaving door open
B: young man enters tower
//: exchange of *grue* for *foutre*
B': young man leaves
A': old woman returns

In the *lai*, the structure is not chiastic:

A_1: old lady leaves room, door is locked
   (Woman's lament and wish for a knight)
B: knight enters through window
   (The real exchange of words revealing the lovers' hearts transpires)
A_1': old lady returns to room, woman claims to be ill
A_2: old lady unlocks door to send for priest
   (knight presumably transforms into woman)
C: priest arrives
   (knight in the form of the lady takes communion)
C': priest leaves
A_2': old lady closes door
B': knight leaves

The structure of the first encounter between the knight and the lady looks nothing like the fabliau's structure. A subsequent meeting, however, corresponds to the structure of the fabliau more closely, but eventually leads to the knight's death.

A_3: old lady pretends to leave but hides
B: knight enters
//: *jeu d'amour*
B': knight leaves
A_3': old lady pretends to return, followed by husband

The matter of surveillance separates this device in the fabliau from its use in the *lai* because the terms A and A_3 are not the same. The A term, which corresponds to the nursemaid's departure in the fabliau, differs significantly from A_3, in which the old woman in the *lai* hides instead of leaving the tower. The B terms of the chiasmus are supposed to constitute the opposite actions of the A terms—the young man or knight would not enter the tower unless his lady were alone. The A_3 terms in the *lai*, however, do not correspond to this condition and consequently do not lead to the same results. The chiasmus in this fabliau creates a closed, circular structure in which the truth (that the girl gave a *foutre* for a *grue*) is not revealed directly to a witness, but rather indirectly through language (the girl tells the nursemaid what happened) and through the presence (and absence) of the bird. Logically, however, there is little reason to connect the bird to the sexual act; the bird does not imply that the couple interacted sexually. Anyone who has not witnessed the scene between the girl and the valet is not capable of interpreting the *grue* as a sign of transgression without an explanation. In the *lai*, the truth (that the lady's love transfigures himself into a hawk) is known directly if surreptitiously by the old woman who hides and witnesses the scene. Although the old woman's interpretation of the scene as a betrayal stands in contrast to the couple's interpretation of it as a union of lovers, both readings of the scene are logical and valid within the text. The lack of a true chiastic structure in the *lai*, however, disallows the possibility of a complete reversal, which would have preserved the couple's secret. In this way, *La Grue* inverts the situation in "Yonec" and creates a reversal in both structure and theme that avoids a witness of the transgression and resolves the dilemma of secrecy. *La Grue* differs from "Yonec" through the use of reversal, both because it reverses the narrative details and because it inverts key parts of the structure of the *lai*. *La Grue* utilizes reversals, especially inversion, in order to highlight the comic and sophistical exchange of *grue* for *foutre*. The structure of similar scenes in "Yonec," however, is not fully chiastic and consequently introduces eyewitness evidence.

In relation to the Eastern collections, *La Grue* both resembles and alters the roles of the main characters in those stories. The relationship between parent and child links these two traditions and distinguishes them from the *lais*. One reversal in the fabliau changes the gender of the child from male to female, thus enabling *La Grue* to draw on both Eastern and Western sources. Similarly, *La Grue* and the Eastern stories present a relationship between mentor/educator and pupil. The role of the nursemaid in *La Grue*, who is responsible for the girl's education and protection, reflects the role of the prince's tutor(s) in the Eastern stories. Moreover, the prince's character in the Eastern tradition furnishes a model for the girl's passive acceptance of her imprisonment, because the prince is also not angry about his isolation. Finally, the fabliau draws on the Eastern tradition to make the tower the site of education, but in the fabliau it is a sexual education. A significant reversal of the Eastern tradition involves the liberated child's exposure to sexuality. In the case of the prince, this lesson is taught when the stepmother tries to seduce the prince and he rejects her. The fabliau reverses this seduction in two important ways: first, by having the girl be the willing victim of seduction; and second, by having the seducer be a man who is an outsider, unrelated to her father. The reversals of gender and of the type of education the child receives allow the fabliau to combine the use of the tower in Eastern collections with its deployment in

Western tales.[45] In all iterations of this tale discussed above, reversal is specific only to the fabliau. Reversal is the feature that makes possible the combination of Eastern and Western versions of the tower motif.

The Manuscript Tradition of *La Grue*

The relationship between *La Grue* and other contemporary texts varies when considered within the work's manuscript contexts. The following section shows how reversals function within the various manuscript contexts of this fabliau. Although the diversity of the manuscripts and their range of organizing principles require individual attention,[46] on the whole they often bring together opposites. Within the codices, *La Grue* may be found among texts that are arranged by structure, by theme, and even by author. In the first manuscript under consideration, the placement of the texts reflects organization by thematic opposition. Yet the fabliaux in the section with *La Grue* are structurally similar. One of the largest and most important codices preserving fabliaux,[47] MS A contains short works exclusively. Copied in a single hand, the codex presents a sequence of texts on more than 350 folios that juxtapose diverse genres. The generic and moral contrasts that the series of texts creates has led S. Lefèvre to remark that "on a l'impression parfois qu'au fil des pages le scribe enfile une perle rouge, une perle noire pour fabriquer une sorte de rosaire paradoxal"[48] [At times one has the impression that the scribe threads a red pearl, a black pearl throughout the pages in order to create a paradoxical rosary]. The placement of texts in segments in MS A reveals and encourages intergeneric comparisons that call into question the message of each text. *La Grue* is preserved among the following series of works in MS A:

fol. 187a	*Les Sept vices et sept vertus*
fol. 188b	*Le Fablel de la Grue*
fol. 189a	*Les Quatre souhais Saint Martin*

The poem *Les Sept vices et sept vertus*[49] distinguishes itself from the two fabliaux by its versification and by its lack of a narrative. Although written in octosyllabic verse like the fabliaux, *Les Sept vices et sept vertus* is divided into stanzas of six lines each following the rhyme scheme *aabccb*. The effect of this versification is to underscore the differences with the flowing narratives of the fabliaux. Even in the *mise-en-page*, *Les Sept vices* stands out. The poem presents definitions of the seven deadly sins. The beginning of this text focuses on sins of the flesh, especially lust. As a morally didactic and even censuring text, *Les Sept vices* stands in stark contrast to *La Grue* that follows. The placement of these two works announces the lascivious content in the subsequent fabliaux, but it also reflects thematic opposition and the *perle rouge, perle noire* contrast of Lefèvre's analysis of the codex.

The combination of the fabliaux *La Grue* and *Les Quatre souhais* does not suggest generic and moral opposition, but rather sets these tales apart from other fabliaux in the codex. As already noted, these fabliaux present chiastic structures, but thematically they underscore the heterogeneity of the genre, because one involves a *pucele* (virgin) and a young valet, the other a married couple; one the daughter of a *châtelain*, the other a peasant; one suggests a certain realism, while the other draws on the marvelous. Although the thematic contrasts exhibited among the two fabliaux and *Les sept vices* suggest a deliberately variegated structure to the codex that calls attention to the distinct nature of each type of work, the grouping of two structurally similar fabliaux indicates the opposite trend, the bringing together of comparable texts. This placement of *La Grue* in MS A next to *Les Quatre souhais* reinforces both works' structural reversals, just as underscores their thematic differences. Yet this juxtaposition of thematically diverse works raises questions about the interpretation of each work, as well as about the interpretation of the manuscript overall. Is the preceding text about vices and virtues intended as a warning to the audience about to read or hear the following salacious fabliaux?[50] Is it merely a device for variety in entertainment? Or is it rather a reminder that the choice of interpretation of these stories is the responsibility of the audience? If the compiler's intention were strictly didactic, why include so many negative, but entertaining, examples as the fabliaux? Like the reversals in the fabliaux, this manuscript anthology plays with opposites and implies that these narratives ought to be read as an exercise in contraries. Just as the fabliaux give no stable ruling on interpretation or morality, MS A offers no explicit code for understanding the organization of the texts it preserves. The fabliaux are scattered throughout the manuscript, sometimes in small groups of similar texts like this one, other times among vastly different poems. Even in the section of folios dedicated to the works of the writer Rutebeuf,[51] his fabliaux are intermingled with his vernacular saints' lives, thus representing a microcosm of the overall organization of the manuscript. The placement of the fabliaux throughout the manuscript indicates that they are given equal weight in the codex as courtly, pious, and didactic works. In this way, the organization of the manuscript as a whole parallels the fabliaux as model texts built on contraries and reversals.

Another of the largest codices of fabliaux, MS D also preserves the *Fables* or *Isopet* of Marie de France, the collection of didactic tales *Le Chastoiement d'un père à son fils*,—to be discussed in chapter 3—some romances and religious texts (for example, the manuscript contains *Partenopeus de Blois* and *La Vie de Sainte Léocade*), as well as other short, courtly narratives. The manuscript, which dates from the late thirteenth or early fourteenth century, was most likely copied by a single hand. According to Tracy Adams, who has studied this codex extensively, "the contents of BNffr 19152 are controlled by an ideology initiated in the set of framed tales with which the manuscript begins, "Le Chastoiement que li Pères ensaigne à son Filz," suggesting that through this set of framed tales, the manuscript promotes and offers instruction in a particular type of intelligence, one that Jean-Pierre Vernant and Marcel Detienne have described as *metis* or 'cunning intelligence.'"[52] The presence of guiding principles of order and interpretation in the anthologies suggests a frame for the stories within. The implicit ordering frames in both MSS B and D promote an association between fabliaux and story collections, one that will reach full fruition in works like the *Decameron* and the *Canterbury Tales*. Although these anthologies may be organized according to larger interpretive principles, the fabliaux they preserve are usually presented as points of contrast in relation to the other works in the codices.

The fabliaux scattered throughout MS D are often linked by authorship and respond to an organizing frame. The microcontext for *La Grue* contains fabliaux exclusively:

fol. 56c   *Le Prestre qui menga mores* (7.191–202)
fol. 56e   *Le Fablel de la Grue*
fol. 57b   *Le Prestre qui ot mere a force* (5.49–69)

Most noticeable among these texts is the presence of priests in this series of fabliaux, but the tales are not specifically anticlerical. In *Le Prestre qui menga mores* a priest riding into town stops at a mulberry bush to eat some berries that he is only able to reach by standing on his horse. After satisfying his hunger, he inadvertently commands the horse to move, but topples and remains stuck in an awkward position. The villagers are concerned when the horse returns home without the priest, and they soon go out to find him, but he will not divulge to them how he came to be in such a predicament.

The text is attributed to Guerin, who is most likely the same Garin of *La Grue*.[53] In this codex, works by a single writer are often placed together, as is the case with the works of Rutebeuf and Gautier le Leu. The placement of these tales suggests that they are in fact from the same Garin. The similarities of the two fabliaux also furnish evidence in support of this claim. The focus on appetite in this tale resembles *La Grue* and highlights in particular the nursemaid of *La Grue*. The nursemaid's concern with the cooked bird and its sauce invites the very act which caused her distress, in much the same way that the priest of *Le Prestre qui menga mores* brings about his own problem of getting stuck in the tree after trying to satisfy his appetite. The act-counteract device evident in *La Grue* is also at play in *Le Prestre qui menga mores*, for in the first instance the priest's speech results in his embarrassment, whereas his subsequent silence in front of the crowd, or rather evasiveness, counteracts and hides his embarrassment. These two fabliaux are related by common devices and themes, and most of all by a common *trouvère*.

The third tale, *Le Prestre qui ot mere a force*, reinforces the notions of exchange and verbal misunderstanding already discussed in relation to *La Grue*, while also exploiting the character of a priest on horseback. The mother of a priest desires money from her son and takes him to court. When the bishop threatens to "suspendre" the priest, she misunderstands this to mean "hang" him, so she finds another priest to blame in her son's place and is soon sent away with him from court. Laden with the old woman, the second priest encounters her real son on his ride home and explains his difficulty. The son offers to take the old woman off his hands for a fee large enough to satisfy his mother. The theme of an exchange of goods and persons—first the mother exchanges her son, then the son exchanges his mother—is similar to *La Grue*. In both instances, a verbal misunderstanding necessitates the first exchange and both stories are circular in structure and return to the nominal status quo by the end.

The placement of fabliaux in this codex clearly displays thematic and structural similarities. More to the point, however, this is the first microcontext of *La Grue* in which the writer Garin is brought to the fore. The first text in the manuscript, *Le Chastoiement d'un père à son fils*, emphasizes the writer by naming him at the beginning of the text. The references to specific writers, as opposed to the suppression of their names, suggests that authorship plays a more dominant role in this codex than in the others studied in relation to *La Grue*. The focus on the writer, in conjunction with the anthology's overall guiding principle of reading for *metis*, implies a growing awareness of authorship in the modern sense and of structural unity that will be addressed by Boccaccio (and Chaucer) in the fourteenth century.[54] If, as Adams has suggested, cunning intelligence is valued in this codex, then the microcontext for *La Grue* offers yet another contrast, since all of the characters in authority in these fabliaux (both priests and the nursemaid) display an absence of guile and barely avoid embarrassment in their respective tales.

On the whole, the manuscripts considered thus far indicate that fabliaux served as a contrasting force in anthologies. One value of the fabliaux in these anthologies relates to their focus on oppositions, which is essential to variegation. The variegated structures of such codices will find echoes in later works like the *Canterbury Tales*, *Les Cent Nouvelles nouvelles*, and especially the *Decameron*, which will be discussed in chapter 3.

The contexts for *La Grue* provided in other codices furnish new insights into the tale and distinguish the role of fabliaux in these manuscript anthologies. MS B, another sizable codex, contains a large number of fabliaux in addition to other short pieces, *Le Roman des Sept Sages de Rome* in prose, which will be discussed more in relation to the verse redactions in chapter 3, and finally Chrétien de Troyes' *Le Conte du Graal/Perceval*. Unlike the other manuscripts, MS B tends to organize texts according to generic and thematic similarity. *La Grue* is preserved in the section of short narratives that are primarily fabliaux, separated from the longer works:

fol. 39c   *L'Esquiriel (La Mere qui desfandoit sa fille vit a nomer)* (6.33–49)
fol. 41a   *La Grue*
fol. 42b   *Les Putains et les lecheors* (6.145–53)
fol. 43a   *La Demoisele qui vost voler*

Keith Busby's discussion of the microcontext of MS B in relation to *La Grue*[55] notes many similarities among these tales. In the first of these stories, a young girl is forbidden to say the word "vit," but does so to excess and to the great distress of her mother. Robin, a young man having overheard their conversation, subsequently invites the girl to pet his "squirrel." When it comes to feeding the squirrel, Robin finds a way for the squirrel to get the nuts in the girl's stomach, much to her delight. This tale with its naive girl is obviously quite similar to *La Grue*. As Busby notes, *La Grue* "depends, like the squirrel-poem, on the discrepancy between a word and knowledge of its meaning. It also illustrates that sex can be obtained . . . by means of an economic transaction."[56] Linking these two contentions, it is precisely a linguistic discrepancy that enables a transaction in each case. Moreover, the discrepancy is itself a type of linguistic exchange. The tales are related topically, whereas their structures vary significantly. In this way, the presentation of *La Grue* in MS B differs from that of MS A because MS B stresses thematic groupings. As Busby notes, the emphasis on euphemism in *L'Esquiriel* highlights an opposition through the contrast of vulgar content and seemly language. Although the specific device of mixing euphemism with sexual obscenity is a type of reversal that differs from the explicit language in *La Grue*, both works exhibit similar themes and an emphasis on opposition, and in this way are further connected.[57]

This thematic grouping contrasts with the next text in this section, *Les Putains et les lecheors*. Although the narrator in this tale refers to his work as a fabliau on two occasions, the text barely has a narrative and it does not contain a trick or a logical fallacy.[58] *Les Putains et les lecheors* deals in generalities, beginning with the creation of the world and the three "orders" of people, namely "clers, chevaliers et laboranz" (6). Forgotten in this system, according to the narrator, are the "putains et lecheors (*jongleurs*)" whom God decides to divide among the other orders, giving the *clers* control of the *putains*, while the *chevaliers* have rule over the *lecheors*. Since the *clers* treat the *putains* well and give them money and clothes, the *clers* are saved, whereas the *chevaliers*, who abuse the *jongleurs*, are damned. This defense of *clers* and *jongleurs* inverts the socially dominant view that rejects *putains* and *jongleurs* as categories, let alone as worthy of treating well at the expense of the knights. As it offers this sociogenic reversal and exploits vulgar themes, this text is related to the other fabliaux in this section and more generally to the larger notion of fabliaux discussed in this chapter. In this microcontext, however, *Les Putains et les lecheors* stands out because it lacks a narrative—it is mostly a descriptive piece—and because the other fabliaux in this microcontext are remarkably similar to each other and all deploy the same theme of innocent young girls who are ostensibly tricked or seduced by a savvy male. Whether or not *Les Putains et les lecheors* is a fabliau, the text's reversal of social norms for the sake of humor links it to the fabliaux tradition, while its generalizations and lack of individualized characters more closely link it to *dits*.[59]

The final work of this microcontext, *La Demoisele qui vost voler*, continues the theme in the other two fabliaux, in which a play on language leads to the alleged seduction of a naive girl. While MS A brought *La Grue* together with a structurally similar fabliau and emphasized lust, the microcontext in MS B reinforces the theme of naive sexuality in *La Grue*. The difference between *Les Putains et les lecheors* and the other fabliaux, between innocence and lechery or *puceles* and *putains*, reinforces thematic oppositions and suggests a deliberately ironic positioning of tales on the part of the compiler. MS B distinguishes itself from other anthologies because it exhibits clusters of similar themes among works.

The fourth manuscript related to *La Grue*, MS E, dates from the late thirteenth century and contains over 200 folios. Among several fabliaux, this codex also preserves many works by Rutebeuf, as well as longer works, such as Jaquemart Gielée's *Renart li nouvel*, Marie de France's *Isopet*, and Huon de Méri's *Tournoiment Antéchrist*. Although the longer texts mention an author, many of the shorter works in the codex have no known attribution. Because the manuscript has some prominent lacunae and was copied in different hands, it would be challenging to argue that the texts it preserves demonstrate a clear *telos* or method of organization, or that it is a deliberately compiled anthology. Despite this lack of unity, the section containing most of the fabliaux, and most especially the sequence of texts with *La Grue*, is found near the end of the codex and maintains a certain consistency and integrity:

fol. 153c   *Le Povre mercier* (8.283–98)
fol. 155b   *Le Fablel de la Grue*
fol. 156b   *Le Blasme des fames*[60]

In *Le Povre mercier*, a poor merchant at a fair reluctantly leaves his only horse in a field where it is killed by a wolf. Having heard the lord will reimburse him for his loss, the merchant goes to the lord and explains his situation. Since the merchant's prayer offered the horse to the protection of both the lord of the land and the Lord God, the lord only reimburses him half the price of the horse and tells him God owes him the rest. When the merchant meets a monk, he demands payment from his Lord. A trial ensues in front of the lord who orders the monk to pay the merchant for half the price of his horse. In similar fashion to *La Grue*, *Le Povre mercier* highlights the notion of exchange. In *Le Povre mercier*, the exchange is fair and equitable (even profitable) to the merchant, but the monk and the lord both lose some money in order to reimburse the merchant; both are at least amused by the spectacle. In this case, it is the naive character who profits. In *La Grue*, the naive girl certainly enjoys herself, but ultimately it is the young man who profits most from the situation, as he gets to keep the *grue*, which has already been cooked for him. Indeed, a reading of *Le Povre mercier* brings attention to thematic issues of exchange, fairness, and profit in *La Grue*. Is the suggestion of this pairing that the girl, the alleged victim, profits in *La Grue*? The works are also similar inasmuch as the young man in *La Grue* receives an altered form of his original bird, whereas the merchant in *Le Povre mercier* receives payment equal to the horse he lost, that is to say, a monetary substitute for his horse. In spite of this resemblance, *Le Povre mercier* does not present a chiastic structure like *La Grue*. Once more, the similarities remain at the level of theme and narrative, but the themes drawn out in this section of MS E differ from the sexual themes highlighted in the other anthologies considered because they focus more on the nature of the characters.

The next work in this microcontext, *Le Blasme des fames*, is considered a *dit* by the editors of a critical edition of this text.[61] Here, there is no narrative, but rather an enumeration of all the vices and base tendencies of women. Particularly striking, and perhaps ironic in contrast to the ostensible naïveté of the *demoiselle de la grue*, are the following lines against women: "Femme fet bien par coverture, / Maudehé ait sa demaine nature; / Femme par sa douce parole, / Atret li home e puis l'afole," [Outwardly she's well-behaved, / But by her nature, she's depraved; / Her words are sweetness sugar-clad / To lure a man and drive him mad].[62] Does *La Grue* serve as a counterexample to these statements, or does this text inform the fabliau, implying that the girl, and perhaps the nurse as well, are guilty of such deception(s)? Certainly the girl's actions in the second half of *La Grue* suggest some deception, a feigned innocence. Nevertheless, there does appear to be a conscious commentary among these three works. If this group is indicative of the rest of the codex, then MS E, or at least the section preserving fabliaux, links works by like themes as they relate to specific characters, as opposed to their overall narrative connections.

The final manuscript context of *La Grue* is MS F, a large codex preserving several romances, two *chansons de geste*, a number of fabliaux, and diverse short texts, as well as the *Isopet* by Marie de France.[63] The fabliaux are integrated among other short works, and therefore shape groupings by form, as seen in the following list:

fol. 277a	*Du Noble lion*
fol. 277c	*Le Fablel de la Grue*
fol. 278b	*La Male Honte* (5.83–134)

Although *Du Noble lion* seemingly has little in common with *La Grue*, it is possible to argue that the works are related through the notion of trickery and opportunism. Both *La Grue* and *La Male Honte*, however, are fabliaux. Since *La Male Honte*, will be discussed in more detail in chapter 2, its mention here in relation to *La Grue* will be brief. The title itself is suggestive of the type of story it presents, a verbal misunderstanding. Just as *La Grue* involves ignorance of the meaning of the word "foutre," so the king of England misinterprets the expression "male Honte" as an insult when it refers to a sum of money in the trunk ("male") of a man curiously named Honte. The character of the king harks back to Noble the lion, but contrary to Noble, the king in this fabliau does not seek to be flattered; instead, he ultimately rewards the man who brings him the trunk for the humor he derived from this misunderstanding. In this way, the similarity between these two fabliaux is evident in their deployment of verbal misunderstanding as the driving narrative force.

The insular version of *La Grue*, known as *Le Héron*, is preserved in MS i; it is the only fabliau in the manuscript by any definition. It is preserved with the very end of the *Chanson d'Aspremont* and another poem on marriage.[64] *Le Héron* occupies less than one folio (fol. 2b–d) in this manuscript fragment. As there is no significant manuscript context in this case, it is impossible to determine how *Le Héron* interacted with other texts.

Overview of Anthologies and Miscellanies of Fabliaux

The previous examinations of the manuscript contexts for *La Grue* reveal the necessity of studying each codex in its entirety in order to understand more fully its organization and the role of the fabliaux in it. To study at least forty codices containing fabliaux is far too large a task, especially because there are approximately twenty manuscripts that contain just one or two fabliaux. By the same token, the larger codices with fabliaux, which have already been studied by several scholars, preserve dozens of fabliaux among many other works of various genres. While studies of the largest codices often promote the deliberate ordering of texts and the value of continuous reading in thematic comparisons, few of these studies focus on the fabliaux specifically because their aim is to explore the inner workings of the codex as a whole and of vernacular compilations in general.[65]

Some notable studies of the fabliaux in their codicological contexts offer a mixture of views on the fabliaux. While the Swiss School of scholars has studied several manuscripts of fabliaux, they do not come to a particular understanding of the role the fabliaux play in codices.[66] In one study of four manuscripts with fabliaux (MSS A, D, M, Z), Carter Revard posits that the texts in MSS M and Z "are not only deliberately variegated, but deliberately placed within the manuscript so as to highlight oppositions and encourage intertextual readings [and] that the scribes deliberately grouped, sequenced, and redacted texts in order to highlight their oppositions and parallels."[67] This assessment generally complements the views presented above on the manuscript contexts of *La Grue*, yet the conclusions Revard draws about these manuscripts, based on a strictly thematic analysis, undermine his premise that the sequence of texts highlights their differences and similarities. While it is true that the texts in these manuscripts include a number of poems about women and clearly demonstrate "'woman' materials," it is less clear why the fabliaux he mentions (*Les Quatre souhaits Saint Martin*, *Les Trois dames*, *Le Chevalier qui fist parler les cons*, and *La Gageure*) are necessarily "antifeminist." Moreover, this assertion that the fabliaux are "antifeminist," even when coupled with a "feminist" text as in the example he gives, negates the latter's role in the sequence. A failure to consider tone and genre further detracts from his arguments about the fabliaux in particular and from the sequence of texts Revard chose to highlight. Even though there is a disparity in the particulars, on the whole Revard's analysis of MSS M and Z complements the examinations of the anthologies of fabliaux above.

In his discussion of the other two manuscripts with fabliaux, MSS A and D, Revard describes them as "anthologies" representing a range "from burlesque to romance, from scabrous or obscene to devout and delicate, from *vilain* to *sainte*, from courtly love to dirty joke to humble prayer."[68] The diversity of texts and their placement within the codices leads Revard to conclude that all four manuscripts in his study must be the result of careful planning.[69] Revard deftly underlines the inherent yet deliberately varied organization of four codices with fabliaux, without specifically pointing to the fabliaux's determining role in these anthologies.

Similar to this account is Alberto Vàrvaro's study of modalities of diffusion of medieval texts, primarily of the twelfth century, which emphasizes the relation between the indifference to generic diversity of manuscript compilations and their relative coherence.[70] Like Revard, he concludes that for MSS M and Z "les compilateurs de recueils ne sélectionnaient pas les genres, comme nous avons tendance à faire" [compilers of collections did not choose genres as we have a tendency to do].[71] Although he touches on other codices containing fabliaux—MSS F and a—the purpose of Vàrvaro's study is to underscore the heterogeneity of the codices as it relates to generic diffusion, and more abstractly to generic definition. His argument supports the notion that generic variety within a manuscript does not denote codicological miscellany or organizational disorder.

Sylvie Lefèvre's study of MS A relates the idea of generic studies to codices. Lefèvre subtly draws out some characteristics of this manuscript, such as the predominance of the octosyllable (only ten of more than 200 works are in alexandrines) and the brevity of the texts, a feature that unites these works and distinguishes this codex from MS D, which, as Revard also notes, finishes with three romances.[72] She agrees with Revard that some aspects of MS A invite reflection on textual groupings and commentary.[73] The focus of Lefèvre's study is a generic consideration of the *saluts* and *complaints*, works preserved almost exclusively by MS A, which she argues are transformed from their lyric models of *langue d'Oc* and here offer a mixture of songs and narrative texts, a fictionalization of lyric that responds to the new anecdotic poetic forms of the north of France.[74] Indeed, the texts in MS A seem to mix and blend genres in a way that undermines strict generic boundaries; what takes over is the short narrative form. Both Lefèvre and Revard propose that the variegated nature of these codices, what Lefèvre refers to as the seemingly paradoxical structure of *une perle rouge, une perle noire*, is comparable to the collections of tales found in the *Decameron* and the *Canterbury Tales*.[75] None of these studies undertakes a close analysis of the organization of the *Decameron* or the *Canterbury Tales*. Manuscript anthologies such as MSS A, B, and D preserve collections of a variety of short works, yet whether or not these anthologies exhibit a guiding principle, as Adams suggests for MS D, is an issue that must be approached through a reading of a single codex in its entirety. Nevertheless, the presence of Eastern frame narrative collections in "fabliaux codices" underscores the resemblance between manuscript anthologies and frame narrative collections.

Finally, in *Codex and Context*,[76] Busby considers a significant number of codices with fabliaux, discussing the manuscripts in their entirety as well as focusing on specific and limited sequences of texts. Busby posits a different structure for each of the manuscripts he studies; these are MSS A, B, C, D, F, H, J. His intertextual analyses, which are usually limited to clusters of three or four texts, argue for various thematic connections among texts. He highlights the "marriage group" in one codex, the comic and burlesque in another, as well as legal satire, to mention but a few examples. As in some of the other studies mentioned, there are often generic and thematic contrasts between specific texts or groups of texts. Although there are far too many points to elaborate here, Busby concludes that the fabliaux serve different purposes in these codices, from that of negative moral *exempla* in MS A, to judicial and anticlerical satire in MS C, to balancing the idealistic *courtoisie* of the non-fabliaux part of MS D. In all of these cases, however, the fabliaux serve as interpretive contrasts to the other texts in the codex.

The manuscripts studied thus far often establish structural irony as an organizing principle, contrasting texts with opposing themes and registers. In the codices for *La Grue*, MSS D and B are the only ones to situate the text exclusively among other fabliaux, and in MS B it was placed among like themes. These groupings provide intertextual commentaries and often expose what was otherwise implicit in the texts. By and large, these microcontexts furnish evidence for the deliberate organization of the codices, extending beyond mere irony and contrast.

This brief examination of sections of a few significant codices for fabliaux also reveals that an understanding of their ordering principles is best considered individually. Most studies of codices preserving fabliaux suggest this need for codicological casuistry by the diversity of their results, but the overriding theme among these studies is that these manuscripts are deliberately ordered collections more often than not and that their variegated structures served as precursors to frame narrative collections like the *Decameron*. In order to have a better sense of the relationship between the "fabliaux codices" and the framed collection of tales, the following chapter will examine a single codex. While there are similarities among some of the codices, no two manuscripts contain exactly the same texts, and even copies of entire manuscripts may vary. The placement of texts has implications for the principles of compilation of a codex as a whole, as well as for a reading of the texts individually. It is the interrelations among the specific texts, and not merely the relations among broad generic categories applied to the texts, that permit an understanding of these anthologies. What emerges from this limited view of the manuscripts is the notion of deliberate, if not implicit, organizational principles behind codices that guide the learned reader. Although the fabliaux are individual texts and therefore do not participate in author-directed compilations, they were often strategically collected and grouped in thirteenth- and fourteenth-century codices as part of the unity of the anthology. The next chapter will analyze the role of fabliaux in a single manuscript: BNF fr. 2173.

2

The Fabliaux in Context

BNF fr. 2173

> Damedex douna le povoir
> Home de faire son voloir,
> Bien ou mal lequel qui li plest.
>
> [The Lord God gave man the power to do his
> will, good or bad, whichever pleased him.]
>
> *IMAGE DU MONDE*

In order to clarify the role of the fabliaux within the larger structure of manuscript anthologies, in this chapter I will examine the inner workings of a single and complete codex: BNF fr. 2173 (MS K).[1] Reciprocally, an intertextual consideration of the works in this codex will furnish a more comprehensive view of the structural preoccupations and organizing principles of an anthology from the late thirteenth or early fourteenth century.

The choice of a codex was based in large measure on practical criteria. Codices with too few fabliaux, fewer than three, do not offer enough examples of the interrelation between fabliaux and other kinds of texts, nor do they adequately represent the variety of the fabliaux. Another consideration was the condition of the manuscript, since incomplete versions and fragments compromised intertextual and intergeneric considerations. There are approximately seventeen manuscripts that meet these conditions: MSS A through O, MS T, and MS l. Although the use of different hands does not necessarily indicate that a manuscript was assembled over time without thought to an overarching structure, manuscripts copied by one scribe, presumably at one time, are more cohesive, and consequently I favored them in choosing a codex. Among these, the strong generic connections between fables and fabliaux—two types of works that share a common etymology—dictated the choice of a manuscript.[2] Of the seven codices that preserve both fabliaux and Marie de France's fables, BNF fr. 2173 is of particular interest.

The images that announce the different texts of MS K distinguish this codex from the other codices preserving fabliaux and serve as interpretive aids to the texts. With the exception of MS l, which is a copy of MS K, there are no other manuscripts with images or illustrations of the fabliaux. Finally, the organization of this codex highlights intertextual and intergeneric questions. Specifically, the placement of two fabliaux among the fables, in addition to the double representation of the "Matron of Ephesus" theme as both a fable and a fabliau, are anomalies of this codex that invite intergeneric comparison and commentary and that distinguish it from the rest of the manuscript tradition of the fabliaux.

MS K is also of special interest because of its likely provenance. Scholars have posited that MS K is of Italian origin, because its particular style of images, with their vivid colors in gouache, is similar to a fragment of the *Proverbia quae dicuntur super natura feminarum* (Berlin, Staatsbibliothek, MS Hamilton 390), which was composed at approximately the same time and written in Venetian dialect.[3] The language of MS K, however, does not betray an Italian scribe. In his study of the codex, Jaap van Os suggests that the manuscript is a collaboration of a French copyist with a Venetian artist, a theory that explains both the quality of the Old French and the drawings, which are unusual in comparison with most manuscripts of the period originating in the north of France, as will be explained below.[4] While it is possible that this team was working in northern France instead of Italy to compose this manuscript, the majority of evidence at this time points to Frenchmen in Italy, such as pilgrims, merchants, *jongleurs*, crusaders, and especially those associated with Angevin rule in the late thirteenth century.[5] Jean Dunbabin has shown that during the French rule of the Kingdom of Sicily, men such as Gui de Dampierre and Robert d'Artois brought their minstrels to Italy, including the *trouvère* Adam de la Halle in 1282.[6] Other noblemen brought with them scribes, schoolmasters, and artists to Italy, particularly to the Regno.[7] In 1240 King Frederick II of Sicily had an unbound copy of the Old French prose *Palamadès* sent to him in Umbria.[8]

Venice, where MS K was probably produced, was a wealthy city because of its international trade and especially because of its connections to the Middle East. The Venetians were involved in shipping trade for the Regno. For this reason, Venice was also likely to have attracted French merchants, noblemen, and their entourages.[9]

Given the strong French presence in Italy, including Venice, in the late thirteenth and early fourteenth centuries, and given the Italian-style images of the codex, the Italian origin of MS K may be considered probable. The argument advanced here actually needs little more than probability because it does not rely on the potential encounter with one specific manuscript, but rather uses that possibility as an indicator of contact. As Old French manuscripts had been brought to, if not produced in, Italy, they and MS K serve as historical evidence that some fabliaux may have been known and even copied in parts of the Italian peninsula in the thirteenth and fourteenth centuries. It is therefore reasonable to conclude that fabliaux may have been available to Boccaccio in written form.

Description and Overview of BNF fr. 2173

In the manuscript tradition of the fabliaux, MS K provides an example of a codex with demonstrable principles of organization. The manuscript is relatively small, only ninety-seven folios of parchment with two columns of approximately thirty-one lines each; it measures 227×175 mm.[10] There are two complete longer works, *L'Image du monde* by Gossuin de Metz and Marie de France's *Isopet*, as well as six fabliaux and the anonymous *Dit de la femme* in the codex. A Latin insert of one folio separates the first text, *L'Image du monde*, from the section preserving the fables, fabliaux, and *dit*:

1. *L'Image du monde* by Gossuin de Metz, ff. 1r–56v
[Latin insert: first-person anonymous confession and John I: 1–4, f. 57]
2. *L'Isopet* by Marie de France, ff. 58r–93v
3. Anonymous fabliaux and *dit*, ff. 93v–97v

The six fabliaux are heterogeneous, ranging from naive and humorous to scatological and bawdy. The placement of the fabliaux in the codex, however, signals an interruption in the unity of the *Isopet*. The first fabliau, *Celui qui bota la pierre*, is situated in the middle of the collection of fables on ff. 78v–79r. Similarly, another fabliau, *La Coille noire* (5.163–89), is placed on ff. 92r–93r, right before the final lines of the *Isopet*. The remaining fabliaux as well as the *dit* are all located after the *explicit* of the *Isopet*. These are: *La Male Honte* (ff. 93v–94v); *Le Dit de la femme* (ff. 94v–95r); *Cele qui se fist foutre sur la fosse de son mari* (ff. 95r–96r and NRCF, 3.375–403); *Le Prestre crucifié* (ff. 96r–97r and NRCF, 4.91–106); *La Vielle qui oint la paume au chevalier* (f. 97 and NRCF, 6.289–99). A note dated 1875 confirms that two fragments were removed at ff. 75 and 77,[11] but these most likely contained fables. According to François Avril and Marie-Thérèse Gousset, the codex dates from the third quarter of the thirteenth century.[12]

The images that distinguish this manuscript from the majority of others preserving fabliaux are of two different kinds. The images corresponding to the first text, the *Image du monde*, are drawings in brown and red ink that illustrate the cosmos—the placement of the planets and the elements in concentric circles—and other natural occurrences Gossuin describes, such as solar and lunar eclipses. The manuscript opens with a drawing of God holding the spherical universe. The largest illustration, placed at the end of the work (f. 56v), outlines the "image du monde," which is the hierarchical placement in the universe of God, the order of angels, the planets and signs of the zodiac, the five elements, and earth at the center. The remaining illustrations of the *Image du monde* are scientific diagrams, but this final drawing, which recalls the illustration of God creating the concentric spheres of the universe at the beginning of the manuscript (f. 1r), serves as the model for the structure of the codex. The order of the codex reflects the descending hierarchy of the concentric levels of the cosmos that the *Image du monde* illustrates. The vanity of man is farthest from God and consequently at the center of the universe.

The second part of the codex presents images of animals and man in 104 color drawings that coincide with and introduce the beginning of most fables and fabliaux; there is not, however, an illustration for every work.[13] These images are remarkable in that they have no frame or border but are merely placed freely in the middle of the text, often running into the margins. The first image in the second part of the codex introduces the *Isopet* with a drawing of a *clerc*—presumably Aesop—with a stylus, showing that he is the author of the work. This image echoes the first illustration of the *Image du monde*, which opens with God holding the universe in one hand and a stylus-like instrument in the other. The drawing of Aesop is slightly smaller in scale than the first illustration of God and His creation. Finally, at the end of the *Isopet*, a similar drawing on a much smaller scale depicts Marie de France composing her translation of Aesop's fables. This sliding scale of images, which is mirrored by the writing that is also slightly smaller in the second half of the codex, connects the two halves of the manuscript and establishes a hierarchy among the texts and among their authors.

Another peculiarity of this manuscript is an insert of one folio (f. 57) written in Latin in a much larger and possibly earlier hand than the rest of the text. Previous manuscript descriptions have not documented this single folio as a text. The insert precedes the part of the manuscript preserving the *Isopet* and fabliaux and follows an undocumented fragmentary folio (56bis) placed after the final illustration of the *Image du monde*. Blank folios such as this typically indicate the end of a text in codices. Although copied in one hand, van Os posits that the two parts of the manuscript may have been separate at one point, either initially or during the period when MS l was copied from it.[14] The only evidence for an apparent separation of the two halves is the existence of the Latin insert, but the role of this folio in the structure of the codex is open to debate.[15] While Barbara Nolan has argued that the moral focus of the Latin insert offers a preliminary guide to reading the remaining fables and fabliaux, it is more likely that the insert was used as scrap to protect the beginning of the *Isopet*, especially since the decorated folios at the end of the *Image du monde* and at the beginning of the *Isopet*, with large and elaborate illustrations, would have needed protection. The hierarchy of texts and images in the codex suggests that the two parts of the manuscript were intended to be joined in order to form a cohesive whole. If the extraneous folio was intended by the compiler as another text, a commentary on the fabliaux to follow, as Nolan suggests, its presence disrupts the unity of the codex established by the hierarchy of images. Although there remains a possibility of the folio's deliberate inclusion and textual integration in the codex, it is more probable that the insert serves only a practical function of dividing and protecting the halves of the manuscript, for which reason its contents will not figure into the following analysis of the codex as a whole.

The texts that form the manuscript range from the didactic *Image du monde* and Marie de France's practical *Isopet*, to some of the most scatological fabliaux. The *Image du monde* is a work on cosmogony, astronomy, and geography. Composed by Gossuin de Metz in 1246, the *Image du monde* survives in three different redactions, two written in verse and the third in prose. MS K contains an example of the first redaction in verse, of which more than sixty manuscripts survive.[16] The version in MS K consists of nearly 6,600 lines arranged in octosyllabic rhyming couplets and is divided into three parts, each of which is further divided into chapters. The text begins with the creation of the universe and the primacy of the Creator. Throughout the *Image du monde*, Gossuin relates the pursuit of knowledge about the universe to the pursuit of knowledge of the Creator, to understanding God through His creation. The second part, made up of nineteen chapters, explains geography as well as the unusual people and animals of different regions of earth. The third part discusses astronomy and the role of the "philosophers" Ptolemy, Vergil, and Plato in the transfer of knowledge—*translatio studii* being an important theme of the work outlined in the first section. In this way, the progression of the text moves from the divine, down to the mundane on earth—a focal point and the lowest position of God's creation—and finally ascends through the cosmos to return once more to the divine.

The remaining texts in the codex respond to the second part of the *Image du monde* by presenting the mundane: primarily animals in the *Isopet*—although there are some people, as will be seen shortly—and people in the fabliaux and *dit*. The use of the octosyllabic couplet is common to all of the texts, further linking them together as components of an ordered compilation. The manuscript mimics the descent at the beginning of the *Image du monde* that begins with the Creator and moves toward the earth. In this way, the fables and fabliaux are subordinate to the *Image du monde* but still a part of the same creation. While the relationship between the *Image du monde* and the *Isopet* evinces a preoccupation with didacticism, if not morality,[17] the rapport between the *Image du monde* and the fabliaux, as well as between the fabliaux and the fables, proves more complex. An analysis of the fabliaux in relation to these texts will expose the implicit structure of the manuscript.

In MS K the fables of Marie de France and the fabliaux are not only preserved within the same part of the codex, they are intermingled. The similarities between fables and fabliaux invite comparison because they are related by their etymology,[18] as well as by their common octosyllabic form and their apparent lessons. The taxonomic imprecision for terms such as fable and fabliau in the Middle Ages often promotes confusion among these works, especially since a few fabliaux are referred to as "fable," even in this manuscript.

MS K specifically calls into question the relation of fables and fabliaux because they are represented similarly throughout the second half of the manuscript: few elements of the *mise-en-page* distinguish the two types of works, they have similar illustrations, and, as previously mentioned, they are linked by the curious placement of certain fabliaux among the *Isopet*. I will attempt to show that the placement of the fabliaux among the fables is intentional for the purpose of thematic comparison and judgment for a medieval audience, and that it also invites intergeneric comparison for a modern audience. The insertion of *Celui qui bota la pierre* (f. 78v) and *La Coille noire* (f. 92r) before the *explicit* of the *Isopet* suggests a deliberate mixing of genres. Moreover, the double representation of the "Matron of Ephesus" theme—the fable, "La Femme qui fit pendre son mari" (f. 69) and the fabliau titled *Cele qui se fist foutre sur la fosse de son mari* (f. 95)—reinforces this intergeneric commentary. An examination of these fabliaux in relation to contiguous fables, and in the larger context of the codex, will highlight the defining characteristics of the fabliaux and their role in the codex. An analysis of the inversions and related poetic devices common to fables and fabliaux will suggest that these devices have different functions in each type of text. In the fables, chiasmus reinforces the message that the tale illustrates, whereas in the fabliaux, chiasmus calls into question the ostensible lessons of the text and invites interpretation.

Celui qui bota la pierre and Fables

The first fabliau in the codex included among the *Isopet* is *Celui qui bota la pierre* (f. 78v), which is preceded by "L'Home qui avoit feme tencheresse" (95), and followed by "La Contrarieuse" (94).[19] These two fables are themselves unusual because they involve humans instead of animals. Pearcy has classified them as fabliaux, albeit transitional ones, and refers to this group specifically as "ruses d'une femme" [women's tricks] tales because of the domestic oppositions they portray.[20] The three texts form a thematic grouping, since they depict a dispute or battle of wills between a husband and his wife. In all three stories, the husband punishes his wife for her wrong-doing. The severity of the punishment differs in each case, as does the role of inversion and chiasmus.

In "L'Home qui avoit feme tencheresse," a man with a contrary wife goes to work with his men, who ask him for some food. The husband replies that they must ask his wife themselves, for it would be worse for them if he asked ("pis lur sereit, s'il i alast," 12). The men ask the wife for food and tell her that her husband does not want any. The wife then offers to bring the men some food with the condition that they alone enjoy themselves ("haiter") and not give any food to her husband. As she brings the food, she tells the men again to enjoy themselves ("pensez del haitié"), to which her husband happily responds that they all will. Angered by her husband's happiness, the wife leaves, but her husband follows her some distance to the river where she falls in. When the other men try to save her, the husband declares that they should look for her upstream, since she was so contrary all her life, even in death she must have fought the current. The final message of the fable warns that people who are contrary and continuously argue against their lord/husband will eventually incur his bitter revenge (f. 78r, 51–58).[21]

In Pearcy's reading of this text, the husband tricks the wife into bringing the food by taking advantage of her contrariness and telling his men to say that he does not want anything.[22] The harsh lesson of the tale invites the audience to side with the husband, a conclusion which is supported by the wife's behavior against her husband. The husband's humorous comment about the wife's floating upstream is very much like a fabliau commentary inasmuch as a witty remark is used to defuse the seriousness of the situation. The objectionable wife has received her comeuppance, which in this case is severe: death. The primacy of oppositions in the text relates it to fabliaux, but the severity of the punishment by drowning removes any levity common to the fabliaux. The audience's sympathy lies with the husband precisely because the narrator mentions that the wife is "mult tenceresse, / De male part e felenesse" (3–4). Her own words and actions against her husband confirm this description; not only does she conspire (or attempt to conspire) with the other men not to let her husband eat and enjoy himself, but she also mockingly reminds the other men of her plan in his presence: "pensez del haitié" (26). The word "haiter" appears in the text in different forms, as an *adnominatio*, which forms part of a chiasmus. After the men have asked the wife for food:

A   Cil s'en alerent *l*̈*ement*,
     Elle les sui hastivement,
     Viande et boivre leur porta;
B   Que <u>haitié</u> fussent, ceo lur proia.
// Ensemble assistrent au manger.
B' "Pensez," fait ele, "del <u>haiter</u>!"
     "Si ferons nos," fait ses barons,
     "E grant merci [que] nos l'avons."
A' Quant ele vit son seignor *lié*,
     Mult ot le cuer triste e irié. (f. 78r, 21–30, emphasis added)

[The men went away happily and she followed them hastily and brought them food and drink; she beseeched them to be joyful. They sat down to eat together. "Remember," she said, "to be joyful!" "We will," said her husband, "and many thanks that we are." When she saw that her lord/husband was happy, her heart was sad and angry.]

Both *adnominationes* of the chiasmus *l*̈*ement*/<u>haitié</u>//<u>haiter</u>/*lié* highlight the idea of happiness; "lié" is from the Latin LAETUS meaning "joyful," and "haitié" is of Germanic (Frankish) origin and also means "joyful."[23] The chiasmus presents a transition from the men, to whom the terms A, B, and B' are applied, to the husband (A') who is finally "lié." The pivot of the chiasmus unites the men, including the husband, when they all sit down to eat together ("ensemble"), and in this way supports Pearcy's reading of the text where tricks played by the husband punish his wife. Not only does the husband's happiness contradict the wife's intention, but it stands in contrast to her own sadness ("mult ot le cuer triste e irié"). In Old French, the word "irié" may mean both "angry" and "sad," the second meaning, in conjunction with "triste," provides a fitting parallel to the two terms of joy, "lié" and "haitié," used for the men. The rhyme "lié/irié" reinforces the contrast between husband and wife, showing their opposition to each other because his happiness corresponds to her sadness.

The wife's contrary nature is further illustrated in another chiasmus, after she has fallen into the river. As the other men search for her:

A *aval l'eve corent* adés
   . . . .
B, C Contre l'eve **la** doivent **quere**,
// [La] la pourront trover a tere,
C' La **la querunt**, si feront bien;
B' [Tant ert] encontre toute rien
A' [Qu'*aval*] *l'eve n'est pas alee*. (38, 43–47, emphasis added)[24]

[They immediately run downstream. . . . They should search upstream for there they will find her on the ground; they would do well to search for her there; she was so contrary to everything in life that she did not go downstream.]

The antonyms "aval" and "encontre" denote the opposition in this chiasmus. These two prepositions also suggest a transition from the men to the wife; in the first term of the chiasmus, the men are running "aval l'eve," but in the second instance it is the wife who is said not to drift "aval l'eve." This chiasmus echoes the previous one because the application of the terms of the chiasmus shifts from the men to the wife, just as it shifted from the men to the husband in the previous example. The word "encontre" also indicates a transition, because in the first instance it refers to the water and in the second to the wife who was "encontre toute rien." In this way, the structure of the verses supports the husband's triumph over his mean and contrary wife.

The motion in this passage expresses the idea of opposition. The negation in the final line "aval l'eve n'est pas alee" and the pivot of the chiasmus, "la la pourront trover a tere," refer to the wife's being motionless in death, which stands in contrast to both the water's movement and to the men's running and searching for her. Her immobility underscores her opposition to the other characters and to the natural world. The final line is an example of *adynaton*, a figure of exaggeration that passes beyond the limits of possibility.[25] The single *adynaton* of the fable serves a comic function and shows that the wife, according to her husband, is in opposition to nature. This impossibility remains verbal, for it is the husband's indirect conjecture about his wife and is never actualized.[26] Throughout the poem the wife is shown as out of place and in opposition to others and to nature, so her punishment is justified. As Pearcy has argued, the husband takes advantage of reversals in logic in order to punish his wife. The syntactic reversals in this story reinforce this reading and close the text to different interpretations. The structure and the syntax both encourage the audience to understand the husband's point of view. In this way, the fable embodies the message of the final lines concerning argumentative people who incur punishment, which is supported throughout by the use of chiasmus.[27] Thus, the use of chiasmus in this fable does not open the text to interpretive possibilities, but rather it indicates and supports a single interpretation.

The fabliau that follows this fable of the contrary wife, *Celui qui bota la pierre*, shows consequences for wrong-doing that are less severe than in the fable. The story begins with a child "molt medisans" (2) [very untruthful/malicious] who sits by the fire observing his oblivious mother ("de lui mie ne se gardoit" (18) [she hardly took care of him or she was hardly aware of him]). One day while the husband is out working, a priest, who is an acquaintance of the wife, passes by the house. The wife starts to push a rock with her foot; the priest then threatens her by saying that if she does not stop this, he will take advantage her ("foutre"). The wife is only too willing to defy the priest and the two of them go into the house, where the couple's young son witnesses the entire scene. When the husband returns home and tries to move the rock, the child quickly warns him of the consequences that befell his mother and thus reveals her misdeed. The husband beats his wife, and the moral of the story is not to trust children or fools (109–14). In the other version of this fabliau in MS B, there is no question of a physical beating, the tale merely ends with the child's warning, which is essentially humorous.[28] The version in this manuscript emphasizes the wife's punishment, thereby assimilating it more with the fables.

The first deception in the tale between the wife and the priest, as Pearcy states, "is clearly meant to obfuscate the distinction between imposed punishment and voluntary compliance," and constitutes the text's first sophistical *mise en jeu*.[29] The child then continues this linguistic inversion by repeating it and applying it falsely to his father. As in the preceding tale, the wife receives her comeuppance, this time for making her husband a cuckold. At the end of the fabliau, the husband "pour chasti ne pour ses cous / Ne remaindra qu'il ne soit cous" (107–8) [even with reprimands and blows, he couldn't not be a cuckold]. The rhyme "cous/cous" (coup/cocu) [blow/cuckold], while imitating the sound "coucou" signifying the cuckold, also reinforces the idea that beating his wife will not change his being made a cuckold, the real coup of the tale. The final "cous" [blow] is also an echo of the "coup" of the sexual act—which is represented metaphorically throughout the tale as the beating of a drum—because the priest "la bese a chaucun cop qu'il fiert" (51) [kisses her with every blow he strikes]. Considering the lesson about not trusting children or fools, there is a seeming disparity between the punished character and the one to whom the moral applies. The tale does not embody one interpretation of the proverb as it did in the fable.[30] The punishment of both the husband and wife supports the ambiguity of the final message and the inversion the tale thereby creates.

At the beginning of the fabliau, the narrator informs the audience that the husband:

A Ala un jor en son *labor*.
B La dame, qui ot le tabour
B' A coi li prestres tabouroit
A' Que que li preudom *labouroit*,
    Fu soule remese en maison. (9–13, emphasis added)

[One day, he went to work. The lady, who had the drum on which the priest would drum while the man was working, remained alone in the house.]

The chiasmus involving the *adnominationes labor*/tabour//tabouroit/*labouroit* establishes the parallel between the husband's work, "labor," and the metaphorical "tabour" of the wife and the priest. The word "tabour" literally refers to a drum, but here the act of drumming serves as a metaphor for the sexual act. In the chiasmus the husband and wife are in opposition. Through the use of the word "tabour," the chiasmus shifts focus from the husband to the priest. Later in the tale, another chiasmus opposes the priest and the husband:

A li preudon *s'en vint courant*
B De la ou il ot labouré;
B' Et cil, qui avoit tabouré
    Au tabor qui resonne quas
    Pour ce qu'il est fendus trop bas,
A' *S'en fu alés* tout maintenant. (70–75, emphasis added)

[The man arrived at a run from the place where he had been working; and he who had drummed on the drum that sounds muffled because it is cut too low, left right away.]

Since the previous chiasmus established a parallel between "labouré" and "tabouré," the poetic opposition is no longer between husband and wife, but between the two men. The verbal antonyms signifying arriving ("s'en vint courant") and going ("s'en fu alés") reinforce the opposition of the men; one man fully serves as a substitute for the other, which was only suggested in the preceding chiasmus.

The substitution of working for drumming hinges in part on the rhyme "labour/tabour." The expression "boute la pierre," which becomes the wife and priest's metaphor for the sexual act, almost rhymes with "foute ma mere,"[31] the phrase the child uses to describe what he has witnessed. The interplay of rhyme and semantic substitution is specific to this fabliau, for in the fable "L'Home qui avoit feme tencheresse," the rhyme "lié/iriée" merely reinforced the contrast between husband and wife; the two emotions were never reversed or exchanged. Nolan notes the interplay of the sacred and profane in this fabliau, explaining that the rock ("pierre") "will be the material device by which the priest wins the lady's assent to go to bed with him. At the same time, the rock as 'pierre' reminds us of the priest's sacred vows ... *moving* the rock thus becomes, in the priest's sacrilegious game, a 'sin' for which sex will be the penance."[32] Nolan also calls attention to the language of the priest as an extension of the sacred metaphor for the profane act; when the priest is ready to leave, he tells the wife: "a vos soupli / Autresint comme a un autel" [I bow to you as to an altar] (54–55).[33] What Nolan refers to as mere jokes and puns in the fabliau are also the distinguishing characteristics of the tale's discourse, where words have both literal and metaphorical meanings. The misunderstanding of these meanings allows the wife to entertain the priest and the child to pass this information along to his father.[34] Even though the semantic reversals and substitutions of the fabliau echo the *adynaton* of the fable, the language of the fabliau surpasses the literal level of meaning employed in the fable. The fabliau already exploits ambiguity of meaning at the level of the single word.

The final lesson of *Celui qui bota* is ambiguous in that it may be applied to almost all of the characters. At first it would seem that in order for the final proverb to fit the narrative, it must be applied to either the wife or the priest, since they ought to have been aware of the child. The lesson at the end of the fabliau warns "que l'en se gart dou petit eulg" (110) [that one should beware of the small eye]; the verb "garder" repeats a word from the beginning of the story where the audience learns that the mother "de lui [l'enfant] mie ne se gardoit" (18) [she hardly took care of him or she was hardly aware of him]. The repetition of this verb suggests that the lesson is best applied to the mother, and this reading is reinforced by the fable "L'Home qui avoit feme tencheresse," where the final lesson and the punishment concern the wife. The ambiguity of the verb also lends itself to different interpretations, for the mother is either oblivious to her child, or else she does not think he poses a threat to her enjoyment. In any event, the fabliau inverts the relationship established in the previous fable between unsympathetic woman and practical lesson, since the lesson of *Celui qui bota* concerns a (somewhat) sympathetic female character, who is not portrayed as quarrelsome like the woman of the fable.

Although the lesson may also correspond to the priest's situation, the primary theme of opposition between husband and wife found in both the preceding and following fables, as well as in this text, suggests that the lesson ought to be applied to one of them. Moreover, since the priest does not receive any punishment for his actions, it follows that the lesson should not apply to him. Nevertheless, if the moral exemplifies the husband's situation, meaning that he should have been on his guard against what the child said, the result is a contradiction between the events of the story and the lesson derived from it. The child is being honest, if a bit eager, when he tells his father what his mother has done, and so he should be believed. The child's tale is essentially a recapitulation of the narrator's own tale, of the fabliau. It is possible to understand the lesson broadly and apply it to the husband because his believing the child does little good to him or his wife. In this example, vengeance serves little or even no purpose. Nevertheless, the ambiguity of the lesson indicates that the fabliau does not necessarily moralize, or at least it does not do so directly.

As the tale does not illustrate the lesson, at least not without some interpretation of the lesson, it thus constitutes the second type of inversion outlined in chapter 1. The use of an ill-fitting proverb is visible in the broader fable tradition of antiquity, where it was more strictly relegated to jokes.[35] The child in this tale unwittingly relates a joke through his warning to his father: "Laissiez la pierre toute, / Que nostres prestres ne vos foute, / Ausint com il fouti ma mere," (89–91) [Leave the stone alone so that our priest does not screw you as he screwed my mother]. The joke has been made the object of the narrative and in this way differs from the preceding fable where the husband's "joke" or comic commentary illustrated his wife's contrariness and served the final message. In this fabliau the joke, which is the literal interpretation of figurative language, is the narrative end, not the means.[36] In spite of the weight given to punishment in this version, the combination of the erotic elements, including language, the use of chiasmus to enable semantic substitutions, and the deliberately ambiguous and nonmoralizing lesson of the story all distinguish this work from the fable.

The fable that follows is "La Contrarieuse," which resembles the previous fable, "L'Home qui avoit feme tencheresse," because it also involves a disagreeable wife. While out walking one day, a man comments on how evenly scythed ("fauchez") the grass in the field is, whereas his wife maintains that it was cut ("tunduz") with shears. The two go back and forth and the argument escalates until the husband cuts out his wife's tongue and then mockingly asks her again if the grass was sheared or scythed, to which she responds by gesturing with her fingers that it was cut with shears. The moral of the fable is not to correct a stupid person ("fols") who says something foolish, for it will only make him angry and more forceful in imposing his lie.

Continuing the thematic unity of the previous two texts, this fable shows that the consequences for a woman's disagreement are also physical, but more severe than in the fabliau. The idea of stupidity ("folie") and specifically of a stupid person ("fols") is introduced by the lesson of the fabliau: "De fol et de petit effant / Se fait touz jors mout bon garder" (112–13). The husband himself in this fable calls his wife a "fole provee" (13) [proven fool], and the narrator introduces her as "contrarïouse" (2) [contrary]. Not only does the wife respond "hastivement" (8) [hastily] to contradict her husband, but even after her tongue is cut out—cut just as she insists the meadow is—she continues to argue. The argument is based on contraries; Pearcy claims that "La Contrarieuse" involves an irresolvable problem where cutting a lawn with a scythe or with shears are mutually exclusive practices. Their dispute does not involve "any shift in the system of truth-values," which is central to his definition of a fabliau, but rather this dispute "establish[es] the characters of the protagonists."[37] During the argument, the husband says to his wife:

> A   tu iés si *engrese* e fole
> B, C   [Que avant] velz metre **ta parole**,
> C', B'   **La moie** velz faire remaindre,
> A'   Par *engresté* la vels esteindre. (15–18, emphasis added)[38]

[You are so mean and stupid that you want to promote your remark and discredit mine, you want to stifle it (my remark) with anger.]

The opposition between husband and wife apparent in this chiasmus shows the wife's "engresté" [anger] as the cause of the dispute. The mirrored syntax of the phrases "avant velz metre **ta parole**/**la moie** velz fere remaindre" suggests that the wife's "parole" precedes her husband's, but this chiasmus is part of his direct speech and in the text he is the first to speak. The husband's direct speech reinforces the narrator's earlier description of the wife. The second line of this passage, introduced by the adjective "fole" of the preceding line and referring to the wife, echoes the end of the fable where the "[fols] veut sa **mençonge** metre avant" (35). This line reverses the syntax of the husband's speech while changing the wife's "parole" into a "mençonge" and thereby suggests that she is in the wrong. Nevertheless, the epimythium may also refer to the wife because of her husband's anger. At the beginning of the fable, "s'est li vilains *irascuz*" (12) when his wife contradicts him, and at the end, the moral states that a foolish man does not know reason when he hears it and "ainz s'en *aïre*" (33). While it was the wife who was "iriée" in "L'Home qui avoit feme tencheresse," here it is the husband. The narrator does not explain how the meadow was cut, so there is no external evidence to prove one character's position, except the final lesson that implies that the husband was wrong. Given that the husband enacts his anger so violently against his wife, it appears that the lesson could also be applied to the wife for arguing with him. Just as the lesson of the fabliau was applicable to more than one character, so the message of "La Contrarieuse" is valid for both husband and wife. The fable does not instruct by providing an example to be emulated and followed, but rather functions as a negative *exemplum* illustrating how not to act. Moreover, the lesson of the fabliau *Celui qui bota*, "que l'en se gart dou petit eulg / Autresint bien comme del grant" (110–11), is applicable to this fable, if not even more appropriate than for the fabliau. The phrase introducing the lesson of the fabliau, "par ceste fable moustrer voilg" (109) [by this fable I want to show], is identical to the types of phrases Marie routinely uses to introduce her fables. Consequently, the placement of this fable after the fabliau, following its particularly relevant final lines, suggests a deliberate interlude and intratextual commentary in this manuscript between fables and fabliau that underscores the inappropriateness of the lesson in the fabliau. Moreover, the generic interplay of these texts also suggests that the fable, like the fabliau, is perhaps more fluid and ambiguous than previously considered.

The prevalence of small thematic groupings observed in other anthologies of fabliaux discussed in chapter 1 is also common to MS K, but in this instance the group of "punished wives" is inserted among the *Isopet*, where two of the texts form part of Marie's fable collection and where *Celui qui bota* intrudes. The placement of *Celui qui bota* deliberately exposes these thematic relations among the texts as it also highlights the similarities between fables and fabliaux more than the generic differences. Indeed, the ending of this version of *Celui qui bota* strongly resembles the fables, while the fables expose oppositions, often through chiasmus, in a manner similar to the fabliaux. Pearcy argues that these types of fables are proto-fabliaux and show a phase of the genre's development.[39] Although the manuscript organization deliberately blends fables and fabliaux at this juncture, there are still some observable differences.

One of the differences in these examples involves the severity of the punishment as well as the correspondence between the narrative and the stated lesson. The women in the fables either die or are tortured, though the morals tend to favor the husbands, whereas in the fabliau the situation is reversed because the husband also receives a form of punishment in being made a cuckold. At the semantic level, the fabliau contains words related to the erotic, such as "foute" and "le tabour" that are not found in these fables, but it also capitalizes on *aequivocatio*[40] and uses the words metaphorically, as opposed to the literal usage of language in the fables. What further distinguishes this fabliau from the fables is the specific usage of the devices *adnominatio* and chiasmus.

The deployment of rhetorico-poetic devices in the fables "L'Home qui avoit feme tencheresse" and "La Contrarieuse" differs markedly from their use in *Celui qui bota*. In the fables, chiasmus reveals the opposition between husband and wife, whereas in the fabliau it exploits linguistic inversions and substitutions, which both render the husband and the priest interchangeable and also place them in opposition to each other. In this way, the fabliau uses chiasmus for character and plot development whereas the fables use it merely for character exposition. Furthermore, the use of rhymes and *adnominationes* in the fabliau emphasizes the interplay of the opposing pairs sacred and profane, a level of opposition that is absent from the fables. Words in the fabliau function simultaneously on a literal and metaphorical level of meaning, so that "labour" becomes a metaphor for the sexual term "tabour," which is itself already a figurative expression; in "L'Home qui avoit feme tencheresse," however, words, such as "labour," retain their literal meaning. Most significantly, these types of texts differ because the lesson of the fabliau is not the immediate result of the events of the story, whereas in the fables, the moral explains and even provides the logical conclusion to characters' behavior. As Jürgen Beyer asserts, at the center of the fables is the message or the proof of how the world is, whereas at the center of the fabliau is the plot and the unfolding of the narrative, not a message.[41] Perhaps more to the point, at the center of the fabliau is a message about the nature of narrative. The child's "joke" in *Celui qui bota* is the joke of the whole fabliau and creates a kind of mise en abyme, which is absent from fables, but which will become integral to the way the *Decameron* operates.

La Coille noire and Fables

The second fabliau that precedes the epilogue of the *Isopet* is *La Coille noire* (f. 92r). Inserted near the end of the collection of fables, after "Le Chat mitré" (f. 91v) and right before the last fable "La Femme et la poule" (f. 93r), *La Coille noire* is one of the more scatological fabliaux. The titles of the works alone signal a remarkable difference between these fables and the previous two considered in association with *Celui qui bota*, namely the presence of animals. This grouping of texts does not suggest the same thematic unity as the previous section of fables and fabliau. As opposed to the previous grouping where the boundaries between fable and fabliau were blurred, in this grouping there are few similarities between the two types of stories. Whether *La Coille noire* was intentionally placed among these fables, or whether this placement signals a copyist's error cannot be known for certain. The following analysis, however, will feature the generic disparity between fables and fabliaux.

The first fable, "Le Chat mitré," illustrates a cat's attempt to trick and eat a pair of mice. Lying in wait all day until he sees a couple of mice, the cat charmingly calls them over and explains that he is their bishop and that they would do well to receive a blessing (or the sacrament of confirmation) from him. The mice exclaim they would rather die than be caught between the cat's claws, so they run away and hide in a wall, unable to move. The moral explains that: "Nus ne se doit mestre en justise / De celui qui mal lui velt querre, / Mes destorner en autre terre," (20–22) [No one should place himself in the hands of someone who seeks to do him harm, but instead should turn to another place].

Unlike the fables previously discussed, this fable has no punishment; instead it shows an unsuccessful trick. In spite of the cat's mellifluous words, the mice are saved by their innate mistrust of the cat, "car il le sevent a felon" (18) [for they know him to be a traitor]. The inherent contrast in the rhymed pair "beneïçon/felon" (17–18) [benediction/traitor] reinforces the notion of a trick. The opposition between cat and mouse needs little explanation, since it is in their nature as the following chiasmus shows:

A asez *voloient mielz* **morir**
B Que **desouz ses ongles venir**.
C <u>Les souriz s'en tornent fuiant,</u>
C' <u>E li chaz les [vet] enchaçant.</u>
B' En la paroi **se sont fichiees**:
A' *Mielz [i] veulent* **estre muciees**. (9–14, emphasis added)

[They would much rather die than come beneath his claws. The mice turn and flee and the cat chases them. They are caught in the wall: they prefer to hide there.]

The mice are at the center of the chiasmus, or rather their escape from the cat is, as "morir" becomes "mucier." The pivot of the chiasmus also marks the central point of the narrative—it is the midpoint of the twenty-two-line text—because the mice "s'en <u>tornent</u> fuiant." The verb "torner" reinforces the idea of a narrative and chiastic pivot, while shifting the focus from the cat to the mice. The repetition of the verb "destorner" in the final line confirms the application of the lesson to the mice. The terms "morir" and "desouz ses ongles venir" are practically synonymous in the context, as are the terms "se sont fichiees" and "estre muciees." The parallel between these two pairs of synonyms further highlights the opposition between the cat and the mice. This chiasmus establishes semantic substitutions that are euphemisms for death. The entire fable depends on the substitution of one word for another, often with a more sinister meaning. Thus, the cat's "beneïçon" could only be associated with killing and eating the mice. Such figurative use of language is made explicit not only through the situation but also by the narrator who explains that the cat "dist que leur eveques fu" (5) [said he was their bishop] and by the chiasmus that highlights the cat's intentions. As in *Celui qui bota*, this fable mixes the sacred and profane, where the cat's hunger is equivalent to the priest's sexual appetite, but unlike the priest, the cat does not have his appetite satisfied. In this respect, "Le Chat mitré" shares elements common to one fabliau in the manuscript, while still retaining the essential characteristics of fables by using animal characters and illustrating their nature.

In the fabliau *La Coille noire* "une mout orguelleuse dame" (2) [a very disdainful lady] discovers that her husband's sexual organs are black. She seeks a divorce from him for this abnormality and she embarrasses him in court before the bishop of Paris with this revelation, even claiming "que por ce ne puis concevoir" (67) [that for this reason I cannot conceive].[42] The husband, however, avenges himself by accusing his wife of using too much straw for "torchons" (101) [rags for bathroom use], to which she responds that she has not used straw or anything else in over a year, hence, as the husband explains, the reason his organs are black. The final lesson of the tale explains: "Que fame ne fait pas savoir / Qui son seignor a en despit, / Por noire coille et por noir vit, / Car autant de force a une noire / Comme a une blanche por voire" (116–20) [That a woman who scorns her lord/husband for having a black testicle and a black member, not make it known, since a black one truly has as much force as a white one]. This fabliau offers an inversion of justice through language. In addition to the reversal of justice, however, the fabliau turns on an inversion, or rather perversion, of nature, since the husband's genitals should logically be white. In this tale the wife receives her comeuppance in the form of an embarrassing remark. Although the mention of a bishop connects this tale to the fable "Le Chat mitré," the bishop plays little part in the meting out of justice in this text. The verbal quid pro quo between the husband and wife establishes a balance not present in the preceding tales, with the possible exception of "La Contrarieuse." While the situation in itself may be considered comic, the humor derives from the character's own words. The discourse belongs to the court and legal matters as the characters speak of their "afaire," "plait," as well as "ancuser," "semondre," and "tesmoigner" to mention but a few examples. In this fabliau the characters and the narrator emphasize their truthful words in unlikely or implausible situations. The wife's immediate reaction to her husband's abnormality extends more than a dozen lines—the entire text is only

120 lines—during which she exclaims, "honie sui et morte . . . dolante en sui et esgaree" (20, 24) [I am ashamed and dead . . . I am mournful about it and disoriented]. Even the husband's victory depends on the wife's own words; "plus a d'un an que ne fu ters / Mes cus de fain ne d'autre rien" (104–5) [it has been more than a year since my bottom was wiped with straw or anything else]. The wife thereby incriminates herself. In this way, the narrative reversal is achieved through spoken language.

The question of justice in the story relates to the question of truth, specifically through the wife's speech, in which she not only assures the court that she is speaking the truth, "iceste est verité prouvee" (66) [this is proven truth],[43] but seeks it from her husband, "et verité li demandasse / Por qu'ele [la coille] est plus noire que blanche" (97) [and she asked him for the truth about why it was more black than white]. The narrator also tells the public that "c'est or la voire" (6) [now this is the truth] in reference to the wife's disdainful reaction, and again at the end of the tale he concludes, "ce sai de voir" (120) [I know it to be true], that black organs have as much "force" as white. Truthful words, this time from the narrator, incriminate the wife in order to serve the ironic justice of the story against "une mout orguelleuse dame." This fabliau differs from the others because within the tale an audience, the court of justice, reacts with laughter to the wife's words. Thus, the (courtly) audience of the fabliau parallels the courtly audience within the tale, and both are asked to judge the case.

Although it also capitalizes on natural oppositions, there is no call to judgment in "Le Chat mitré," and consequently no question of debate. While the appeals to truth throughout the fabliau distinguish it from "Le Chat mitré," in both instances the lying characters—the cat and the wife through exaggeration—are contradicted by the narrator. These characters are ultimately disappointed in their claims. Linked by the theme of lying, *La Coille noire* and "Le Chat mitré" nevertheless clearly set themselves apart as fable and fabliau respectively.

The final fable revisits the theme of nature because it illustrates that one cannot change one's habits. In "La Femme et la poule," a woman offers to give her hen as much grain as she would like so that the hen will not need to scratch and search for food on the ground. The hen replies that regardless of her needs, she would act the same way because it is in her nature to do so. As the moral explains: "plusors genz puent trover / [Manaie e] ce qu'il ont mestier, / Mes il ne puent pas changier / Lor nature ne lor usage; / Touz jors [avive] en lor courage" (22–26) [Many people can get money and what they need, but they cannot change their nature nor their habits; these always intensify in their hearts]. This fable mixes humans and animals, putting them on the same level inasmuch as they speak to each other. There is not so much a lesson here as an explanation of behavior. The repetition of the words "us" and "usage" underscores the role of habit and nature. These are further linked through the hen's explanation about looking for food which she does "selonc ma nature, selonc mon us" (20) [according to my nature, according to my habit]. The even rhythm and balance of this line are repeated in the final lesson, reinforcing the notion that people cannot change "lur nature ne lor usage." The language is remarkable for the use of puns, such as the pair "us/us" (2, 20) meaning "door/habit," as well as the pair "grant/grant" meaning "big/give." If the story demonstrates that people will follow their natural inclinations just as the hen does, then it seems a fitting introduction to the fabliaux on the following folios where natural appetites abound.

In this grouping of texts, the fabliau clearly deploys a narrative reversal, when the wife is humiliated for embarrassing her husband, and a logical fallacy that connects the husband's discolored genitals to his wife's statement about being unclean. The black "coille" represents an anomaly of nature. The two fables, on the other hand, resemble each other in that each conforms to the audience's expectations of nature. These fables depict the instinctive sagacity of the weaker character; the mice know not to let the cat/bishop "bless/confirm" them, while the hen is aware that her nature and habits are stronger than culture. In this way, the fables support logical conclusions about the natural world, whereas the fabliau defies them. Moreover, both of the fables involve animals, making them more typical fables than the previous two examples, but also distinguishing them further from the fabliau. *La Coille noire* relates a playful verbal trick between a husband and wife, whereas neither fable has a successful trick. If anything, *La Coille noire* resembles the previous grouping in which husbands counteracted and punished the "ruses d'une femme." In this respect, the inclusion of *La Coille noire* among the fables lends itself to comparisons with the previous grouping, while also underscoring the distinction between the fables and fabliaux.

Intratextuality in MS K: The "Matron of Ephesus" Theme as Fable and Fabliau

The second remarkable feature of this codex, in addition to the two fabliaux inserted among Marie de France's *Isopet*, involves the theme of the "Matron of Ephesus," which is represented in two distinct versions, one fable, "La Femme qui fit pendre son mari" (25), and one fabliau, *Cele qui se fist foutre sur la fosse de son mari*. Since the topos is essentially the same in both cases with only a few minor plot variations, the substantial generic differences are not played out thematically but rather in the language of the text, or more specifically, in the poetic devices. In the fable, chiasmus is self-reinforcing, while chiasmus in the fabliau undermines the narrative. Pearcy has shown that this is one of a few fabliaux whose source in fable literature is known. Uncharacteristically, both the fable and the fabliau take advantage of logical fallacies. For this reason, looking beyond the notion of logical fallacies reveals the distinctive characteristics of each type of text.[44]

The "Matron of Ephesus" theme concerns a widow who is seduced by another man at her husband's gravesite. The topos was widely known in the twelfth and thirteenth centuries and existed in various forms.[45] The two versions of the topos in MS K share some striking similarities, most notably in the role of the young man as seducer, as opposed to other versions where the widow is the seductress.[46] Marie de France's fable, which is relatively short at forty lines, begins with the widow grieving night and day at her husband's tomb and mentions that nearby is the body of a hanged-man (a thief). The penalty for burying the hanged-man is death by hanging, but in spite of this interdiction, one of the thief's relatives, a knight, buries the body and soon needs to extricate himself from a death sentence. The knight returns to the cemetery, quickly seduces the widow, and then explains his situation to her and asks for her help, lest he be hanged or forced to flee. The widow offers to use her husband's body in place of the hanged-man's, justifying this action by an appeal to the rights of the living over those of the dead: "delivrer doit on par le mort / Le vif dont on atent confort" (35–36) [Through death we ought to free the living from whom we receive comfort].

The other version of this topos, the fabliau *Cele qui se fist*, is slightly different: a young woman is suddenly left widowed and very noticeably demonstrates her grief to all, refusing even to leave her late husband's tomb despite the efforts of her family to console her. While she laments her loss at the cemetery, a knight and his squire pass by and witness the scene. The knight expresses his pity for the woman to his friend. The squire, however, not only feels no pity, but makes a wager with the knight that he can seduce the widow in a few minutes. The knight accepts the wager and hides nearby while the squire approaches the widow and explains that he is even more upset than she is because he killed his lady "en fotant" [in screwing]. The widow responds by asking the squire to kill her in the same way and the story ends with the narrator's comments on the inconstancy of women.

The fabliau differs from the fable in three significant (narrative) respects:

(1) there is no hanged-man and consequently no exchange of corpses. The only corpse in the story is that of the husband and it remains buried throughout the fabliau; (2) in addition to the knight there is also a squire. It is he who seduces the widow, but in this version the widow very willingly allows herself to be seduced; and (3) there is no threat of death for any character—except for the widow who vows not to leave her husband's tomb until she is dead[47]—only a wager between the squire and the knight over the seduction.

Both the fable and the fabliau employ chiasmus at crucial narrative points, but the structural effect of the device differs sharply in the two cases. The first chiasmus in the fable establishes the exchange of corpses while demonstrating the knight's motivation behind the exchange.

>   D'un home conte li escris
> A Qui estoit mors et <u>enfouis</u>,
>
>   ...
>
>   Pres d'ilec avoit un larron
> B Qui **pendus** fu par mesproison.
>   *Par la contree fu crié:*
>   *Qui le larron auroit osté,*
> // *Son jugement meisme auroit,*
>   *S'il ert ataint pendus seroit.*
> B' Un chevaliers le **despendi**;
> A' Ses parens ert, si <u>l'enfoui</u>.
>   Dont ne sot il ***conseil trover***,
>   Com il s'em peust ***delivrer***. (1–2, 5–14, emphasis added)

[The written source tells of a man who was dead and buried. . . . Near him was a thief who had been hanged for a crime. It was decreed across the land that anyone who removed the thief would have the same sentence; if he were caught, he'd be hanged. A knight, who was one of his relatives, unhanged him and buried him. Then the knight didn't know how to find help in order to free himself from trouble.]

The chiasmus formed by the paronyms *enfouis/enfoui* and **pendus/despendi** announces the dénouement of the fable. The terms *enfouis* and *pendus* [buried and hanged] are set in opposition, but **pendus/despendi** are not opposed here. The first use of the word *enfouis* (2) refers to the husband whereas the second (12) refers to the thief. This poetic exchange of the husband and thief is enacted later in the fable, such that the narrative order mimics the poetic order. The passive verbs in the first half of the chiasmus (A, B) *estoit enfouis* and *pendus fu* are transformed into active verbs (*despendi* and *enfoui*), the subject of which is the knight. This verbal transformation shows the knight's active, even calculating role in the narrative. The four-line pivot of the chiasmus represents the knight's reason for acting, namely the threatened penalty of death. This chiasmus not only outlines the rest of the narrative and introduces the notion of exchange, but it identifies the knight as the active agent behind the body switching. Within the work's chiastic logic, he who was buried will be hanged, and he who was hanged will be buried.

The rhyme of the two final lines of this passage: "Dont ne sot il **conseil trover**, / Com il s'em peust **delivrer**" connects the *conseil* [advice or help] the knight seeks with the notion of *delivrance* [freedom]. It is through *conseil* that he will be freed from being hanged himself and will be able to enact the substitution made poetically explicit in the preceding chiasmus. It is this parallel between *conseil* and *delivrance* that authorizes the second chiasmus and the dénouement.

> A S'el ne l'en set *conseil donner*,
> Hors dou païs estoit aler.
> La preude fame respondi:
> B "**Desforçons mon baron** deci,
> B' Si **le pendons** la ou cil fu,
> Si n'ert james aperceü.
> A' *Delivrer* doit on par le mort
> Le vif dont on atent confort." (29–35, emphasis added)

[If she didn't know how to help him, he would have to leave the country. The virtuous woman answered: "Let's unearth my husband from here and hang him where the other man was; no one will ever notice. Through the dead man we ought to free the living from whom we receive comfort."]

The second chiasmus is dependent on semantic substitutions established in the first chiasmus. The second terms, B and B' [unburying and hanging] reflect a semantic union and represent the physical exchange of bodies. The reversal is complete with the "undoing" of the prefix "des-" now applied to burying instead of hanging (or *foutre* as in *La Grue*, which uses the same mechanism of reversal). The use of the first person plural suggests the widow's complicity. She allows herself to be seduced by the knight's speaking "cointement" (20). The A and A' terms of the chiasmus refer to the knight's active role in seducing the woman, since he sought and found *conseil* in order to be freed. The second chiasmus plays out the substitution of burying and hanging presented in the first chiasmus. Each chiasmus serves to prefigure and reinforce the narrative structure of the fable. Moreover, most of the terms in the second chiasmus are spoken by the widow, not the narrator as in the first chiasmus, although the last two lines are ambiguous and can be attributed to either the woman or the narrator. The effect of the figure, however, is the same, to reinforce the narrative, whether expressed by the (implicit) narrator or by a character's words.

Finally, the message invites the audience to reflect on the obligations of the living to the dead: "par iceste senefiance / Pouons entendre quel fiance / Pueut auoir li mors el uis / Tant est li monde faus et faintis" (37–40) [by this meaning/story, we can understand what faith the dead can have in the living; the world is so false and fake]. The fable furnishes two examples of duty to the dead: the widow who dishonors her husband by allowing herself to be seduced and by unburying and hanging his body, and the knight who honors his duty to his thieving relative at great personal risk. The fable ultimately reinforces the antifeminism of the topos; even though the knight instigated the seduction, the widow's complicity puts her at fault. The image in MS K that accompanies this fable suggests the widow's responsibility, for it shows her lifting her husband's corpse out of a coffin with the knight's help as she eyes the empty noose over the knight's shoulder.

Whereas the fable "La Femme qui fit pendre son mari" warns about fickle women, the fabliau *Cele qui se fist* suspends moral implications in favor of laughter.[48] The fabliau is nearly three times as long as the fable, but still quite short at 117 lines (with one unrhymed line). The detailed descriptions of the widow's theatrical grieving and an increase in character dialogue account for the difference in length. From the beginning, this work lays out the question of truth. While Marie appeals to Aesop's authority at the beginning of her *Isopet*, the narrator of this fabliau places his authority in question by opposing truth to fiction when he states:

> Puisque la volenté me vient
> A, B De <u>fables</u> *dire* et il m'en tient,
> B', A' *Dirai* en leu de <u>fable</u> un **voir**. (1–3, emphasis added)[49]

[Since I have the desire to tell a story and it is my duty, I will tell in place of a fictitious story a true story.]

In this instance the word "fable" must be understood in its broadest sense of "story" or "fiction," since the narrator places it in opposition to "un voir" [a true story/history]. The first person narrator, to which no persona corresponds in the fable, promises his audience a "voir" as opposed to a "fable." Although the word "voir" is not typically a noun, nor does it usually denote a literary genre, here it clearly designates the "truth," or rather "a true story" in a broad sense, as opposed to fiction. The chiasmus of these lines reinforces the notion of fiction and thus undermines the narrator's appeal to truth by contradicting his assertions.

At the midpoint of the story, the key notion of fiction returns to undermine the claim that the narrator made at the beginning. This other evocation of fiction appears in the text as the knight and squire make their wager: "'Si dolente com el se fait, / La fouterai se vos vos traiez / En tel leu que vos le voiez'. . . . 'Mes tu as el cors le deable, / Qui controvee a si grant **fable**.' / 'En ceste **fable** gageroie / Envers vos, se gagier osoie'" (58–59, 63–66, emphasis added) ["As grieved as she seems, I'll screw her if you'll go where you can see it." . . . "You have the devil in you if you invented such a story." "I'll place a bet against you on this story, if you dare to bet"]. The social reversal this scene makes explicit between savvy squire and innocent-minded knight results in another reversal of courtly narrative: it is the squire who seduces the woman, not the knight. The squire's "fable" is precisely that of the entire tale: he seduces the widow by means of a fiction, for it is through the squire's story to the widow, in which he mixes courtly and crude registers by claiming that he killed his lady "en fotant,"[50] that death becomes a sexual metaphor. The squire proves his "fable" true by enacting it and in this way the story contains its own truth; the "fable" of the narrator is also a "voir." To say that the widow is seduced, however, is to misunderstand the character of the widow and the work as a whole. The woman's flamboyant show of grief is also clearly fiction. The work represents a complete reversal where fiction is truth and truth fiction, thereby undermining the narrator's final claim that "dame est de molt foible nature, / De noient rit, de noient pleure. . . . Qui fame croit il est desuez" (113–14, 117) [woman is of very weak nature, she laughs for nothing and cries for nothing. . . . He who believes a woman is deceived].[51] Although the widow's rapid change in behavior is ultimately explained by the inconstancy of women, established in part by the preceding text, the ill-fitting final line could only apply to the dead husband. As Pearcy has argued, the use of *aequivocatio* in this text, where both parties understand death as sex, enables the widow and the squire to indulge their sexual appetites without verbally violating any interdictions.[52]

As witness to the seduction, the knight acts as the courtly audience of the squire's fiction, and in this way parallels the audience of the fabliau. The knight's ultimate response to the squire's storytelling is not a moral judgment, but rather laughter: "qui se paumoit de ris" (103) [who fainted from laughing].

In fainting, he repeats the actions of the woman during grief and sex. Earlier in the narrative, while the widow is grieving, she faints: "Et si se paume a chacun pas" (22) [and she faints at every step], a gesture she mimics at the end of the tale when she asks the squire to kill her: "Atant se laisse cheoir outre / Ainsi com s'ele fust pasmee" (98–99) [at this she let herself fall backwards just as if she had fainted]. Thus, the response of fainting is the same for grief, sex, and laughter.

A second chiasmus sets up a link between death, grief and love:

A Et sa fame <u>qui mout l'amoit</u>
B En fu de sa *mort* mout iriee
    Mes fame s'est lues atiriee
C A plorer et a **grant duel faire**
// Quant ele a <u>un poi de contraire</u>
C' Et tost ra **grant duel oublie**
B' Quant la dame vit *devie*
A' Son seignor <u>qui tant la amee</u>
    Souvent s'est chaitive clamee. (8–16, emphasis added)

[And his wife who loved him very much was greatly saddened by his death, but woman is immediately disposed to cry and mourn deeply when she has a little annoyance and quickly jumps to forget her mourning. When the woman saw her deceased husband who loved her so, she constantly called herself miserable.]

The chiastic rhetorical structure shows that death, grief, and love form the main thematic unity of the text, but at the end all are met with laughter. Love, which causes the widow to grieve, will help her forget her grief. The relation through fainting of grief, sex, and laughter is collapsed into the final moment, thus subverting moral judgment in favor of laughter.

The narrator ends the fabliau with a generalizing statement about the inconstancy of women, but his statement fails to match up to the intricacies of the narrative itself. In the fable, the ending preserves the symmetry of death over punishment; in this text, however, pain and pleasure, the overcoming of grief and the metaphor of sexual suicide, are all joined in a single moment at the end. The moralizing terms of the fable are replaced in the fabliau by the discrepancy between the unreliable narrator and the chiastic devices that undermine the narrator's claims. The fabliau converts the "Matron of Ephesus" topos into a consciously fictional and playful work that substitutes moralizing didacticism with laughter. It also leaves open the question of accountability as to whether the squire seduced the widow, whether the widow jumped at the squire, or whether both are responsible. More to the point, the focus in the fabliau is not (overtly at least) on determining a victim and a culprit, but rather on the enjoyment of the scene as a story. By focusing on levity, the fabliau leaves the question of judgment open.

The use of chiasmus in the fable reinforces the narrative structure and invites the audience to reflect on questions of morality, specifically love, trust, and death, whereas the structure of the fabliau challenges questions of moral judgment by poetically linking the terms of morality—grief, death, and love—to laughter. Within the codex, these two texts validate the substantial ideological differences between fable and fabliau.[53] The presence of these two works in a single codex also pushes to the fore questions of interpretation. Is B. Nolan's opinion that the frivolity of the fabliau is intended as a negative exemplar to reinforce the moral issues of the fable the only valid interpretation? Or is it possible that the life-affirming fabliau questions a pessimistic anecdote by transforming it into laughter? In terms of understanding the topos within the context of MS K, it is the fabliau's deliberate interpretive ambiguity, as opposed to the closed observation and even didacticism of the fable, which encourages accepting multiple possibilities in the individual texts and in their intergeneric context. Perhaps the representation of this theme in two forms intentionally highlights the matter of choice and calls on the audience to judge not just the texts but the assembly of the codex. The generic distinctions between fable and fabliau, however, have never been more apparent than in this example where, although the same theme is exploited in both instances, the playful and comic intentionality of the fabliau distances it from the moralizing nature of the fable through a simple reversal.

The codex as a whole seems to promote judgment. The juxtaposition of didactic and entertaining works calls on the audience to interpret the relationships among the works. Although a didactic encyclopedia, the *Image du monde*, as the epigraph to this chapter shows, supports the choice of man, and thereby the audience, in determining questions of morality. While the actual audience may have been broad, the rhetorical aspects of these works would have been more accessible to a learned audience of readers who could also rewrite and transform the texts.

The "Matron of Ephesus" and Intertextuality

Another substantive difference between this thematically corresponding fable and fabliau is the fabliau's pairing of the "Matron of Ephesus" topos with the scene of Laudine's widowhood in Chrétien's *Le Chevalier au lion/Yvain*. The textual similarities show the fabliau's resemblance to Chrétien's text:[54]

(*Yvain*: Affliction de la veuve)
Mais de duel faire estoit si fole
C'a poi qu'ele ne s'ochioit.
A la feÿe s'escrioit
Si haut qu'ele ne pooit plus,
Si recheoit pasmee jus.
Et quant ele estoit relevee,
Aussi comme femme desvee
S'i commenchoit a deschirer,
Et ses chaveus a detirer.
<u>Ses chaveus tire et ront ses dras</u>,
Et se repasme a chascun pas,
Ne riens ne le puet conforter,
<u>Que son seigneur en voit porter</u>
<u>Devant li en la biere mort,</u>
<u>Dont je ne quide avoir confort:</u>
<u>Pour che crioit a haute vois.</u>
(1150–64, emphasis added)

(*Cele qui se fist foutre sur la fosse de son mari*)
Quant la dame vit devié
Son seignor, qui tant l'a amee,
Souvant s'est chaitive clamee;
De grant duel demener se paine.
Molt i emploie bien sa paine:
Ce semble a touz vers son seignor
Que ainz fame ne fist duel gregnor:
<u>Ses poinz detort et touz ses dras</u>,
Et si se paume a chacun pas.
<u>Et quant ce vint a l'enterrer</u>,
<u>Dont oisiez fame crier</u>
Et dementer et grant duel faire;
Nus ne l'en puet arieres traire.
Ainçois s'escrie desors touz.
(14–27, emphasis added)

[But she was so crazed with grief that she was on the verge of killing herself. All at once she cried out as loudly as she could and fell down in a faint. When she was lifted back to her feet, she began clawing at herself and tearing out her hair like a madwoman; her hands grabbed and ripped her clothing and she fainted with every step. Nothing could comfort her, for she could see her lord dead in the coffin being carried in front of her. She felt she could never be comforted again, and so she cried out at the top of her voice.]

[When the woman saw her dead lord, who loved her so, she often called herself wretched; she pained herself in showing great grief; she really used all her effort. It seemed to everyone that a woman had never shown greater grief toward her lord. She wrung her fists and all her clothes and she fainted at every step. And when it came time to bury him, then you heard a woman scream and grieve and show great grief; no one could pull her away. Thus she cried above everyone else.]

Even though many of the repetitions in these two passages, specifically the crying and fainting, are stock phrases associated with literary representations of widows or of emotionally distraught courtly women,[55] the fabliau is clearly a rewriting, or perhaps a parody of, *Yvain*. There are four key moments of resemblance between these texts: (1) the widow's loud crying; (2) pulling her clothing; (3) fainting at every step; and (4) being inconsolable at the time of her husband's burial. Both texts use the superlative to describe the woman's crying (*Yvain*, 1053 and fabliau, 27). Not only is the rhyme "dras/pas" [cloth/step] the same in both texts, but the two verses are quite similar. Both passages are also followed by a speech from the widow, but with entirely different purposes. The parallel between the situations is clear: Laudine must find a new knight/husband to perform a duty, namely guarding the fountain for her, and the widow of the fabliau must find a new man to perform a duty, which is ideally taking care of her and her child, but more immediately involves sex.

The most remarkable difference in the presentation of the widows' grieving is the order; in *Yvain* she cries first, then pulls her clothing, faints, etc., whereas in the fabliau the woman first pulls her clothing, faints, and then cries. The near inversion of the order highlights the parodic insincerity of the widow in the fabliau, but not without hinting at the violent excess of Landuc's widow. Furthermore, the situational inversion presented in the fabliau reinforces the notion of irony, since Laudine marries a knight, Yvain, whereas the widow of the fabliau is merely seduced by a squire. The substitutions of sex for marriage, and of a squire for a knight, mirror the situation in Marie's fable.[56] Thus, the fabliau *Cele qui se fist* is a composite of different traditions and registers of language. It is a comic reworking of the "Matron of Ephesus" theme precisely because it parodies the scene of the grieving widow Laudine in *Yvain*. The mixture of registers further highlights the use of figurative language that is common to all three fabliaux discussed thus far and which most distinguishes them from the fables. In this way, *Cele qui se fist* combines elements of different narrative forms, the widow topos in romance and in a fable, through inversions that are sociogenic in the case of *Yvain* and rhetorical and structural in relation to "La Femme qui fit pendre son mari." This particular use of inversion as combinative prefigures the fabliaux material in the *Decameron*, which also joins diverse genres together. Through inversions the fabliaux suggest interpretive ambiguity that opposes them to didactic and explanatory forms such as fables and *exempla*. The remaining fabliaux in MS K bear out these defining characteristics.

The Other Fabliaux of MS K

After the *Image du monde* and immediately after Marie de France's *Isopet*, there are a few short texts: four fabliaux and a single *dit*. The fabliaux at the end of the manuscript represent a cross-section of the genre, from the satirical and violent *Le Prestre crucifié* to the humorous and frivolous *La Vielle qui oint la paume au chevalier.* These fabliaux are connected, however, by their focus on figurative language. The first text after the *explicit* of the *Isopet* is *La Male Honte*, which relates a verbal misunderstanding. When Honte, a subject of the king of England, falls ill, he asks his friend to bring his trunk (*male*) of money to the king, as is the law. After Honte's death, his friend goes to London and tries to execute his duty by offering the king "la male Honte," which the king misunderstands to mean "foul shame" and considers an insult. After three failed attempts by the friend to approach the king using this same address, a courtier convinces the king to let the man explain himself. The king is so amused by the man's explanation and by the misunderstanding, that he rewards him with "la male Honte" [Honte's trunk].

The misunderstanding in the tale revolves around the ambiguous meaning of the phrase "la male Honte," for which Richard Spencer understands three meanings: "Honte's trunk" or "foul dishonor" or "trunk of shame."[57] Pearcy observed that this fabliau is another example of *aequivocatio*, since each word has more than one meaning.[58] Indeed, the entire story involves the choice of interpretation for two different words. This codex presents the first of two versions of *La Male Honte*, which differ little from each other in content but are attributed to two different people, a certain Guillaume and Huon de Cambrai. The focus of the tale is clearly its language, more than the situation or even the characters. The phrase "male Honte," which appears some twenty times in the text of 157 lines (the *vers orphelin* at line 29 is replaced in the critical edition), capitalizes on the homophones in Old French. The two couplets near the beginning and end of the text (8–9 and 148–49) are inversions of the same rhyme "conte/Honte" (in these instances meaning "story" and the name "Honte") that frame the events of the narrative in order to emphasize the enclosed fiction and word-play. The story involves nothing more than a play on Honte's unusual name and the ambiguity of the word "male" in Old French.

The misunderstanding is also predicated on oral transmission of information, which the work highlights through the extensive use of characters' direct speech. Nearly half the text takes the form of the direct speech of one of the characters as opposed to the narrator's voice. Ironically, it is the friend's inability to explain himself, or perhaps the king's inability to understand a *vilain* who speaks "en son language" (33) [in his language], that furnishes the subject matter and repetitious language of Guillaume's tale. While the repetition of certain words and phrases, such as "male Honte" and "conte" used to mean both "story" and "count," is essential to the comic play of the text, other terms evoke an underlying disparity between word and action, between courtly and *vilain*. Frequent references to "droit," doing what is right, reinforce the *vilain*'s sense of duty in executing the will of his deceased friend and in complying with the law. In spite of his language, the *vilain*'s actions are *courtois*. Moreover, in sharing the money with his friends, the *vilain* attempts to practice "true courtly *largece*," as Spencer terms it.[59] The opposite is true of the king's behavior, for he ungraciously refuses the gift. The end of the story, however, restores the natural order. The temporary reversals in this text of courtly and noncourtly behavior represent the sociogenic inversions in the tale that establish the basis for the linguistic reversals, ambiguity, and misunderstandings. As Spencer notes, "the king [ultimately] refuses the gift because he is *courtois*, whereas the *vilain* is its natural recipient and indeed in a sense its source, since he represents all the 'non-courtois.'"[60]

Spencer's remarks also imply that the king is, ironically, noncourtly and responsible for the misunderstanding, not that the *vilain* is incapable of relating his story. Not only does the king behave in a *vilain* manner, but the *vilain* adopts two roles out of place for his position. The *vilain* acts as both a courtly knight on a quest on behalf of his friend and as a professional storyteller, a kind of minstrel, when he narrates his misadventure. If the king is noncourtly and the friend courtly, then the characters' inverted behavior also parallels the verbal misunderstanding, or rather linguistic inversion, that is the subject of the fabliau. As a quest parody, the story takes advantage of sociogenic inversions. Nevertheless, the matter remains open as to whether the king has misunderstood the *vilain*, or whether the *vilain* is at fault for not making himself understood.

The inversion is only reversed with the *vilain*'s explanation of his mysterious phrase, one that essentially recapitulates the plot of the fabliau. Still, the *vilain* does not exactly exonerate himself, since his clarification does not take the form of direct speech, but rather is summarized by the narrator. The voice of the *vilain* is replaced by that of the *clerc*, Guillaume, and probably of a real minstrel in performance. The character of the *vilain* now resembles Guillaume, for both have narrated the same tale.[61] Thus, narration itself and the role of the *clerc* are the subjects of the tale; the point of the story is its value as a story that is open to interpretation. As in *Cele qui se fist*, the primary reversal of the tale is a linguistic inversion, but Pearcy remarks that "the distinction between *La Male Honte* and *Cele qui se fist foutre* will consist in the fact that in the former protagonists in the core exchange will fallaciously assume ~(AA) [the two exclusive meanings of the phrase "la male Honte"], while in the latter protagonists in the core exchange will sophistically assume (AA) [the two mutually understood meanings of "ocire"]."[62] In this way, the fabliaux are connected to, but distinct from, the other texts in the narrative because they alone capitalize on linguistic and sociogenic inversions, in different ways, in order to open the messages of the texts to various interpretive possibilities.

The work that follows *La Male Honte* is the anonymous *Dit de la femme* (f. 94v), which is only preserved in this and one other manuscript (the copy of this codex, MS l). Composed in octosyllabic couplets, this nonnarrative text is a mere sixty-two lines. Similar works such as the *Bien des fames* and the *Blasme des fames* are found in other "fabliaux anthologies," notably MS A,[63] suggesting that the placement of such a *dit* in MS K among the fabliaux was a relatively common feature of similar anthologies. In the first half of the *Dit de la femme*, the narrator describes a beast of many colors, which later becomes a simile for woman's inconstancy: "De volentez a plus touz jors, / Que la beste n'a de coulors" (31–32) [she always has more desires than the beast has colors]. The text is not strictly antifeminist, for women are described as multifaceted, and at the end the narrator summarizes his description with moral categories of women: "Fames sont de plusors manieres: / Les unes vilz, les autres chieres; / La vilg tigne l'en en vilté / Et la bone ait l'on en chierté" (59–62) [Women are of many kinds: Some are cheap and we should hold them so; others are precious and we should value the good ones]. While the "ruses d'une femme" group of texts (fables and a fabliau) tend toward antifeminist views through the theme of punishing wives, and the "Matron of Ephesus" texts emphasize the widow's complicity in her ostensible seduction, this *dit* embraces a more ambiguous view of women. Neither strictly antifeminist nor protofeminist, this *dit* thematizes and categorizes women and consequently evidences an ironic placement in the manuscript because it comes immediately after the decidedly "male" fabliau *La Male Honte*. Not only are the characters male in the fabliau, but in medieval literature and art items such as bags and trunks ("male") often represented male anatomy. This *dit* aspires to a type of encyclopedic presentation of the range of female attributes, both physical and moral; it is an "image de la femme." Like the fables, this text reflects the nature of women by offering a playful inventory of female characteristics in a practical and joking manner to demonstrate the divergent nature of women. Like the fabliaux, this text leaves judgment open, arguing that women vary, for some are good and others are bad. In light of this *dit*, *Cele qui se fist*, which follows, arguably responds to the notion of ambiguity, at least in interpreting women's behavior, for the widow may be seen as the victim or the perpetrator of seduction, a loving wife or an unfaithful widow. In this way, the *Dit de la femme* reinforces the ambiguity in the "Matron of Ephesus" theme in its fabliau form.

The penultimate work in the codex, *Le Prestre crucefié*, represents a typical "triangular" fabliau in accord with Nykrog's model, because it involves a man, his wife, and her lover, the priest.[64] In this respect, it resembles the scenario in *Celui qui bota*. In *Le Prestre crucefié*, Messire Rogier an *imagier* [sculptor/

artist], suspecting his wife of infidelity, pretends to go into town so that he may unexpectedly return and catch her with the priest. Surprised by her husband's early return, the wife directs the priest to undress and hide in her husband's workshop as a crucifix. Rogier takes a knife into his workshop and proceeds to "fix" the crucifix by dismembering the priest. The priest runs from the house, but is caught by two men, beaten, and returned to Rogier who holds him for ransom. The moral is addressed to priests, who should not entertain other men's wives lest they leave "la coille en gage" (98) [the testicle as ransom].

 Le Prestre crucefié also lends itself to thematic comparisons with the other texts in the codex. The violence in this work is reminiscent of the fable "La Contrarieuse," while the vulgarity also recalls *La Coille noire*. For Nykrog, this is one of a handful of "fabliaux à triangle" where the husband triumphs precisely because the other man is a cleric.[65] As Pearcy notes, the husband "champion[s] an ultimately triumphant reality that establishes itself in opposition to the artificial and illusory world created by [his wife's] machinations."[66] The comeuppance involves an extension of an illusion, pretending that the lover is part of the crucifix, which is all the more ironic since he is a priest. This text favors the clever husband who, unlike the dead husband in *Cele qui se fist*, is able to seek revenge. The substitution of a priest for a statue becomes an inverted physical enactment of figurative language, since a literal object (the priest) stands in for a representation (the statue). The cutting and dismembering central to the tale create an inversion of the process of artistic creation. The inversions of image and flesh, creation and dismemberment, characterize *Le Prestre crucefié* as a fabliau, in spite of its similarity to fables, as shown in its violence and fitting epimythium. The contrast between the merry widow in *Cele qui se fist* and the wife in *Le Prestre crucefié* recasts the question of adultery in the codex once more in a violent manner. Similarly, this fabliau undermines the role of the priest, who profited in *Celui qui bota*, by presenting a reprehensible and lecherous priest who merits his punishment. Reading these fabliaux together, the manuscript presents a series of oppositions: one fabliau where a priest triumphs and one where a priest is mutilated; stories with an inconstant widow who is either blamed or freed from guilt; women as good and bad; as well as stupid people who are both men and women, peasants and nobles. Yet these texts do not all serve a single purpose. The audience must determine how to understand these oppositions. Ultimately, the contrast created by the fabliaux in this manuscript neutralizes attempts at didacticism in favor of open interpretation.

 The final work in the codex, *La Vielle qui oint*, rivals the fables in its brevity with only fifty-six lines. The tale involves the literal interpretation of an expression, another example of *aequivocatio*, for which reason it resembles *Celui qui bota*, *La Male Honte*, and *Cele qui se fist*. An old woman's cows are confiscated for grazing in the lord's field, so she asks her neighbor for advice about having them returned. When the neighbor suggests she "grease the knight's palm" in order to have them returned, the old woman goes to the knight, makes her request, and slathers his hand with lard. The knight is so amused upon hearing her explanation that he agrees to return the woman's cows.

The dénouement closely resembles that of *La Male Honte* because of the verbal misunderstanding that is met with laughter from the socially higher ranking auditor, in this case a knight. As in *La Coille noire* there is an appeal for justice, but in this case it is favorable to the woman. The final proverb, "provre n'a loi se il ne donne" (56) [the poor person has no justice unless he pays], is contradicted by the outcome. Yet it seems that the entertainment, the laughter the old woman induces, constitutes the payment. In the opening lines of the text, the narrator announces "d'une viele vos voil conter / Un cort fabliaus por deliter" (1–2) [I want to tell you a short fabliau about an old lady to amuse you], which is significant both because he refers to his work as a fabliau as opposed to a fable, and because of the claim that the purpose of the fabliau is to amuse. If, as critics have attested, fabliaux were sometimes recited as payment for food or lodging, then the idea follows that laughter or amusement is the basis of a transaction.[67] Within the text the old woman accomplishes the transaction through her humorous, though unintentional, play on words that reverses the perceived injustice of her losing her cows. The stylistic simplicity of *La Vielle qui oint*, with few, if any, rhetorical devices or a chiasmus, betrays the rhetorical and poetic richness of the other fabliaux in MS K. Similarly, the role of the *clerc* is minimal in this work, the last of a codex in which the majority of texts highlight clerical importance in the transmission of knowledge and entertainment. The last two fabliaux reveal the topical mainstay of the genre: comeuppance and laughter. In this respect, *La Vielle qui oint* resembles *Cele qui se fist*, in which another knight reacts with laughter to the transaction between his squire and a widow.

Among the fabliaux considered, *La Male Honte* and *La Vielle qui oint* stand out as the only nonsexual works. The role of the narrator in all of these fabliaux is echoed by one of the characters, who, directly or indirectly, relates his or her adventure/story. The retelling of the episode is also the subject of the fabliaux: the child in *Celui qui bota* acts as narrator when he explains to his father what his mother has done; the couple, particularly the husband, in *La Coille noire* narrate their misadventure in court, in the form of a complaint; Honte's friend, in explaining himself, acts as narrator; the squire in *Cele qui se fist* renders true the fable he constructs to the knight; and the old woman in *La Vielle qui oint* narrates her misunderstanding when she explains it to the knight. Thus, in these fabliaux, the act of narration carried out by a character parallels that of the narrator and of the content of the entire tale. The emphasis on narration suggests not only that fabliaux call attention to their being fiction, but that fiction and narration are values in themselves. The ambiguity inherent in all of the fabliaux of MS K further emphasizes the value of this fiction in forcing judgment.

Conclusion

In considering the overall organization of the codex, the remarkable diversity of genres and ideas that it contains still offers a coherent whole. In the first half, the *Image du monde* presents a summary of the scientific knowledge of the world and cosmos in the mid-thirteenth century. The work is punctuated with useful and practical explanations and illustrations of natural phenomena with the intent to instruct. The intention of the *Isopet* is also to illustrate the nature of man through the veil of the animal world, as well as to instruct. Finally, the fabliaux are intended to entertain and perhaps incidentally to instruct, but the thrust of the texts in the codex has moved from moral to mundane, from highly didactic to almost strictly narrative. The conjunction of these three types of works reflects not only the cosmos, but an encyclopedia of human understanding; the world, animals, and man are presented in instructive, moralizing, and entertaining ways. The codex as a whole is vernacular and encyclopedic,[68] for it represents the concept that the order of the cosmos is reflected in all levels of creation, even in man and animals.

The creation of the universe, as outlined in the *Image du monde*, thus parallels the structure of the codex. Beginning with the most scientifically and morally important text, the *Image du monde*, and finishing with the least ornate, least sophisticated fabliau, *La Vielle qui oint la paume au chevalier*, the codex displays an overall shift toward the mundane. In terms of scientific and moral importance, the placement of the *Image du monde* first underscores the importance of the knowledge it transmits, which concerns divine creation and the nature of the world. The purpose of Gossuin's text is primarily didactic, to teach one how to live. As the longest text in the codex, the *Image du monde* belongs first in the hierarchy. Furthermore, Gossuin is also the most notable and important *clerc* of the codex, responsible for much of the scientific content and innovations of his text. In the *Image du monde* Gossuin establishes his role as *clerc* as concomitant with the transfer of knowledge. At the middle level is Marie de France, who carefully names herself at the end of the *Isopet*. Her work also instructs, giving both moral and practical lessons about human nature. Although the individual fables are brief, the collection known as the *Isopet* is second in length only to the *Image du monde*. At the innermost level of the hierarchical spheres of creation are the fabliaux and *dit*, most of which are without attribution. The historical importance of the *clercs* for this codex follows the pattern of descent, and the role of the *clerc* in each text is successively reduced. The last two texts, among the shortest fabliaux, again emphasize a progressive descent toward the heavy, sinful center of earth. In most of these fabliaux, a mise en abyme of the act of narration has the characters in the tale repeat the narrative events, essentially narrating the tale, except in the last two texts where the narrators all but disappear. Certainly the scientific and moral lessons diminish in the fabliaux section of the manuscript and the final texts offer little rhetorical interest.

In terms of the vernacular, the *Image du monde* and the *Isopet* are both based on Latin originals, the *clerc* Gossuin de Metz and Marie de France have translated and imbued the originals with their own innovations, reflections of their own understanding. The fabliaux distinguish themselves in the codex as the only truly vernacular works, neither translations nor direct adaptations of Latin models, with the exception of the "Matron of Ephesus" theme.[69] Nevertheless, a collection of such works in the vernacular suggests that this manuscript was both instructive and popular; most likely not intended for the most educated or most devout of audiences, which would explain the absence of Latin and of prayers or saints' lives. By reason of this vernacularization, the Latin confession and incomplete Gospel inserted near the middle of the codex ought not to be considered integrally with the other works. The care devoted to the execution of each half of the manuscript suggests that the content of the Latin folio was not intended to inform the rest of the codex.

Within the second half of the codex, the relationships between fables and fabliaux are deliberately rendered ambiguous. The lessons of the fabliaux more often than not inform the audience about the work at hand rather than about a generally applicable characteristic or rule. In this, the lesson of the fabliaux distinguishes itself most from that of the fables, for the fables embody a message that illustrates a truth external to the text, whereas the fabliaux self-reflectively proclaim their own role as fiction, a "truth" internal to the text. While the differences enumerated throughout this chapter between fables and fabliaux are substantive, the structure of this codex and the placement of certain fabliaux among the *Isopet* promote the notion of intergeneric fluidity characteristic of the fabliaux. The compiler of this codex carefully sought to emphasize the similarities between fables and fabliaux, whether through common topics or through the use of final lessons, which, on one level, the tales illustrate.

While the *Image du monde* and the *Isopet* point to historical figures as *clercs*—in as much as Marie is a *clerc*—and narrators, the fabliaux in this codex overlap the roles of narrators and characters. This type of overlap and consciousness of the role of narrator and narration points to a deliberate attempt to advance a fiction as the truth of the work and to shift focus away from illustrations of external truths. Nevertheless, the descent in the codex from the large, didactic, and historically and morally significant *Image du monde* to the small, trivial, and poetically and thematically simple *La Vielle qui oint* suggests a codicological structure that follows the rules of hierarchical organization. In this way, these diverse texts are united by an overriding principle of the codex, which takes its inspiration from the concentric circles of the universe illustrated in the *Image du monde*. Whether the fabliaux are to be understood as negative examples to avoid, or as a part of the variety of creation that Gossuin accentuates in the *Image du monde*, is never made explicit, since the choice belongs to the audience. This appeal to judgment and interpretation is the hallmark of the fabliaux.

In MS K, the fabliaux represent a diverse range, including scatological and erotic themes, mildly misogynist and anticlerical characterizations, and finally violent and frivolous outcomes, but they are primarily linked by their emphasis on inversion through figurative language. Figurative language denotes a detachment between literal objects and the language used to refer to them, often leading to faulty logic. The contrast between the allegorical sophistication of *La Male Honte* and the economic simplicity of *La Vielle qui oint* shows a progressive decline in the rhetorical richness of the texts that stands in contrast to the continued deployment of structural and linguistic reversals that restore these narratives to the status quo. Within the codex, the fabliaux represent the least didactic compositions, but they are nonetheless the most open to interpretation. Indeed, the variety of the fabliaux and the inversions they display not only distinguish them from the other texts in the manuscript, but they also encourage rereadings and variant interpretations of individual fabliaux and of other narratives within the anthology. While antifeminist sentiments seemingly dominate the first part of the manuscript, the reversals of logic and values inherent in the fabliaux call into question these views and invite the public to reevaluate the texts. In this way, it is the role of the fabliaux in MS K to challenge singular interpretations and reveal alternatives.

As shown here and in chapter 1, "fabliaux anthologies" may exhibit principles of collecting and organizing diverse material in ways that often call attention to thematic similarities or else highlight differences that encourage interpretive possibilities. Still, these anonymously compiled anthologies bear witness to broader questions of genre and interpretation explored in other types of collections, such as *Dolopathos*. Such story collections from the late twelfth to the fourteenth centuries reveal the preoccupations of this period with genre and the practice of collecting diverse materials into a coherent, uniform, single entity bound by a frame. An examination of some of these collections, culminating in the advent of the novella in Boccaccio's *Decameron*, will illustrate how compilations of short stories evolved and how the fabliaux influenced both the compilations as single units and the various texts of which they were composed. The following chapter will posit that the principles behind the organization of most anthologies preserving fabliaux have a similar function as a framing device.

3

Medieval Story Collections and Framing Devices

> Le cose che sono senza modo non
> possono lungamente durare.
>
> [Nothing will last for very long unless it possesses a definite form]
>
> DECAMERON, INTRODUZIONE:95

The first and second chapters showed that the fabliaux are distinct from other medieval short stories because of their use of reversals on rhetorical, thematic, and structural levels, while also interconnected with other genres, often as combinations or parodies of them. The reversals in the fabliaux allow these texts simultaneously to converge with and diverge from other types of narratives. In this way, the fabliaux may resemble and adapt to other short stories, whether fables, *dits*, or even edifying tales and *exempla*, while still retaining their essential character.[1] In this chapter I seek to elaborate the ways in which the transmission of the fabliaux in manuscripts is linked to the practices of story collecting and framing in the thirteenth and fourteenth centuries. More specifically, this chapter situates the fabliaux as central to Boccaccio's transformation of received short story collections from both the Eastern and Western traditions. Certainly specific *novelle* trace their origins to the fabliaux, yet Boccaccio's treatment of the fabliaux tradition extends beyond the level of the individual story to the very structure of the *Decameron*.[2] As Boccaccio's models for the *novelle* in the *Decameron* and for the work's overall structure derive from different literary traditions, Boccaccio often brings the divergent material together using the same mechanisms of combination and inversion deployed in the fabliaux. In addition to the genre's influence on the *Decameron*, the manuscripts preserving fabliaux reveal similarities to the *Decameron* that will be explored below.

Pinpointing the particular contributions of the manuscript collections of fabliaux to the overall structure of the *Decameron* depends in part on understanding the relationship of these anthologies to contemporaneous collections of short stories, as well as to intermediate collections: those produced in the time between the composition of the fabliaux beginning in the late twelfth century and the appearance of the *Decameron* in the mid-fourteenth century. The question arises: Why give so much credit to anthologies of fabliaux for influencing and even shaping the *Decameron* when there are other collections of stories that seem to have more in common with Boccaccio's work? After all, these are collections that Boccaccio may have known more intimately, and that, in some instances, demonstrate similar principles of generic variegation to the "fabliaux codices." As more carefully arranged compilations of works, especially short works, were common practice in this period and did not always involve fabliaux, why give primacy to those codices with fabliaux? Scholars have already analyzed the significant influence of the *exemplum* on the *Decameron*, and Vittore Branca with Chiara Degani proposed *exempla* anthologies as models for Boccaccio.[3] How do collections of *exempla* differ from collections of fabliaux? Proceeding in chronological order, this chapter will examine the types of story collections that were most likely available to Boccaccio before exploring the structure and framing of the *Decameron*. This order of examination will highlight Boccaccio's innovations in relation to previous collections, while also underscoring similarities to anthologies in which fabliaux abound.

The first distinction concerning story collections available to Boccaccio as models for the *Decameron* involves geographic origin: the difference between collections from the East and those from the West. The Eastern collections are more properly speaking Middle Eastern, primarily of Arabic and Persian provenance, but other collections such as the *Panchatantra* can be traced back to India.[4] Of course, Boccaccio could only have known these collections through Latin or vernacular translations, and not in their "original" Eastern forms. Similarly, some Eastern works had been transmitted to Europe and Latinized (or Christianized) centuries before the writing of the *Decameron*, including the tradition of Aesop's fables and the story of *Barlaam et Josaphat*. For these collections, their Eastern connections are more remote than those collections translated during the same period in which the fabliaux flourished. In the twelfth, thirteenth, and fourteenth centuries, the influx of works of Eastern origin coincided with the trend of encyclopedism and the increased dissemination of Western short stories in collections; the two types of corpora overlapped and arguably influenced each other. This overlap obscures the direction of influence and renders some distinctions between Eastern and Western works a bit unclear. In spite of uncertain influences in some cases to be discussed below, the Eastern and Western traditions in this period can generally be separated along organizational as well as thematic lines. Some of the texts indicate their origin, such as *Barlaam et Josaphat*, which takes place in India. It is unclear the degree to which Boccaccio would have been aware of and concerned with distinctions between Eastern and Western literary traditions. The most significant distinction to be made based on geographical origin concerns frame narratives in contrast to nonframe narratives. If the geographic origins of each type of collection were not always known to Boccaccio through the texts themselves, differences in organization and themes at least signaled divergences in the types of collections, which he most likely recognized and exploited.[5] This is not to suggest that Boccaccio considered framed and unframed narratives to be opposite types that he brought together, but rather that he recognized a distinction of some sort and consequently mixed narratives and framing devices from each type of collection.

Eastern Collections

The use of a frame characterizes the Eastern compilations transmitted to Western Europe beginning in the twelfth century.[6] A frame narrative unifies the stories in these collections and distinguishes them from Western anthologies. There are three major collections from which the majority of the others derive. The first, Petrus Alfonsi's *Disciplina Clericalis* (c. 1110), an adaptation of Arabic and Persian works, constitutes one of the earliest extant translations of Eastern short stories from Arabic into Latin.

In the overarching narrative of the *Disciplina Clericalis*, a father instructs his son by relating anecdotes that illustrate a moral or more often a maxim of a philosopher. The son as interlocutor asks questions or else answers his father's questions in a way that transitions to another series of anecdotes and proverbs. The content of the lessons is moral and practical living, as Christianized by Petrus Alfonsi, who was himself a convert from Judaism. As a series of lessons and warnings, the stories and proverbs educate the boy and the audience, who are presumed to be clerics, as the work's title suggests.[7] In sum, the frame is a conversation used as a pretext for a series of didactic stories and proverbs. Still, the collection most likely did not exist as such in its Eastern forms, since Petrus says he "brings together" (*compingere*) the stories, proverbs and castigations of philosophers and Arabs. As one editor of the text claims, "at no time in the prologue does he [Petrus Alfonsi] infer [*sic*] that the work had any prior unified form, and, judging from the multiplicity of its sources, it is probable that he collected material before rendering it into Latin and unifying it into a single work."[8] While the content of the *Disciplina Clericalis* is of Eastern origin, the compiling, organizing, and framing are more likely the work of Petrus Alfonsi himself. As the framing device has much in common with the other collections of Eastern origin, the idea of the frame, of using a conversation to link disparate material, probably hails from the East. Nevertheless, it is also possible that the bringing together of disparate material reflects the practice of *compilatio* developing in the West at this time, to be discussed below. In this respect, the *Disciplina Clericalis* seems to offer a mixture of Eastern and Western material and practices.

Whether or not Boccaccio was directly familiar with this Latin composition would be difficult to prove because the *Disciplina Clericalis* inspired vernacular translations and adaptations in the second half of the twelfth century that were as popular and accessible to Boccaccio as the Latin text.[9] Though Petrus Alfonsi lived in Spain, he most likely produced the *Disciplina Clericalis* in England, for which reason it is probable that the dissemination of the text began in the Anglo-Norman area. Indeed, the earliest extant vernacular translations are in Old French (Anglo-Norman): the *Fables Pierre Aufors* and *Le Chastoiement d'un père à son fils* date from the late twelfth or early thirteenth century.[10] A French prose version emerged at the end of the thirteenth or beginning of the fourteenth century, while a Tuscan version was also produced by the end of the thirteenth century. The acceptance of the *Disciplina Clericalis* into medieval culture meant that stories and proverbs from the collection, though separated from their original context, circulated in various forms, whether as explanatory anecdotes or as *exempla* in sermons in the thirteenth-century Latin compilations of Vincent de Beauvais or Jacques de Vitry,[11] or else as popular tales, both in oral and written transmission. For the most part, as the tales were integrated into the West, they retained their didactic intent, especially in Latin versions.

The *Disciplina Clericalis* and Old French narrative, however, arguably exerted a mutual influence on each other that affected the nature of the stories in vernacular translations. In the vernacular adaptations of the *Disciplina Clericalis*, this influence often shifted the focus from moral lesson to amusing anecdote, particularly where fabliaux were involved. The *Fables Pierre Aufors* and *Le Chastoiement d'un père à son fils* reduced the didactic portions of the *Disciplina Clericalis*, rendering the narratives less antifeminist and more like fabliaux in some cases.[12] As Edward Montgomery notes in his edition of *Le Chastoiement*, the French adaptation is more than twice as long as the Latin text, even though it is missing some *exempla* and didactic portions. In the French version, judgment is rendered and the adaptor's chief concern is not the didacticism but rather the "attractiveness" of the narrative.[13] These emendations suggest a preoccupation with the entertaining content of the stories over that of the frame. Furthermore, the introduction of judgment in the tales in *Le Chastoiement* assimilates them to other Old French works, especially the *jeu parti* and the fabliaux. In this way, the frame was retained and the overall didactic thrust of the collection remained intact, but the substance of some of the individual stories was altered to make them more entertaining and less overtly didactic.

In the opposite direction, the *Disciplina Clericalis* served as the direct source for one anonymous *fableor* who composed *Le Chevalier qui recovra l'amor de sa dame* (7.239–53), since he names "Pierres d'Anfol," a corruption of Petrus Alfonsi, as the first to write this "fablel."[14] Since the *Disciplina Clericalis* furnished sources for fabliaux, and the fabliaux ethos infiltrated Old French translations of the *Disciplina Clericalis*, it seems that there was a certain parity among the stories of Petrus Alfonsi's text and the fabliaux, which frequently resulted in their being brought together in collections. Cristiano Leone notes that translations of the *Disciplina Clericalis* were often transmitted in codices with thematically similar fabliaux,[15] suggesting that even manuscript compilers sought to bring together fabliaux with the tales in Petrus's collection. *Le Chastoiement* is preserved in both MSS D and Z of the fabliaux tradition, and Hilka claims that another witness, MS London, British Library, Harley 527 substitutes the fabliau *Le Cuvier* for the tenth *exemplum* in *Le Chastoiement*.[16] *Les Fables Pierre Aufors* is also preserved alongside fabliaux in MSS X and Y, reinforcing the conflation of the two traditions. While Busby asserts that English-produced MS M, which includes four fabliaux within the *Disciplina Clericalis*, served as a model for the continental anthologies that mix fabliaux and Eastern-inspired works, both types of codices (continental and English) were produced around the same time, rendering problematic any conclusions about the direction of influence.

As already mentioned, the *Disciplina Clericalis* was diffused and translated both as a compilation and as individual stories and proverbs. If the East introduced the story collection, the West dissected and extracted the stories in order to repurpose them and even reinsert them into different collections, while also introducing new narratives into the existing frame. According to Marcus Landau, Boccaccio derived four *novelle* from the *Disciplina Clericalis*, or rather a French translation of it.[17] In spite of the isolated retelling and recopying of certain parts of the *Disciplina Clericalis* by Boccaccio and others, it is still possible for Boccaccio to have known the work as a compilation. In this way, the *Disciplina Clericalis* furnishes a model of a story collection of Eastern (Arabic and Persian) origin with a linking frame narrative, in which there are stories that resemble or even integrate fabliaux. Nevertheless, Boccaccio's *cornice* varies significantly from the educative dialogue between father and son that strings together the proverbs and tales of Petrus Alfonsi's translation.[18]

The second model of a story collection originating in the East was the *Book of Sindbād*. In the Eastern tradition, which includes Syriac, Greek, Hebrew, Arabic, Persian, and Castilian versions, the collection is known as *Sindibad* or *Sendebar*, whereas in the Western tradition it bears two distinct names: *The Seven Sages of Rome*—in Latin, French, Italian, English, Swedish, Dutch, and Welsh versions—and the derivative *Dolopathos* (in Latin and French).[19]

The skeletal narrative common to all versions relates the story of a prince who is sent away to be educated. While away, his widowed father marries an evil woman who decides after a time that she wants to meet the prince. When it is read in the stars that the prince will die upon his return to his father if he speaks before the eighth day, he decides to remain silent. After his curious, silent arrival, his stepmother tries to seduce him, but the prince refuses her advances. Angry, the stepmother then accuses the prince of attempting to seduce her and tries to convince the king through storytelling to kill the prince. As the prince is held captive, his tutor(s) arrive(s) to narrate stories to the opposite effect of the queen in order to spare the prince's life. On the final day, the boy speaks the truth, thereby freeing himself and condemning his stepmother to death. Although both the Eastern and Western traditions involve a frame narrative, Sindbād is the boy's tutor in the Eastern tradition only, whereas in the Western tradition the Seven Sages of Rome are his tutors and also narrate the stories that will save the young prince's life. The number of tales narrated by the sages and the queen varies significantly from version to version, as do the specific tales and their order. Mary Speer has pointed out that only four stories are common to the Eastern and Western traditions: *Canis, Aper, Senescalcus,* and *Avis*.[20] The means of transmission of the collection from East to West also remains shrouded in mystery. Nevertheless, the Western versions retain the frame narrative and the concept of a collection of stories even as they diverge from the Eastern collections in the content of the stories. While the Eastern versions originate in the eighth century and continue until the fourteenth century, the oldest surviving Western versions date from twelfth-century France.[21]

Among the Western versions, Old French figures prominently, but there are also Italian renderings of the Seven Sages tradition that may have been available to Boccaccio, as well as some thirteenth-century Spanish adaptations with which Boccaccio was less likely to have had contact.[22] The Old French verse redaction of *Le Roman des Sept Sages de Rome* (1155–90) is the oldest extant version of the tradition and is preserved in two manuscripts.[23] Although Gaston Paris's claim that the Seven Sages tradition came to Europe through Italy may be valid, the modest manuscript evidence suggests a voyage from France to Italy, a route familiar from much of French literature's influence on the Italian peninsula and one that mimics the trajectory of the *Disciplina Clericalis*.[24] Prose versions in Old French follow the verse translations in the thirteenth century, as do the first Italian versions in the fourteenth century, which are essentially translations of the Old French adaptations.[25] Later Italian redactions differ significantly from the French texts, including adding black magic to the stepmother's talents, but the Italian versions that precede the composition of the *Decameron*, and to which Boccaccio may have had access, resemble the French adaptations.[26]

In the Old French *Roman des Sept Sages* preserved in BNF fr. 1553[27]—a manuscript which will be discussed below in more detail—some of the sages' stories have moved away from the openly antifeminist, didactic force of the rest of the collection toward a fabliaux ethos. For example, the third sage narrates a version of *Puteus*, in which the wife of a rich Roman sneaks off at night to visit her lover, only to be found out by her husband and locked out of the house. When her husband will not let her back inside, she threatens to kill herself, but instead throws a rock in the well in order to make her husband believe she has drowned. As the husband rushes out to save her, the wife runs into the house and locks her husband out. She then accuses him of the very act she committed and mocks him in public; in the aftermath, the husband goes to trial. Rutebeuf's fabliau *La Dame qui fist trois tors entor le moustier* (5.337–57) most likely used a version of *Puteus* as its source, yet the tale in the *Sept Sages* already exhibited narrative elements characteristic of the fabliaux. The reversal of the situation in *Puteus* where the trickster is tricked, the references to "Renart,"[28] and the trial at the end all suggest the influence of Old French narrative generally and fabliaux specifically on this version. Unlike the fabliaux, however, the frame narrative renders justice to the husband, who was merely the victim of a conniving wife. The message to the king in the frame narrative is clear: do not believe your wife and spare your son's life. Thus, the frame narrative prescribes one interpretation of the tale, whereas the fabliau has been removed from a frame narrative and consequently is open to other interpretations, such as rewarding rather than condemning the wife's ingenuity.

There are other similarities to fabliaux, particularly in the version of *Le Roman des Sept Sages* preserved in BNF fr. 1553, which includes the tricks wives play upon their husbands in the fourth and fifth sages' stories. Although these tales are found in later redactions of the Seven Sages tradition in the West, they are not common to the Eastern collections.[29] The stories are *Tentamina* and *Avis*, which are the first and third tales respectively in MS Chartres, B. M. n° 620. In the fourth sage's tale, a young woman married to an old man wants to take a "dru," but her mother warns her not to unless she first tests her husband. The girl says she wants "Guillaume le chapelain" to be her "dru," (2675–704). If not a sign of the direct influence of fabliaux, this reference to a priest-lover at least reflects a convention of Western narrative.

Finally, the sixth sage's story shows the influence of Western literature because it presents yet another version of the "Matron of Ephesus" topos, this time with a fully antifeminist ending where the wife defiles her husband's corpse, and the man subsequently rejects her for her inconstancy.[30] *Le Roman des Sept Sages* offers pairs of opposing tales, the message of those recounted by the sages contrasting with the message of the tales told by the queen, that ultimately call the king to judge them. In spite of this call to judgment, the tales retain their exemplary nature because they propose to instruct the king and elucidate the truth, leading him to the morally correct conclusion. The pairing of opposites in the collection, however, suggests a shared feature with the fabliaux more generally.

As one branch of the Seven Sages tradition, *Dolopathos* exists in two languages: a Latin version from the late twelfth century (1184–1212) composed by Cistercian monk Johannes de Alta Silva; and an Old French translation of Johannes's text by Herbert, composed between 1207 and 1212.[31] While the *Seven Sages* is the primary source, only four tales from the Western tradition were used in *Dolopathos*: *Canis*, *Gaza*, *Inclusa*, and *Puteus*.[32] In this adaptation, the seven sages narrate stories, but not the stepmother. Additionally, *Dolopathos* is a Christianized text, much like the collection *Barlaam and Josaphat*. The Old French text is also considered a *roman*,[33] and even evidences the influence of Old French literature by referring to "fablel" and "Renart" in the text. Whether these words reflect the vocabulary of the writer/translator or of the scribe(s) is not of great importance here because the century separating the date of composition from the date of the manuscript compilation preserving the work is still chronologically prior to Boccaccio's *Decameron*. In this way, the work may have been available to Boccaccio, and it furnishes a precursor for the conflation of Eastern story collections with Western material.

Furthermore, *Dolopathos* transforms the *Puteus* narrative by combining it with another narrative of the Seven Sages tradition: *Inclusa*. In addition to its topical similarity to *La Grue* as discussed in chapter 1, the version of *Inclusa* in *Dolopathos* provides the motivation for the wife, who is locked in the tower, to take a lover and subsequently be locked out of the house or tower in order to inaugurate the *Puteus* narrative. In this version, the wife forgives her husband for locking her out after he promises to destroy the tower and let her live as she wishes. Isolated from a didactic context, this tale from *Dolopathos* does not share the same antifeminist message of the version in *Le Roman des Sept Sages*, because it rewards the wife at the end. The narrator in the frame narrative, however, furnishes an interpretation of the tale that preserves the antifeminist tenor of previous versions by stating that the queen is even more "evil" than the woman in the story.[34] The combination of two narratives and the ending that seems more favorable to the wife suggest that the *Puteus-Inclusa* story in *Dolopathos* succumbed to the influence of Western vernacular narratives, including the practice of combining narratives that is recurrent in the fabliaux. In spite of this plausible influence, the reduction of tales to those narrated solely by the sages, thus eliminating the queen's opposing voice from the text, reveals that *Dolopathos* removes the balance of opposites in favor of a single-path didacticism in which all stories work toward truth and justice to spare the prince's life. Altering the content of the stories in this tradition does not alter the meaning of the frame.

Both *Le Roman des Sept Sages* and *Dolopathos* suggest some influence of Old French narrative and of fabliaux more specifically within the individual tales, just as a small number of fabliaux share themes with stories in the Seven Sages tradition. The influence of this tradition on the fabliaux and on individual *novelle* in the *Decameron* has already been explored by Landau, Branca, and Bédier.[35] As these three traditions share some stories, it is likely that the *Sept Sages* was a source for certain fabliaux and *novelle*, but also that there was mutual influence of Old French and Italian literature on the stories in the Seven Sages tradition as they were received and transmitted in Western Europe, particularly after the thirteenth century when continuations of the Seven Sages cycle appeared.[36] A fifteenth-century Italian version, known as the *Storia di Stefano*, has three stories—more than any other version—that resemble fabliaux, namely *La Housse partie* (3.175–209), *Les Perdrix* (discussed in chapter 1), and *Les Trois dames qui troverent l'anel* (2.215–40).[37] That some stories in the later versions of the Seven Sages tradition resemble fabliaux and romance suggests the mutual influence of Eastern and Western works in the thirteenth, fourteenth, and even fifteenth centuries. The Seven Sages tradition furnishes the most likely model of a frame narrative for Boccaccio, one that involves different narrators telling tales on different days that respond both to a theme and to each other. The mixture of this Eastern material with fabliaux and other Western narratives is analogous to the generic mixtures that characterize the *novelle* in the *Decameron*.

Finally, the didactic collection known as *Barlaam et Josaphat* has a long tradition of emendations. Originating in the East as the story of Gautama Buddha, *Barlaam et Josaphat* reached the West when it was translated from Greek into Latin in the eleventh century.[38] The first French versions, however, date to the beginning of the thirteenth century, after *Dolopathos*.[39] Jacobus de Voragine also included a version of *Barlaam et Josaphat* in his *Legenda Aurea*, a collection of saints' lives organized by the calendar, which will be discussed in more detail below in relation to Western collections. The substantial frame narrative of *Barlaam et Josaphat* involves an Indian king who wants to keep his son from Christianity and the ills of the world by locking him in a palace. When the hermit Barlaam arrives disguised as a merchant, he is able to meet the prince and instruct him in a dialogue about his Christian Lord through a series of anecdotes and parables. Although predicated on a dialogue like the *Disciplina Clericalis*, *Barlaam et Josaphat* offers a much more detailed dialogue with a focus on conversion; it is supremely didactic and the most Christianized of all the Eastern works. The stories it contains are parables and *exempla* which all lead to the prince's religious awakening and conversion. Although the dialogic form has little in common with the frame narrative of the *Decameron*,—except possibly for the conversations among the *brigata* narrators—the premise strongly resembles the "hundred and first" novella of the *Decameron* told outside the frame in the Introduction to Day IV as the story of Filippo Balducci.[40] Unlike the other collections from the East, *Barlaam et Josaphat* reveals little if anything in common with fabliaux, but instead retains a strictly exemplary and didactic form in the West.[41]

These Eastern-origin story collections as received in the West witness a notable degree of conflation and mutual influence with Western short stories. The earliest extant Latin translations of the Eastern story collections barely predate the emergence of the fabliaux, the branches of the *Roman de Renart*, Marie de France's *Lais*,[42] as well as other types of short stories from the second half of the twelfth century. Moreover, the codices that preserve the vernacular adaptations of the Eastern collections were produced in the same areas and at the same times as the anthologies containing fabliaux; indeed, in many cases these are the same manuscripts. The issue of sources notwithstanding, did the translation of these Eastern story collections influence the organization of manuscript anthologies, or is it rather that a predilection for compilations of vernacular texts precipitated the translation of similar collections from Eastern sources into the vernacular? The chronology and the direction of influence between these traditions are probably less clear-cut than has previously been suggested, but it is certain that Boccaccio relied on the frame devices from the East for the overall framing of the *Decameron* tales. The implicit organization of certain days, however, probably derives from some Western sources to be discussed below.

As for the frame narrative, the *Decameron* has more parallels with the Seven Sages tradition than with the *Disciplina Clericalis* and its derivatives or *Barlaam et Josaphat*. The *Seven Sages* and the *Decameron* are both story collections organized around a set number of days, with a limited number of stories narrated each day. Both collections have a number of narrators, as opposed to the father and son of the *Disciplina Clericalis* or the teacher in *Barlaam et Josaphat*, and both have a mixture of male and female narrators, except for *Dolopathos* where all the narrators are male. While the *Decameron* arguably does not share the overt antifeminism of the Seven Sages tradition, where the only woman, the evil stepmother, is sent to death at the end for her lies, both collections are based on a premise of storytelling as a means to escape from death. Specifically, in the Seven Sages tradition, the prince is freed from a death sentence by the persuasive stories his tutors tell his father, whereas in the *Decameron*, the *brigata* of ten young men and women flee to the countryside and tell each other stories to escape the threat of death by the Plague that has ravaged the city of Florence. Even though Boccaccio's *cornice* is the sum of many parts and many types of stories and historical narratives (which will be referenced below), these common threads with the Seven Sages tradition support the Eastern origin of the frame device. Still, the Eastern collections use the frame in order to promote a didactic (and often antifeminist) message, but when they reach the West, the content becomes more malleable, as evidenced by the interaction with fabliaux. The use of opposites in the Eastern collections helps to underscore a single point rather than to open the text to interpretive possibilities. In the Eastern framing tradition, even as the content of the tales veers from the central message of the work, the frame reasserts the collection's overall didactic function, whereas the frame in the *Decameron* is arguably more ambiguous.[43] This disparity in framing is similar to the function of chiasmus as a framing device in fables and fabliaux as shown in chapter 2, since the use of chiasmus in the fables reinforces the structure and moral didacticism, whereas in the fabliaux these are undermined.

Western Collections

Among the Western medieval collections of short stories that predate the *Decameron*, there are two main types that may have influenced Boccaccio: collections of a single genre often attributed to a single author, whether miracle stories or pious tales, saints' lives, fables, and *lais*; and second, the so-called miscellanies such as the "fabliaux manuscripts," which contain a mixture of different material brought together in various ways. Certain *exempla* collections, however, fall in between these two categories, revealing the thematic diversity of the *exemplum*, while still maintaining a formal and generic consistency imposed by a compiler. None of these collections contains a frame narrative as the Eastern collections do, but rather attain justification and structural coherence through other means.

Collections of stories attributed to a single writer, such as Marie de France's *Lais* and *Isopet* or Gautier de Coinci's *Miracles Nostre Dame*, offer significant parallels with the *Decameron*, mostly because of their generic uniformity and authorial control.[44] The generic and stylistic homogeneity of this first type of Western collection differs little from the Eastern collections, except for the absence of a frame narrative. Nevertheless, the Western collections sometimes have a kind of frame, whether topical defenses of the work, as in the Prologue to Marie's *Lais*, or other explanations, such as Gautier de Coinci's justification of his translation of miracle stories, in which he claims to translate the miracle stories so that "cil et celes qui la letre / N'entendent pas puissant entendre," [those who do not know how to read can understand].[45] In most instances, there is an authorial intervention at the beginning of the collection that indicates the cohesion of the series of stories to follow, much like the introduction to *exempla* collections. The pious collections differentiate themselves from secular collections like fables and *lais* because of their exemplary texts and overall moralizing intention. The *exemplum* is necessarily didactic, while *lais* and even fables are less rigid categories. The manuscripts more often than not attest to this division. As single works made up of various stories, pieces like the *Lais*, the *Isopet*, and the *Miracles Nostre Dame* constitute the first type of medieval collection of Western origin available to Boccaccio. Such works offer rhetorical but not narrative frames for a set of texts of a single genre and more frequently of a single theme or didactic purpose. The manuscripts in which the pious collections are preserved focus on moral instruction, rarely mingling with profane works like the fabliaux.

As concerns manuscript culture, the thirteenth century witnessed an increase in the writing and compiling of encyclopedias and summas in Latin and vernacular works. While these genres are outside the focus of this study on narrative, the principles behind summas and encyclopedias transferred to narrative collections. Compilers of *exempla* used in sermons, like Jacques de Vitry and Étienne de Bourbon, unified their material through the practices of *collectio, compilatio,* and *ordinatio*. These concepts constitute the framework for coherent principles of organization, bringing together disparate and often fragmentary pieces. As outlined by Alastair Minnis, *ordinatio* involves subordination in the structure of a book.[46] *Compilatio*, on the other hand, is a two-part activity that involves locating excerpts from different authorities (*auctores*) on a given subject and then ordering these excerpts (*ordinatio*).[47] According to Minnis, Vincent de Beauvais gave the *compilatio* a literary dimension when the practice had previously been reserved for canon law.[48] Finally, *collectio* is a collection of different texts, whether fragments or complete works, but it differs from *compilatio* in that *compilatio* has *ordinatio* but *collectio* does not.[49]

Although begun and modeled in Latin works, the concepts of *ordinatio, collectio,* and *compilatio* were endemic to thirteenth-century culture. As Malcolm B. Parkes has described, the dissemination of *compilatio* as a kind of writing and book led to writers "both in academic circles and outside adopting and adapting the form to suit their own academic or artistic purposes."[50] Parkes observed that, "as a literary form *compilatio* influenced works in vernacular literature. The process of *ordinatio* at the higher level may be detected in the general schemes of the *Decamerone*, the *Confessio amantis, Les Cent balades* and the incomplete *Canterbury Tales*."[51]

The practices of organizing *exempla* also reflect the notion of *ordinatio*. Collections of *exempla* suggest somewhat more variation than the single-author and single-genre collections. Jean-Thiébaut Welter posits that the *exemplum* continued to expand as a form in the twelfth century to include a wide variety of sources from works like the *Disciplina Clericalis, Barlaam et Josaphat*, the Seven Sages tradition, and even fabliaux, although fabliaux were often condemned by compilers of *exempla*.[52] Like the fabliau, the *exemplum* has the capacity to assimilate different sources while still retaining a clear generic identity. Yet this wide thematic variety in the *exemplum* presents a range of subtypes.[53] Beginning in the second half of the thirteenth century—the same period that saw the advent of "fabliaux codices"—compilers created collections of *exempla* that were no longer framed by sermons or treatises, but rather by logical guidelines summarized in the introductions.[54] Within the manuscripts that preserved *exempla* collections, the stories could be organized "logically," alphabetically, or else in moralizing terms, but often still displaying a range of subtypes.[55] One trend in *exempla* compilations in the thirteenth century, however, aimed to limit the variety of the genre. Humbert de Romans prescribes only seemly language in *exempla*, as well as the need to make the lesson fit the circumstances of the *exemplum*, with no political controversies, and no names of great people;[56] very much the opposite of the fabliaux and the *Decameron* stories. More to the point, the variety of the *exemplum* only admits of a didactic and moralizing intent, whether in isolation or in the context of a compilation. Although similar to the manuscripts preserving fabliaux to be discussed below in more detail, *exempla* codices do not reveal the same degree of generic variegation as the vernacular collections, but rather variation within a type.[57] Like the *Decameron*, however, they do evidence practices of *ordinatio*.

Jocabus de Voragine's *Legenda Aurea*, a collection of saints' lives composed in the 1260s, reflects a similar, though slightly different, structuring principle from the majority of *exempla* collections of this period. The *Legenda Aurea* shows a "logical" organization by the liturgical calendar, so that each day gives the story of a different saint. Unlike other pious collections of the thirteenth century, the *Legenda Aurea* integrates Eastern and Western story collections by including a version of *Barlaam et Josaphat* as saints celebrated on November 27, creating a sort of mise en abyme of stories. This mixture of East and West recalls the interweaving already discussed in relation to the Seven Sages tradition and other Eastern collections. Jacobus derived the lives from a variety of sources so that, although all are stories of saints, they display some thematic diversity. According to Landau, Boccaccio was familiar with the *Legenda Aurea*, so it could also have served as a precedent for a mixture of Eastern and Western stories.

In vernacular literature and in Italian specifically, only the *Novellino* offers a collection of one hundred stories that reveals a greater thematic variety than any other compilation addressed thus far, including collections of *exempla*. Yet the stories in the *Novellino* are more properly speaking plot outlines and are significantly less developed than the *novelle* in the *Decameron*. While Boccaccio certainly owed much in the *Decameron* to the *Novellino*,[58] the frame and overall organization of the *Decameron* are indebted to other sources, since the thirteenth-century *Novellino* has no frame or distinct narrator(s). Like the vernacular translations of Eastern collections, the *Novellino* brings together stories and anecdotes of Eastern and Western origin. In spite of the diversity within the *Novellino*, the work is still composed of a single genre and the anecdotes all possess a similar form. As the *Novellino* is composed of *novelle* like the *Decameron*, all of the Western collections discussed so far offer stories of a single generic type, such as fables or *exempla*, saints' lives or *novelle*.

Most of these collections, whether secular or pious, were composed beginning in the late twelfth century and continuing in the thirteenth and fourteenth centuries, the same period that witnessed the translations of Eastern story collections and the fruition of the fabliaux. In this way, there seem to be several types of collections that could have influenced Boccaccio in integrating Eastern and Western material in the *Decameron*. The Boccaccian *novella*, however, draws on a greater variety of sources than any of the Western or Eastern collections already mentioned and unites them in a frame. For this reason, no single source explains all of the elements of the *cornice* and the hundred tales. While *exempla* collections show the greatest thematic variation of the collections studied thus far, unified by a type of frame, they were not the only models for compiling diverse narrative material. The second type of Western collection that may have influenced Boccaccio in composing the *Decameron* furnishes a model whose narrative variety equals that of the *Decameron*. Medieval manuscript anthologies, especially the larger anthologies that preserve fabliaux, offer a mixture of Eastern and Western works, of narrative and logical frames, that display a range of themes and genres comparable to the *Decameron*.

"Fabliaux Codices"

In their manuscripts, fabliaux are often found alongside fable collections, as shown in chapter 2, and with other short narratives in the vernacular, but less often with other vernacular collections. For example, only one manuscript contains fabliaux and Marie de France's collection of *Lais*, inasmuch as these tales constitute a collection.[59] Similarly, fabliaux often figure in codices with pious tales but not with collections of pious tales. When they are not the only piece in a manuscript, collections of pious works tend to figure into codices with specifically didactic and moralizing outlooks. The *Miracles Nostre Dame* and similar collections may be found in manuscripts dedicated to the Virgin.[60] Profane works, on the other hand, tend to be found in miscellanies or anthologies, which present a range of texts.

The codex known as MS J (BNF fr. 1553) resembles MS K, which was examined in chapter 2, because it also contains Gossuin's *Image du monde* and a small number of fabliaux. As both the *Image du monde* and the fabliaux were popular and widely copied in the thirteenth and fourteenth centuries, their sharing more than one manuscript is neither necessarily significant, nor indicative of any substantial thematic or generic connections. Indeed, MS J differs from MS K in a number of respects, not the least of which is its length. Although MS J preserves just five fabliaux in over 500 folios, all of the fabliaux are grouped in a section of short stories between ff. 488 and 514, near the end of the codex. As is the case in other codices preserving fabliaux that have already been described, the taxonomy of MS J blurs the distinctions between the fabliaux and other short narrative works, in some cases by designating them as *lais* in the *incipit*.[61] Since the other texts in this section of the manuscript are mostly *lais*, this microcontext offers a grouping by relative length, and arguably by type, rather than by theme.

The longer romances and other types of works in MS J are preserved at the beginning of the codex in different sections from the fabliaux and are generally organized thematically. There are sections on saints, a series of romances, and a section on Roman emperors, that all precede the fabliaux/*lais* section, and that attest to generic and thematic groupings. MS J constitutes a variegated assemblage of short and long, pious and secular, didactic and entertaining texts, composed by a variety of writers and copied in different hands at different times: a true miscellany.[62] While the interconnections of the fabliaux to other works in the microcontext function much the same way that they do in other manuscripts of fabliaux already discussed, the fabliaux's relationship to the macrocontext of the entire codex proves not as readily discernable.

The relationship of the parts to the whole in this instance suggests no framing device. While the compilers of *exempla* collections usually identified the schemes by which the texts were organized, there is no explicit statement of intent in the organization of vernacular miscellanies or anthologies. The lack of an explicit structure does not necessarily rule out the possibility of an implicit structure. Indeed, the same practices of *ordinatio* found in the *exempla* codices may also be at work in many "fabliaux codices." Diverse narrative material, whether in Latin or the vernacular, may be brought together and arranged according to scholastic models of organization. Since some *exempla* collections bring together a range of themes, other assemblies of varied narratives may reflect the same type of arrangements. As already shown, MS K revealed a very specific *ordinatio*, as do (sections of) MSS A, B, C, and D, among others (see chapter 1). For MS J, a collection of diverse texts does not necessarily imply a lack of relationship among the parts. It is precisely the relationship of typology, of similar works, that unites the fabliaux/*lais* section of MS J and that ties together the different parts of the entire codex. It is thus possible to situate manuscripts preserving fabliaux within this scholastic tradition, to say that *ordinatio, compilatio,* and *collectio* infiltrated vernacular narrative and especially vernacular compilations of the thirteenth and fourteenth centuries. Unlike the *exempla* collections, however, MS J and similar codices bring together different genres and themes that contrast with each other; the principles behind these collections remain implicit for the reader to interpret. As Sylvia Huot has remarked, "the tension between fragmentation and wholeness remains unresolved."[63]

Remarkably, in modern accounts, the few fabliaux of MS J dominate the categorization of this codex.[64] With the exception of *Trubert* (MS j), no single extant manuscript contains fabliaux exclusively, whereas many manuscripts contain nothing but *exempla*. This means that the written transmission of the fabliaux necessarily involved other genres, compiled in collections. The "fabliaux" label for manuscripts suggests that these stories constitute a notable identifying element of the codices, at least in their reception. Why should the fabliaux seem more noteworthy than the other texts in these collections? In essence, this question recalls the value of the fabliaux as a genre: What is their purpose and what is to be gained from them? It is arguable that the language and themes of the fabliaux—their vulgarity, obscenity, and arguable perversion of social and moral norms—explain their overdetermined mark on manuscript culture as negative exemplarity. In terms of genre, the fabliaux do represent a kind of anti-*exemplum* because they insist on multiple readings and interpretations removed from a moral framework. Thematically, and even socially, the fabliaux exhibit a preoccupation with the nature of language and narrative. For this reason, the fabliaux are not *exempla-in-malo*, studies of how not to live and behave, but rather examples of how to read. Although there remains a possibility to understand fabliaux as models to avoid, this is one possibility among many, a feature to which the texts themselves point. Furthermore, these same "fabliaux collections" occasionally contain other ostensibly subversive texts that are equally vulgar and obscene. Such works as the *Dit de la femme* in MS K and the farcical prayers in MS A—including "La Patenostre a l'userier" on fol. 219—also serve as contrasting elements in the codices, but they still manage to elude critical attention and fail to categorize an entire collection. Unlike the Seven Sages tradition where the anti-*exempla* of the evil queen failed to overturn the overall message of the text, the fabliaux do pose threats to the interpretation of other texts in the same codices. The essence of the fabliaux and their role in codices must be understood in two parts. On the level of the individual story, the fabliaux highlight the fiction they create and the subsequent impossibility of a single reading. The fabliaux call attention to their own polyvalence by bringing opposites together through reversals. Within manuscripts, and unlike any other type of collection, the fabliaux often function as the *élément perturbateur*, leading the audience to question and even reinterpret other works in the collection.

A consideration of other parts of MS J signals a preoccupation with the short story. In addition to romances, the first part of MS J also has two story collections: *Barlaam et Josaphat* (as "De Josaphat, ki fu fiex, et de Balaham l'ermite ki le converti," ff. 198–254) attributed here to St. John Damascene, and *Les Sept Sages de Rome* (as "Des .vii. Sages," ff. 338–67). As discussed above, both of these are collections of stories from the East with a moralizing intent. Together with the section of fabliaux and *lais*, these works suggest the primacy and variety of the short story in this and similar vernacular manuscripts, like MSS A, B, C, and D. Moreover, all of the texts in MS J represent the two main types of material, Eastern and Western, that Boccaccio will combine in the *Decameron*. Before Boccaccio, vernacular manuscripts constituted the milieu for combining these traditions.

MS J is not the only "fabliaux codex" to preserve story collections of Eastern origin alongside Western tales. MS B also contains a prose version of *Le Roman des sept sages*, while a fragment of *Dolopathos* appears in MS q, the same codex as the fabliau *Les Trois aveugles de Compiegne* (2.151–84), and a version of *Le Chastoiement d'un père à son fils* is preserved in MS Y, just three folios before the fabliau *Jouglet*.[65] Some of the larger codices also preserve single tales extracted from the Eastern tradition along with fabliaux. In the fabliaux tradition, MSS D, O, X, and Z preserve a mixture of story collections adapted from Eastern models with at least one fabliau. Although most of these collections (except MS D) contain a single fabliau, these are the very types of codices that call into question generic boundaries, as well as indicate the popularity of fabliaux and their adaptability to a variety of contexts. MS Z transmits two "English fabliaux" not affiliated with Chaucer, while many of the tales in the Eastern story collections of these manuscripts have been broadly adapted to resemble fabliaux more closely, as discussed above.[66] Moreover, the number of fable collections associated with codices preserving fabliaux also attests to this juxtaposition of Eastern and Western texts, as the *Isopets* never lost their connection to Aesop and consequently with the non-Western world in the history of their transmission. In addition to MS K, which preserves Marie de France's *Isopet*, MSS D, F, H, and I are among the other large anthologies of fabliaux that contain fable collections.[67] These codices suggest not only that the fabliaux participated in the scholastic practices of collecting and compiling, but that the thirteenth- and fourteenth-century compilers who brought them together with Eastern story collections recognized a kinship between these two traditions and sought to associate the fabliaux specifically with Eastern collections of stories. In this way, the Old French codices preserving fabliaux bring together Eastern and Western tales, both separately and as collections, and compile them using scholastic principles of organization to create generically diverse narrative books.

Unlike the Eastern story collections and unlike single-genre collections of stories in the West, only variegated manuscripts like the "fabliaux codices," and to a lesser extent some *exempla* collections, produce the thematic and generic diversity that will come to define Boccaccio's *Decameron*. Even though Boccaccio's tales are all *novelle* and thus of one genre, he clearly drew from different genres, as will be discussed. The tragic tales of Day IV are not of the same ilk as the scandalous, fabliaux-related stories of Day III, for example.

If the fabliau and the *exemplum* are opposite genres, the manuscripts preserving each genre share some common structuring features. More to the point, the anthologies of fabliaux are the only collections to combine in a single place the types of Eastern and Western material that Boccaccio used as sources for the *Decameron*. As Boccaccio may have deployed the same concepts of organization and structure as well as similar combinations of diverse material as those that characterize anthologies of fabliaux, surely these codices must be considered one vernacular precedent or rather model for the *Decameron*.

Boccaccio's work as a collection of one hundred stories differs most from the manuscript anthologies preserving the fabliaux in its generic homogeneity—all the tales are *novelle*—and in its authorial supervision, just as it differs from more homogeneous collections because of its thematic variety and its overarching frame narrative linking all of the stories. While it may seem that other precursors to the *Decameron* more closely resemble these key aspects of homogeneity and authorial presence than do "fabliaux manuscripts," the *Decameron* successfully marries these two types of collections.

Frames and Structure in the *Decameron*

The following analysis of the structure of the *Decameron* will suggest the work's connections to the fabliaux and the anthologies that preserved them. Specifically, this study will elaborate that the fabliaux and the *Decameron* both highlight reversals as a means to show the open nature of storytelling, that the fabliaux and the *Decameron* both mix different types of works through reversals, and finally that the "fabliaux manuscripts" modeled the bringing together of Eastern frames and Western compilations for the *Decameron*.

As a complex work, the *Decameron* functions on many levels and therefore is to be understood on many levels. The polyvalence of the *Decameron* limits any claims concerning *the* value of the text because it necessarily offers more than one value. One of the values the text proposes, however, is multiple possibilities of meaning. In this view, which is espoused by Guido Almansi,[68] the *Decameron* addresses the nature of writing and storytelling, as it calls on the reader to judge it. Discussing the *Decameron* as an aesthetic text places "the burden of interpretation on the reader,"[69] as Millicent Marcus has stated, but it also reveals crucial elements of the structure related to the fabliaux. The structure of the *Decameron* lends itself to analyses by levels and frames, moving from the outermost layer of the frame down to the nucleus, which is the level of one hundred *novelle*.

Studies of the *Decameron* typically divide the work into narrative segments, which Michelangelo Picone outlines as four levels: the first is the author's address to his audience of lovesick ladies and his critics—what he refers to as the extradiegetic level—that comprises the *Proemio*, the *Introduzione alla quarta giornata*, and the *Conclusione dell'Autore*; the second level, the intradiegetic level, encompasses the *Introduzione*—that is, the actual frame narrative that introduces the character/narrators—and the introductions and conclusions to each day; the third level consists of the hundred stories narrated by the *lieta brigata*; and finally the fourth level of narration, the metadiegetic level that marks a further mise en abyme, occurs in individual stories where a character within a narrative tells his own story.[70] Although all of the levels interact in myriad ways, it is primarily in the first two levels that Boccaccio establishes his *ars narrandi* and provides the unifying elements for the hundred *novelle*. The third and fourth levels of narration described by Picone correspond more directly to specific fabliaux and the fabliaux material more generally.

In contrast, Joy Potter offers another series of five narrative frames: the first is the book as experienced in the outside world by the reader and Boccaccio as writer; the second is Boccaccio's story about the *Decameron* addressed to the fictional ladies; the third level is the account of Florentine society during the Plague; the fourth is any narration about the *brigata*; and the fifth level refers to the hundred tales told by the *brigata*.[71] The systems offered by Picone and Potter are in many respects complementary. Potter's levels one and two correspond roughly to Picone's extradiegetic level, except that Potter's second level or world draws attention to the fiction of the audience of ladies whom Boccaccio as narrator addresses in the *Proemio*, the *Introduzione alla quarta giornata*, and the *Conclusione dell'Autore*. The contrived audience of lovesick ladies is a fiction that is reflected in the innermost level of the *Decameron*, the stories told by the *brigata* for which the other members of the company serve as audience. Picone's intradiegetic level approximates Potter's worlds three and four and focuses on the *Introduzione* and on any narration about the *brigata*. Once again, Potter's levels call attention to the fiction of the *brigata* as placed in opposition to the historical events of the Plague. Finally, Potter notes that the last world is that of the hundred stories, presumably combining Picone's diegetic and metadiegetic levels.

While Picone's frame model applies narrative classifications to the organizational categories of the *Decameron* designated by Boccaccio (*Proemio*, *Introduzione*, *novelle*, mise en abyme, etc., each corresponds to a narrative level in Picone's system), Potter's frame system highlights the different literary functions and interrelations among the structural designations, such that the different worlds are often brought together in narrative commentaries, or what she refers to as frame shifts and breaks.[72] Both systems offer useful views of the narrative metatextuality and interrelations in the *Decameron* for understanding the role of the fabliaux.

In addition to these (mostly) narrative levels, two further structural levels relate to the fabliaux material in the *Decameron* as they contribute to practices of organization. Since the majority of the ten days in the *Decameron* are organized around a theme, there is arguably a coherent order to the days and their respective themes. At no point in the *Decameron* does any narrator articulate any unifying principle related to the days or the themes they treat, so any order is necessarily implicit. Yet the interrelationships of the ten days of narration and the themes they explore suggest relevance to the notion of framing stories. In addition to the order of the days, there is also the sequence of stories within each day that constitutes another level of organization. Since these structural levels of the narratives do not correspond exactly with the content, nor with the interpretive frames applied to them in Potter's system, the following discussion of the metatextual levels will draw primarily on Picone's narrative categories because they mimic the author's rubrics, adding the insights of Potter's frames where applicable.

Although the various narrative levels Picone describes are interrelated, treating them separately will reveal their roles in the whole work and then subsequently suggest the ways in which they interact. The first level of narration (the extradiegetic level), which includes the *Proemio*, the *Introduzione alla quarta giornata*, and the *Conclusione dell'Autore*, establishes Boccaccio's reasons for undertaking the *Decameron*, his *ars narrandi* as Almansi calls it, and provides a defense of his work. As Picone remarks, it is the level about writing.⁷³ As such, the allusions in these segments of the text evoke literary genres and conventions more than historical events or even social problems.

Like *Dolopathos* and most medieval works, the *Decameron* begins with an explanation of the work's intent and utility. The *Proemio* also introduces the primary rhetorical devices that will permeate the work. Robert Hollander notes the symmetry of the *Proemio*, where the first half is devoted to Boccaccio's experience of love, and the second half addresses the lovesick ladies.⁷⁴ The balance in the *Proemio*, which is constructed of "antithetical pairs,"⁷⁵ will guide the rest of the text, which is built on symmetry and antithetical pairs or the joining of opposites. After opening his text with an expression of his own personal suffering in love, the author then addresses his audience of *donne amorose* and states that the purpose of his work is to offer *consiglio* and "alcuno alleggiamento prestare . . . in soccorso e rifugio di quelle che amano" (*Proemio*, 7 and 13) [to offer some solace . . . [to provide] succor and diversion for the ladies, but only for those who are in love, 3]. From the beginning, Boccaccio inscribes an audience in the *Decameron*, but this audience reflects literary concerns more than the historical fact of his real audience or even his intent, who he wanted his audience to be. The idea of the text as an aid to lovesick ladies, which recalls Ovid's *Remedia Amoris* and the medieval tradition of courtly literature more generally, emphasizes the literary intentionality of the text. Love, a theme central to many of the *novelle*, is invoked from the beginning through a personal and individual experience that is then opened up to a larger audience of women. The audience of ladies also recalls another medieval convention, the courts of love that Andreas Capellanus described in his *De Amore*.⁷⁶ As Potter has noted, this reference to love in conjunction with the invocation of God in the early part of the *Proemio*, "is an indication of a literary intent. Both are allusions to known codes."⁷⁷ These codes will be mixed throughout the *Decameron*, and brought together with other codes and narratives.

The first words of the text, "Umana cosa è . . ." (*Proemio*, 2) [it is human/a human thing] are a literary allusion and interpretive pole from which to analyze the *Decameron*. As the first word ("umana") indicates, the text concerns human affairs, not divine ones. While the role of divine, moral, and transcendental matters in the *Decameron* is less clear than that of the human aspect presented in the *Proemio*, the contrast between "human" and "divine" suggests yet another literary allusion: to Dante's *Divina Commedia*. If Boccaccio is offering a "human comedy," he does so in part by referencing and manipulating literary constructs.⁷⁸ In this way, the *Decameron* establishes itself in the vernacular (and courtly) literary tradition and emphasizes its own literary and aesthetic concerns.

In addition to a classical and courtly notion of love, the *Proemio* introduces the question of genre when the author states his intention to "raccontare cento novelle, o favole o parabole o istorie che dire le vogliamo" (13) [narrate a hundred stories or fables or parables or histories or whatever you choose to call them, 3]. Branca summarizes the generic distinctions of each type named:

> Novelle sono genericamente narrazioni di ogni argomento; favole rammenta l'uso francese di 'fabliaux'; parabole accenna a esempi e probabilmente alla volontà didascalico-allegorica che non di rado è presente nei prologhi e negli epiloghi delle singole novelle, e qualche volta in racconti moralizzati per via di paragoni . . . storie indica infine specialmente le narrazioni a sfondo storico, di personaggi illustri.
> [Novellas are generically narrations of every argument; fables recall the French use of 'fabliaux;' parables touch on *exempla* and probably on a didactic-allegorical desire that is not infrequently present in the prologues and epilogues of single novellas, and sometimes in moralized stories owing to comparisons . . . finally, (hi)stories indicate especially narrations with a historical background, of famous people].[79]

Although in making this statement about his tales Boccaccio only hints at some generic distinctions, the stories are clearly of mixed material. The generic nature of each tale is not expressed by either Boccaccio or any of the character/narrators, so that each novella's type must be determined by the reader. As Pamela Stewart notes, most of the tales are designated as *novelle* and this term encompasses the other three, *favole, parabole*, and *istorie*.[80] This being the case for Boccaccio's *novelle*, the stories in any mise en abyme of the fourth level of narration often demonstrate the generic distinctions that Branca noted, such that these categories exist for the characters created by the *brigata* and possibly for the *brigata* as well, but Boccaccio as author consciously subsumes these categories into his new narrative form, aptly named the novella.[81] This use of generic terminology among the *brigata*, which is not explicitly shared by the author, parallels the references to the god of Love who exists within the narratives, but not in the author's commentary. Boccaccio's new narrative form is dependent on courtly love only as a literary device.

If the fabliaux correspond to the *favole*, as Branca suggests, then they form only a part of the tradition and generic material from which Boccaccio developed his *novelle*. Similar to the fabliau, the novella brings together other short narrative forms. Like the *exemplum*, the novella supersedes the variety of themes and tones represented in the hundred tales by uniting them under a common form and common generic designation. Within the *Proemio* there is no indication of how the fabliaux material, nor the exemplary material, which is put on the same level, specifically pertains to the work's purpose. Nevertheless, the thematic breadth of the *novelle* suggests a generic flexibility similar to, but greater than, that of the fabliaux.

The predominantly (Western) literary allusions in the *Proemio* meet with an Eastern influence in the *Introduzione alla quarta giornata*. Only in the Introduction to Day IV does the author defend the role of fables and the entire *Decameron*. While the introduction to *Dolopathos* involved both an explanation of the utility of the work and a defense of the content, Boccaccio has separated these functions and dispersed them over the *Proemio*, which explains the work's utility, and the *Introduzione alla quarta giornata*, which defends against accusations. The *novelle* will later mimic the device of dividing functions between two different parts, as will be seen in chapter 4.

The *Introduzione alla quarta giornata* interrupts the narrative sequence of the days in order to posit a defense of the stories against real or imagined critics. The defense is delivered in two manners: through the author's direct address to the critics and through the *exemplum* of Filippo Balducci. Potter remarks that the defense's position in the work as an interruption, placed outside the parallel framing elements of the *Proemio* and the *Conclusione dell'Autore*, reinforces its metanarrative purpose because it is seemingly integrated within the narrative contents of the frame, among the other *novelle*.[82] Moreover, a significant part of the defense involves a story often referred to as the hundred-and-first novella of the *Decameron*, thus linking the function of the story with the structure of the whole. Boccaccio once again begins by addressing the *donne*, an address that reinforces the connection of this *Introduzione* to the *Proemio*. His initial claim that his *novelle* are humble, "non solamente in fiorentin volgare e in prosa scritte per me sono e senza titolo, ma ancora in istilo umilissimo e rimesso quanto il piú si possono" (IV: *Intro.*, 3) [(These little stories of mine) which bear no title and which I have written, not only in the Florentine vernacular and in prose, but in the most homely and unassuming style it is possible to imagine, 284], does not denote a literal excuse, but rather refers to the Classical tradition of the affected modesty topos.[83] Other literary references in this section to Ovid, Dante, and the *Novellino*[84] suggest that the passage clearly continues the literary and rhetorical system of interpretation established in the *Proemio*, here for the purpose of defending the author's work.

The alleged detractors of the *Decameron* contend that the author enjoys and pays excessive attention to women, particularly for a man of his age, that he would do better to write poetry, "dicono che io farei piú saviamente a starmi con le Muse in Parnaso che con queste ciance mescolarmi tra voi (le donne)" (IV: *Intro.*, 6) [(The critics) say that I would be better advised to remain with the Muses in Parnassus, than to fritter away my time in your company, 284], that he ought to "earn his bread" through some other pursuit, and that he is guilty of misrepresentation in his work. In response to the critics, or at least to the first objection that he is overly fond of women, Boccaccio narrates a story, "non una novella intera, acciò che non paia che io voglia le mie novelle con quelle di cosí laudevole compagnia, quale fu quella che dimostrata v'ho mescolare, ma parte d'una, acciò che il suo difetto stesso sé mostri non esser di quelle" (IV: *Intro.*, 11) [not a complete story (for otherwise it might appear that I was attempting to equate my own tales with those of the select company I have been telling you about), but a part of one, so that its very incompleteness will set it apart from the others, 285]. Boccaccio's emphasis on the unfinished nature of this *exemplum*, even though it is finished, may be an attempt to distance it from his "real *novelle*," but it actually only reinforces its resemblance to the other *novelle* within the frame. Since it is also among the most famous and widely distributed stories of the period, its position as extradiegetic interruption calls attention both to its metanarrative quality and to the utility of stories in general.[85]

Based on an *exemplum* found in *Barlaam et Josephat*,[86] the story of the Introduction to Day IV concerns Filippo Balducci, a Florentine who, having lost his wife, retreats from the world with his only son. At the age of eighteen, the son accompanies his father for the first time to the city where he marvels at all that he sees, asking his father to name everything. He is particularly compelled by the sight of women, but his father tells him not to look, explains that they are evil, and when pressed reluctantly gives them the name "goslings" (*papere*). The son insists that he has never seen anything so beautiful and would like to take one and feed it (put something in its bill), ("le darò beccare," IV: *Intro.*, 28). The father's response continues the metaphor: "'tu non sai donde s'imbeccano,' e sentí incontanente piú aver di forza la natura che il suo ingegno; e pentessi d'averlo menato a Firenze" (IV: *Intro.*, 29) ['Their bills are not where you think they are, and require a special sort of diet.' But no sooner had he spoken than he realized that his wits were no match for Nature, and regretted having brought the boy to Florence in the first place, 287].[87]

As the story illustrates, the son's natural desire for women ultimately triumphs over his father's plan to avoid them. The narrative emphasizes the association between Filippo and Boccaccio's detractors. As Marcus has explained, "in Filippo, Boccaccio is enacting his critics' injunction to abandon women in his dotage. Filippo takes his young son with him to a mountaintop, actualizing

Boccaccio's critics' suggestion that the writer repair to Mount Parnassus."[88] The limited world of the cave imposed on the son is only a part of Filippo's fabrication; the rest becomes apparent through his language when he deliberately misnames women *papere*. Filippo's fear that the very name of women will arouse his son's desire, "il padre, per non destare nel concupiscibile appetito del giovane alcuno inchinevole disiderio men che utile, non le volle nominare per lo proprio nome, cioè femine, ma disse: 'Elle si chiamano papere'" (IV: *Intro.*, 23) [Not wishing to arouse any idle longings in the young man's breast, his father avoided calling them by their real name, and instead of telling him that they were women, he said: 'They are called goslings', 287], shows that he assumes a literal understanding of words, at least for his son if not for himself. This assumption about the literal nature of language further associates Filippo Balducci with Boccaccio's critics.

Later in the narrative, literal becomes metaphorical when Balducci continues the metaphor of the *papere* that his son has seemingly understood literally. As Marcus notes, "Filippo's strategy of denial becomes one of disclosure through metaphor," disclosure about the sexual appetites of women, and consequently "Filippo learns that figurative language, far from masking its referent, can convey a truth with an efficacy superior to any equivalent literal expression."[89] Thus, the story of Filippo Balducci illustrates both the practical use of narrative and the power of Nature.[90] The story's focus on figurative language reinforces its exemplary position in the author's defense of narrative.

As an *exemplum*, however, the story of Filippo Balducci is problematic. Removed from the original frame narrative story collection of Eastern origin, Boccaccio has repurposed this antifeminist tale from *Barlaam et Josaphat* by reversing its message. Instead of offering a reason to avoid women and remain chaste as the story suggests in the Christianized frame of *Barlaam et Josaphat*, the story of Balducci justifies the author's desire for women as natural. The traces of antifeminism remain in Filippo, but the message of the tale in this context clearly undermines the work's traditional lesson. While Boccaccio's version of the story of Balducci resembles other versions of the *exemplum*, he replaces the typical misogynist reference to women as demons by referring to them instead as goslings.[91] The substitution of goslings for women is authorized by the common notion of appetite related to both sex and food. This substitution removes the work from the moral/misogynist context of the *exemplum* and places it into a metanarrative commentary on the nature of language and storytelling. Indeed, the interpretation of the entire story seems to hinge on a single word. This tale has the form of an *exemplum* with a fabliau ending. The text retains the didacticism and the codified language of the *exemplum*, but not its moral intent; instead, it defends storytelling.

Like the novella that precedes it (III:10, the story of Alibech and Rustico to be discussed in chapter 4), the story of Filippo Balducci also narrates a conversion: the linguistic conversion of women to goslings that enables Filippo's joke at the end, and the son's figurative conversion from ascetic to worldly and sexual young man. Through this notion of conversion, the story of Filippo Balducci retains, in an altered form, the conversion of Josaphat in the frame narrative of *Barlaam et Josaphat*. As in the story of Alibech, Boccaccio has inverted, or perhaps overlapped, spiritual conversion with sexual awakening. In this way, the story of Filippo Balducci may be seen as a partner, if not a gendered reversal, of the Alibech narrative that precedes it. While one story is arguably a fabliau and the other arguably an *exemplum*, the juxtaposition of the two suggests the malleability of literary forms. Both depict conversions, both draw on similar types of rhetoric, both mix Eastern and Western material, and both defy the moral expectations of the literary systems to which they belong.

Even though many scholars have contended that the tale is a parody of the *exemplum* through which Boccaccio intended to challenge religious asceticism and make obsolete the *exemplum* as a genre,[92] Potter astutely remarks that, if this were Boccaccio's intention, he would not have used an *exemplum* to defend his work.[93] Instead, Boccaccio transforms the *exemplum* to suit a literary purpose, and in this way validates vernacular literature on its own terms, without recourse to a moral or religious context. The story of Balducci paradoxically represents both the opposite of the Alibech tale, and the same lesson about conversion and the unfixed character of narrative that the rest of the *Decameron* will suggest in other ways.[94]

Finally, the *Conclusione dell'Autore* takes up the defense of the work begun in the *Introduzione alla quarta giornata*, while also returning to the precepts of the *Proemio*.[95] The criticisms Boccaccio mentions in this section are literary and touch specifically on his use of language. He denies the claim that he has "nello scriver queste novelle troppa licenzia usata," by appealing to his "honest" language, "niuna [novella] sí disonesta nè, che, con onesti vocaboli dicendola, si disdica a alcuno" (*Conc.*, 3) [in writing these stories . . . taken too many liberties (and) no story is so unseemly as to prevent anyone from telling it, provided it is told in seemly language, 798]. While Branca notes that this excuse is a traditional defense in medieval poetics, it also highlights the *courtoisie* of Boccaccio's language, and for Potter suggests a reference to the story of Filippo Balducci.[96] Boccaccio also states that even if the tales are unseemly, it is not his fault because it is part of the nature of the stories themselves, which he has only rendered faithfully; he later adds that he is not "lo 'nventor" (*Conc.*, 17) [the inventor] of the tales. While this response harks back to the allegation in the *Introduzione alla quarta giornata* of his dishonesty in presenting these tales, it also suggests the autonomy of fiction.[97] Yet the story of Balducci and a number of tales in the *Decameron* point to the opposite of this claim: that the stories are adaptable and modifiable to different contexts and diverse ends. This variable nature of the stories implies that they cannot have one purpose, one meaning, but rather that they must be open to interpretation, just as they are open to multiple renderings.

The mutability of the *novelle* finds a parallel in the mutability of the single term. In regards to the language of the stories, Boccaccio claims that "forse a spigolistra donna non si conviene, le quali piú le parole pesan che' fatti" (*Conc.*, 5) [(maybe the expressions) are too unbridled for those prudish ladies who attach more weight to words than to deeds, 798]. The statement that facts are of more weight than words is yet another allusion to the lesson learned by Filippo Balducci, and it also equates the autonomous stories with fact, as if they existed outside of his work. Continuing the argument that promotes the independence of his stories, Boccaccio explains that the *novelle* "chenti che elle si sieno, e nuocere e giovar possono, sí come possono tutte le altre cose, avendo riguardo all'ascoltatore" (*Conc.*, 8) [like all other things in this world, stories, whatever their nature, may be harmful or useful, depending upon the listener, 799]. This seems to be one of the central messages of the *Decameron*, one which it shares with the fabliaux. In this way, Boccaccio asserts the openness of his *novelle* by placing the responsibility of interpretation on the audience.[98] In stating that "niuna corratta mente intese mai sanamente parola" (*Conc.*, 11) [no word, however pure, was ever wholesomely construed by a mind that was corrupt, 799], Boccaccio equates the interpretation of stories with the interpretation of a single word, once again by evoking the story of Filippo Balducci. In this way, he also places the onus of interpretation on the reader, not the writer. As a work that focuses on the nature of language and open-ended narrative, the *Decameron* has much in common with the fabliaux. Using and referring back to the story of Filippo Balducci, an *exemplum* that Boccaccio altered through a fabliau-style reversal, integrates an Eastern-origin *exemplum* with predominantly Western allusions, for the benefit of Western detractors, and announces more profound combinations of Eastern and Western collections in other levels of the narrative.

Therefore, the outermost level of the frame where Boccaccio explains the import of his *Decameron* not only mixes Eastern and Western traditions, it also points to the work's need to be interpreted and to the responsibility of the reader to weigh and judge the material without authorial direction. This mixture of East and West recalls the "fabliaux codices" just as the reversal in the defense story of Filippo Balducci is reminiscent of the fabliaux as a genre. The fabliaux and the manuscripts that preserved them influenced the *Decameron* beyond the level of themes in the individual *novelle*; both the fabliaux and the *Decameron* point to the multiplicity of narrative meaning and the need for interpretation. The different narrative levels of the *Decameron* reinforce this message and the text's relationship to fabliaux.

The *Cornice*

The frame narrative or *cornice*[99] of the *Decameron* establishes a coherent context for Boccaccio's collection of one hundred stories. Boccaccio centers the narration of the tales around a *brigata* of ten young men and women, who leave plague-ridden Florence and escape to the countryside, where they pass the time by each narrating one story every day over ten days. The three young men and seven young women take turns presiding over the storytelling, each serving as king or queen for a day and usually designating a theme for the day's stories (the exceptions being the stories of Days I and IX which are "free"). Each day concludes with a song, a type of lyric finale performed by one of the *brigata*. At the end of their sojourn, the young men and women return to the city. The frame combines Eastern and Western frames, primarily by using a narrative derived from Eastern sources with the organization of the days within the frame and their *novelle* evoking the Western practice of *ordinatio*.

Boccaccio encloses the Eastern-inspired *cornice* with allusions to traditional (Western) literary topoi in the extradiegetic frame. Yet the narrative of the *cornice* also draws on Western literary material, combining this and other traditions with the Eastern device in a seamless description that begins with the historical event of the Black Death. While the sections of the first level of narration as described by Picone are to some extent considered part of the frame, the *cornice* proper distinguishes itself from the level of writing and address because it sets up the narrative that will make the *novelle* possible, depicting not only the history of the Plague, but also the introduction of the *brigata*, and the scenes describing the activities of the *brigata* at the beginning and end of each day.

As mentioned above, the *cornice* corresponds to the framing devices of Eastern story collections, although it does not re-create a specific frame from one of the collections discussed; rather it is an amalgamation. Unlike the Eastern collections, the multiple narrators form a harmonious group where none threatens the life of any of the others, as in the Seven Sages tradition or *Barlaam et Josaphat*, but rather they exist primarily through their dialogue with each other, as was the case in both *Barlaam et Josaphat* and the *Disciplina Clericalis*. The members of the *brigata* constitute an ideal audience, a rather courtly one, which highlights the literary intent of the work. That the audience also serves as narrators reinforces this intent. The *brigata* is a specific Western institution in an Eastern frame device.

Tracing the elements of the *cornice* to earlier collections, Picone formulates three types of frames and demonstrates their application to the *Decameron cornice*.[100] The first type of frame inserts stories into a larger narrative for the purpose of avoiding or delaying an action, such as in the *1001 Nights* or the *Septem sapientum*; the second type of frame furthers the main narrative by using stories to prove a point or defend a position, as in Josaphat's conversion in *Barlaam et Josaphat*;[101] the third type of frame presents stories narrated *in itinere* as in the *Canterbury Tales*.[102] As Picone explains, these three types of frames are found "nel *Proemio*, dove si scopre la presenza non solo del primo tipo di incorniciamento (le cento novelle vengono raccontate per liberare le donne dalla loro malinconia amorosa) ma anche degli altri due (del secondo, in quanto le novelle offriranno "utile consiglio" alle donne; e del terzo perché le aiuteranno ad attraversare il "cupo pelago" della vita)" [in the *Proem*, where one discerns the presence not only of the first type of framing device (the hundred stories will be told to liberate the ladies from their amorous melancholy) but also of the other two (of the second, in which the *novelle* will offer "useful advice" to the women; and of the third because they will help them to cross the 'cupo pelago' of life].[103] While the third frame only fits metaphorically into the structure of the *Decameron*—arguably because the first example of its use is in Chaucer's *Canterbury Tales*, which postdates Boccaccio's work—the first and second types are clearly combined. For the *brigata* the tales function to ward off death and to entertain, creating an idyllic, ordered society that stands in contrast to the destruction in the city;[104] while for the audience of *donne*, as Picone explains, the stories help them ease their sufferings in love and offer them advice.

Picone's study highlights Boccaccio's combination of the different models for the frame narrative. Moreover, the content of the frame is also taken from various sources, thereby furthering this notion of combination. Boccaccio places the events of the *cornice* in the recent past, the Black Death of 1348 in the city of Florence. In this way, the scenario of the *cornice* is original and historically anchored; consequently, it is not a translation or adaptation of a frame from one of the Eastern collections of stories. The Plague of 1348 in Florence serves as the true historical impetus, and Branca insists that Boccaccio's use of the plague is based on the description of the pestilence in Italy in the eighth-century *Historia langobardorum* (II. 4) by Paul the Deacon.[105] To this allusion, Giovanni Getto adds Livy's description of the plague during the siege of Syracuse in *Ab urbe condita* (XXV. 26); Gaetano Braccini and Simone Marchesi have demonstrated Boccaccio's reliance on this passage by citing a number of similarities in the language of description in the *Decameron* and in Livy's text.[106] Furthermore, Joseph Gibaldi has noted the pastoral influence in the *cornice*, where the pastoral genre serves as the nostalgia for a past that never was.[107] Therefore, the content of the frame is the result of a combination of historical and literary sources, much like the allusions of the extradiegetic level of narration. The frame further reflects Boccaccio's *ars combinatoria* by mixing Eastern-inspired structural devices with content from Classical models. It is precisely this relationship, pairing the structural models of one type with thematic models of another that reflects the connection between the generally Eastern-inspired frame and the Classical and vernacular story content.

As shown in relation to the story of Filippo Balducci, *Barlaam et Josaphat* furnishes Boccaccio with a model for a specific story as well as for the frame. The same is true to some degree of the other collections of tales, for they provide sources for individual stories and serve as a model for the frame, as is the case for VII:4 which is a version of *Puteus* from the Seven Sages tradition, or for X:8 from the *Disciplina Clericalis*.[108] Since these frame narrative collections function on both macro- and micro-textual levels, may the same be said of the inverse situation? Do narratives such as fabliaux that provide source material for individual stories also serve as organizational models in their codicological contexts? Are the Eastern and Western narrative traditions that are combined to form the *Decameron* used analogously? Compilers of Old French manuscript anthologies brought together disparate texts in order to form codices. Boccaccio's use of the frame brings together similarly disparate materials and links them through narrative. Both the "fabliaux codices" and Boccaccio's *Decameron* are attempts to collect and reassemble the narrative traditions of the East and West.

The Ten Days of the *Decameron*: Themes and Order

The *cornice* serves a structural function by bringing together different narrative levels while also providing a context for, and intermittent respites from, the narration of the hundred *novelle*. The frame announces the ways in which the tales will be organized: by day and by theme. The *cornice* is integrated with the *novelle* and, as Almansi explains, the *cornice* "serves pre-eminently to instruct the reader as to how the stories are to be read and understood, since they do not exist as separate entities but are conditioned and reflected by the stories that precede and follow them, by the themes for the day and the personality of the individual story-teller, and even by the young company's own jokes, comments, tears and sympathy for their fictional creations."[109] Despite this integration, the *cornice* remains a fictional exterior commentary to the *novelle* as it highlights the *novelle*'s role as fiction.

As the narrative thread that links the stories of the ten days of the *Decameron*, the *cornice* provides a unifying, ordering design, but it does not explicitly participate in the sequencing of the days. The only direct indications that the days are sequenced within the text issue from the discussions of the *brigata*. The interrelationships of the days are primarily thematic. Although the organization of the ten days may parallel the organization of the ten stories within each day, exploring these levels separately will suggest the various ways in which structure and thematics interlock in the *Decameron*.

Unlike the tales of the Seven Sages tradition, the tales narrated on a single day in the *Decameron* usually concern a single theme designated by the ruling king or queen of that day. There are only two exceptions to this thematic structure: The first day has no explicit theme, and is therefore "free," and the ninth day similarly suspends the rule in favor of variety, giving no thematic constraints. Because the other days are unified by a theme, they form thematic narrative units reminiscent of the thematic groupings in some of the Old French manuscripts discussed previously. In order, the themes for the remaining days are:

> Day II = "di chi, da diversi cose infestato, sia oltre alla sua speranza riuscito a lieto fine" [Those who after suffering a series of misfortunes are brought to a state of unexpected happiness]
> Day III = "di chi alcuna cosa molto da lui disiderata con industria acquistasse o la perduta ricoverasse" [People who by dint of their own efforts have achieved an object they greatly desired, or recovered a thing previously lost]
> Day IV = "di coloro li cui amori ebbero infelice fine" [Those whose love ended unhappily]
> Day V = "di ciò che a alcuno amante, dopo alcuni fieri o sventurati accidenti, felicemente avvenisse" [The adventures of lovers who survived calamities or misfortunes and attained a state of happiness]

Day VI = "di chi con alcun leggiadro motto tentato, si riscotesse, o con pronto risposta o avvedimento fuggí perdita o pericolo o scorno" [Those who, on being provoked by some verbal pleasantry, have returned like for like, or who, by a prompt retort or shrewd manoeuvre, have avoided danger, discomfiture or ridicule]

Day VII = "delle beffe, le quali o per amore o per salvamento di loro le donne hanno già fatte a' suoi mariti, senza essersene avveduti o sí" [The tricks which, either in the cause of love or for motives of self-preservation, women have played on their husbands, irrespective of whether or not they were found out]

Day VIII = "di quelle beffe che tutto il giorno o donna a uomo o uomo a donna o l'uno uomo all'altro si fanno" [The tricks that people in general, men and women alike, are forever playing upon one another]

Day X = "di chi liberalmente o vero magnificamente alcuna cosa operasse intorno a' fatti d'amore o d'altra cosa" [Those who have performed liberal or munificent deeds, whether in the cause of love of otherwise].

From the outset, the themes for the days reveal not only the tastes of the *brigata*, but their often contrary reactions to the storytelling. For example, Pampinea declares "per questa prima giornata voglio che libero sia a ciascuno di quella materia ragionare che piú gli sarà a grado" (I: *Intro.*, 114) [I desire that on the first day each of us should be free to speak upon whatever topic he prefers, 23]. At the end of the day when the rule is passed to Filomena, she deliberately deviates from Pampinea's rule by requiring a theme: "io il voglio cominciare a fare: cioè a ristringere dentro a alcun termine quello che dobbiamo novellare" (I: *Conc.*, 10) [I do however wish to initiate a practice ... namely to restrict the matter of our storytelling within some fixed limit, 67]. This shift from narrating the desires of all to the desire of one individual, from personal freedom of narration to a limiting theme, from extemporaneous narration to well thought-out storytelling, constitutes in many ways a series of oppositions that contrast Days I and II. Hollander notes that the first story of Day II counterbalances the first story of Day I, while Marcus sees similarities between Day I and the "wheel of Fortune" that governs Day II.[110] In the case of I:4, Almansi disagrees with the assertion of Padoan, who finds that the tales in Day I result in the opposite of what the protagonist wants, whereas on Day II the results are the opposite of what the protagonist expected.[111]

Similarly, the happy endings owing to Fortune in the *novelle* of Day II differ markedly from the "industria" and self-reliance of the tricksters on Day III. The clash between the notable concupiscence of Day III and the tragic love of Day IV continues the *perle rouge perle noire* thematic pattern established by the previous days' divergent narrative material. The days of the *Decameron* resemble clusters of stories related by theme, whose disparities among the clusters recall the variegated structures of Old French anthologies. Even in this small sample of *Decameron* themes, the third day functions as the *élément perturbateur*.

The opposition between the themes of Days IV and V offers arguably the most striking contrast in the *Decameron*. While Filostrato asks the *brigata* to tell stories about unhappy love ("infelice fine"), Fiammetta commands the opposite ("felicemente avvenisse"). Fiammetta, "la quale meglio dell'aspra giornata d'oggi, che alcun altra, con quella di domani queste nostre compagne racconsolar sapr[à]" (IV: *Conc.*, 3) [knowing that (she is) better able than any other to restore the spirits of our fair companions tomorrow after the rigours of the present day's proceedings, 363], becomes responsible for recuperating the *brigata* from Filostrato's error of leading them into unhappiness. The direct opposition of these two days plays out in the language of the stated themes, where the pair "infelice/felicemente" strongly suggests opposition, even though the forms of the words—one adjective and one adverb—downplay the polarity. The language of the tales on these days also reflects this opposition. As Marcus has suggested, the tragic tales of Day IV, especially IV:1, show the literalization of metaphor, whereas the comic tales of Day V, especially V:4, use a metaphor to represent the literal.[112] As much may be said of the juxtaposition of the linguistic modes of Days III and IV, since many of the stories on Day III involve similar plays on the nature of figurative and literal language. Although Marcus argues that the tragic mode of Day IV is incongruous with the rest of the *Decameron*, the tone of the stories on Day III, which is one of the most indebted to the fabliaux, also sets these works apart in the first half of the *Decameron*.

Victoria Kirkham suggests that a "longer narrative unit starting with the third day and extending through the fifth"[113] unites the *novelle* on these days. Although Kirkham admits thematic similarities between Day I and Day II, she argues for a moral interpretation of the sequence of days in order to justify the licentiousness of Day III, "for if we now ask where the adultery and fornication of the third day lead in the *Decameron*, we find a pattern that recalls thematic motifs of Boccaccio's earlier works. Carnal desire (III), while humanly natural (Intro. IV), leads to tragedy and death (IV) unless legitimized by the life-affirming institution of matrimony (V)."[114] Since in this interpretation these days are dependent upon each other, their order must be observed and their sequencing becomes a part of their interpretation. This justification-of-marriage group recalls similar groupings in codices of fabliaux like MS B. Kirkham's observations, an exclusively moral reading of the *Decameron*, limit the purpose of Day III, of the fabliaux material in general, to *exempla-in-malo*. Although a valid reading, Day III, and by extension the other days (VII, VIII, and IX) in which the stories are predominately inspired by fabliaux, propose more than negative exemplarity, but rather the numerous possibilities of narration and interpretation, as an analysis of some *novelle* on these days will suggest in chapter 4.

The transition from Day V to Day VI offers not so much a thematic contrast as a stylistic one. Many of the tales on Day VI serve as metaliterary commentaries on the whole work. Marcus posits that Day VI "reflects the organizing principle of the entire *Decameron*."[115] Hollander notes that Days I and VI are both beginnings, are both Wednesdays, and are related by witty remarks.[116] Indeed, the days of the week also relate the Days of narration to each other. Since Days I and VI are Wednesdays, then Days II and VII are Thursdays, Days III and VIII are Sundays, Days IV and IX are Mondays, and finally Days V and X are Tuesdays. Yet the days of the week do not furnish too many thematic parallels. Janet Levarie Smarr has charted the symmetry of Days I–IX in a "9 + 1 pattern"[117]:

> Days I and IX are parallel because they have a free topic.
> Day II is topically linked to Day III just as Day VII is linked to Day VIII. Days III and VII both have new locations and Fiammetta and Dioneo sing together. The garden and *valle delle donne* on Days III and VII respectively are "farther removed from the plagued city, more protected and more naturally ideal."
> Days IV and VI have interruptions in the intradiegetic narrative and are the only days on which the king/queen sings. Moreover, the interruptions on Days IV and VI "form a matched pair in which for men and for women sex is proclaimed the uncontrollable natural instinct."
> Day V is central to this structure and is symmetrical with Day X.[118]

Yet this perfect symmetry does not hold for the juxtaposition of the days, which reveal other relationships. For example, Days VII, VIII, and IX, which all have many tales based on fabliaux, form a subgroup about trickery and are related by many intertextual references. The intertexts of these days support the variability of the themes, thus opening them to multiple interpretations. Under Dioneo's rule, Day VII concerns *beffe* that wives play on their husbands. Although Day VIII continues the theme of *beffe*, at the end of Day VII the new queen, Lauretta, almost commands the opposite of Dioneo's theme: "se fosse che io non voglio mostrare d'essere schiatta di can botolo che incontanente si vuol vendicare, io direi che domane si dovesse ragionare delle beffe che gli uomini fanno alle lor moglie" (VII: *Conc.*, 3) [but for the fact that I do not wish it to be thought that I belong to that breed of snapping curs who immediately turn round and retaliate, I should oblige you, on the morrow, to talk about the tricks played on wives by their husbands, 548]. By opening the theme to tricks men and women play on each other in general (as well as tricks men play on men), Lauretta avoids creating an opposing theme and instead promotes thematic unity. Still, the chiastic structure of the topic she provides suggests opposition between her Day and Dioneo's, as well as the oppositions between characters in the tales themselves: "di quelle beffe che tutto il giorno **o donna a uomo o uomo a donna** o l'uno uomo all'altro si fanno," (emphasis added). Opposition on and between these days highlights interpretive poles. While Day IX is "free," it arguably continues the *beffe* of the previous days and connects to some tales on Day VIII through the repeat occurrence of Calandrino tales. Finally, Day X is as enigmatic as the first day. Hollander has focused on the myth of order that the sequencing of these tales creates and the notion that the structure is actually open-ended.[119] His assertion that Day X is the "inverse companion piece to Day IX" continues the pattern of opposition observed in the previous days.[120] After the freedom from narrative constraints on Day IX, Day X marks a return to law and order, and as such constitutes the opposite of Day IX. In the "9 + 1" symmetrical pattern, however, the stories of Day X are concerned with sexual renunciation and thus represent the opposite of the other days.[121] Once again, the days reflect the same type of thematic and stylistic oppositions familiar from the anthologies of fabliaux.

While there is a case to be made for the progression from best to worst, moving from *novelle* I:1 to X:10, the intermediate days do not follow the same progression, but rather resemble the variegated structures found in the Old French codices. Whether subgroupings of similar themes, as in Days VII, VIII, and IX, or contrasting subgroups that inform one another, as in Days III, IV, and V, the sequencing of days of the *Decameron* reflects the frameless textual patterns of the "fabliaux codices." Within the Eastern-inspired *cornice*, the organization of the days resembles Western manuscript collections, thus combining Eastern and Western sources for the structure.

The Order and Sequencing of *Novelle*

For the *novelle* within the days, the same question of order applies, except for the last story of Days II–X, which is consistently narrated by Dioneo. Yet Dioneo's privilege already indicates a precise structure for the *novelle*. Picone has suggested that Boccaccio's separation of the tenth story of every day is derived from the structure of *Barlaam et Josephat* where the tenth story is the exception, the negative *exemplum* of the collection.[122] This observation shows that the order of the *novelle* is determined by some organizational principle that may vary from day to day but still maintains a "9+1" pattern for the central days. The intertextual relations of the *novelle* are of two types: the interplay of stories within a single day and the interplay of stories across days. The majority of these interrelations are thematic or else metanarrative commentaries. Similar to the Old French codices, the structure of each day demands individual consideration because not all days are structured in the same way. In particular, the "free" days, those without thematic designations given by a member of the *brigata*, conceivably display implicit organizational principles, and in this way mimic the implied structure of some "fabliaux codices." The following analysis will focus on Days I, III, VII, VIII, and IX because they display the strongest rapport with the fabliaux.

The first day is in many respects the most enigmatic, for there is no specified theme under Pampinea's rule. The disparate source material and the variety of themes and characters in the first day, however, do not immediately suggest any principles of organization.[123] In this, Day I resembles the "fabliaux codices." Given the lack of an explicit connection among the stories, Day I of the *Decameron* leaves the reader with the same types of organizational questions as many anthologies preserving fabliaux: Are these stories related? If so, how? What coherent principle of organization links these texts? For example, the grouping of *novelle* three, four, and five of the first day demonstrates the range of themes and sources. The third story relates the parable of Melchisedek the Jew and the question of the one true religion, followed by the fabliaux-inspired tale of the monk and the abbot who are guilty of the same sin of concupiscence with the same girl, and finally the fifth tale, borrowed from the Seven Sages tradition, illustrates the clever remark of the Marchesana di Monferrato used to deter the passions of the king of France. Thus, this small assemblage of *novelle* reflects three different themes and three different types of sources, and concerns three vastly different societies. Such thematic disparity among the tales is reminiscent of a codex like MS A. For example, in MS A the moralizing text *Les Sept vices et sept vertus* is coupled with the bawdy fabliau *La Grue* (see chapter 1), and in the section of Rutebeuf's works in this same manuscript, his *Ordres de Paris*, a satire against the mendicant orders, is followed by the scatological fabliau *Le Pet au vilain*, and finally by the renardian fable about the stag *Brichemer* (ff. 314, 315, 315). MS E similarly presents Rutebeuf's works: the

Complainte de Saint Amor is followed by the *Pet au vilain* and then *Brichemer* (ff. 70, 71, 72). In the *Decameron*, the focus on order established in the *Proemio* and in the *cornice* by the author implies that the rest of the *Decameron* follows some similar type of organization.

Scholars have often argued for a thematic current to unify the stories of Day I: "Si è così ipotizzata la presenza di un filo tematico che percorre l'intera prima giornata iniziale, e che consiste secondo alcuni interpreti nella 'riprensione aspre ed amara dei vizi dei grandi' e secondo altri nella 'esaltazione della parola astuta e intelligente'" [It is hypothesized that the presence of a thematic thread runs through the entire first day and according to some critics consists of the "bitter and cutting censure of the vices of great people" and according to others of the "exaltation of the witty and intelligent word"].[124] The first of these interpretations implies a moral intent of the stories, one not necessarily in keeping with the first story of Ser Cepparello, while the second, the relation of *buoni motti*, responds more appropriately to the metaliterary question of language, but as Timothy Kircher remarks, it "fails to account for the developments in either Panfilo or Neifile's narratives, the first two tales, nor does it point out the object of this wit."[125] Another reading of the first day, which is valid for all of the *novelle*, is the transformative role of language. That many of these stories also present a mise en abyme or highlight the role of narration by one of the characters (I:1, 3, 7) points to the central role of language in the first day. As Picone explains, "l'unità della prima giornata non è di tipo tematico ma funzionale, non è un'unità narrativa ma metanarrativa" [the unity of the first day is not of a thematic type but of a functional type, it is not a narrative unity but a metanarrative unity].[126]

Because of the variety of *novelle* told on Day I, it may be argued that the first day is the most representative of the genre and of the company of *novellatori*. Significantly, the first novella, which arguably frames the rest in conjunction with X:10, revolves around linguistic opposition. Getto has argued that Ser Ciappelletto's confession is a systematic reversal of his lifetime of sin as described by Panfilo.[127] That the first novella turns on linguistic reversals validates the significance of this device in the *Decameron* and calls the reader's attention to further play on opposition in the remaining *novelle*, if not in the structure. Indeed, reversals and narrative combinations will shape the reading of the rest of the *Decameron* by showing ambiguity as open to interpretation. In this way, the *novelle* offer a similar lesson about the nature of reading to that of the fabliaux.

Dioneo's tale (I:4), the first in the *Decameron* to break from the (pseudo-) spiritual tenor of the preceding tales, announces his inclination for fabliaux-related themes. These themes are fully realized under his rule on Day VII, one of the days most indebted to fabliaux. Similarly, Elissa's first story (I:9) is the shortest of the first day and involves terse verbal play—a rebuke to a cowardly king—that yields extraordinary results and reverses the king's attitude. Day VI when she is queen is likewise marked by the brevity of the tales, certainly the shortest in the *Decameron*, and the focus on the power of wit and verbal play. In this way, the stories of the first day are sometimes indicative of the different types of narrators, such that every member of the *brigata* has a distinct personality that is reflected in the thematic bent of their individual tales and of the days under their rule. Yet the relationship between the stories of the first day and their reflection in the themes of the remaining days does not necessarily hold for all of the characters because the ninth day, which is also "free," is overwhelmingly related to fabliaux material and to the interplay with stories from Day VIII, most notably those that concern Calandrino.

The third day involves tricks, specifically those demonstrating how characters' *industria* helps them to attain what they desire or to recover what is lost. As already mentioned, the word "industria" falls into the same semantic field as the word "ingegno"; both are closely tied to the wit of fabliaux themes. The third day is also related to the second because they both deal with Fortune.[128] In comparison with the first two days, the structure of the third day is elaborate and symmetrical because "Boccaccio offers five pairs of closely related stories in which there exist both a male and female counterpart."[129] The pairs of tales, as Marina Brownlee shows, are 1-10, 2-5, 3-7, 4-8, 6-9. The stories of each pair use the same type of *industria*, with one featuring a male, the other a female protagonist.[130] For example, in the first story, Masetto di Lamporecchio's feigned stupidity allows him to satisfy his sexual desires with a convent of nuns, whereas in the tenth tale, Alibech's real naïveté leads her to pursue her sexual desire, nominally in the service of God, with the hermit Rustico. The other pairs function in a similar way, but rather than focusing on the gender equality and symmetry in these tales, these pairs highlight narrative inversions of the type demonstrated in fabliaux. The inversion of the first and last tales forms a chiasmus that frames the rest of the stories on Day III. In this way, both the theme and the structure of Day III emphasize fabliaux. The themes of trickery and inversion common to fabliaux and the *novelle* of Day III are both realized in the structural inversion represented by a chiastic frame. Furthermore, Day III, as Brownlee has noted, descends from the "Paradiso in terra" at the beginning of the day, through Ferondo's Purgatory in III:8, and finally culminates in Alibech's metaphorical Hell.[131] While Purgatory and Hell are shown in the diegetic level of narration, Paradise on earth exists only for the *brigata* since it is presented in the intradiegetic level of the Introduction to Day III. In this way, the stories of Day III demonstrate a frame shift with the world of the *brigata* and call attention to their fiction. The order of the tales on Day III does not resemble the variegation in anthologies of fabliaux, but rather reflects the chiastic pattern of paired opposites of the fabliaux themselves. In this instance, the structure of the day has been borrowed from structural aspects of the content. These reversals of themes indicate the variability of interpretation for these stories, which may be written and interpreted from opposing perspectives.

Why should Day III, which up until the midpoint of the *Decameron* has been the most highly structured day, also be the day with the bawdiest tales? The order presented in the extradiegetic level of narration and in the *cornice* anticipates organization of a similar kind for the individual narratives. Yet the first day to point to its own contrived structure is Day III, the fabliau day. This structure reinforces the notion that the narrative material of the fabliaux points to its own structure and its own purpose as fiction. The more contrived the structure of a tale or a day, the more that structure calls attention to itself as a creation, as fiction. The stories of Day III participate in a metanarrative commentary about the nature of storytelling; consequently the days that present fabliaux mimic this metanarrative reflexivity by calling attention to their own structure. More than any other day, however, the fabliaux material on Day III suggests narrative and interpretive possibilities through opposite pairs of tales. The device used in individual fabliaux to open up a single text to variant readings has been transformed by Boccaccio into an organizational level that includes narrative more generally. The organization displayed on the predominantly fabliaux-inspired days and the metanarrative quality of this material, will be examined through specific examples in chapter 4.

Smarr notes that Day III is one of the most removed from reality, since the *brigata* move to the paradisiacal garden. On Day VII, a day that parallels Day III, the *brigata* move to the equally perfect *valle delle donne*. While the tales on Day VII are largely related to fabliaux, they also draw on Eastern sources. *Novelle* VII:1, 4, and 6 all have analogues in the *Disciplina Clericalis*, and VII:8 in other Eastern collections. *Novelle* VII:2, 5, 7 have fabliaux analogues. Day VII brings together the tales of Eastern story collections with the fabliaux tradition, highlighting the analogies between the two traditions as many of the previously considered "fabliaux manuscripts" do. The tales are unified by the theme of the trick, rather than the antifeminist message of the Eastern frame narratives. Boccaccio's frame is for the benefit of women, not their condemnation. The stories do not have the same message here because the frame has been changed, suggesting that the context alters the value of the tales.

Although the tales of Days VII and VIII are in large part indebted to fabliaux, they do not display the same systematic organization as Day III. The intratextual connections and references among some *novelle* on these days will be discussed in more detail in chapter 4. As the tales are united by theme, they do not demonstrate the same type of variegation seen in some anthologies of fabliaux, but they do underscore analogies between tales from the Eastern collections and the fabliaux.

The alternation of fabliaux and nonfabliaux stories of Day IX evokes the *perle rouge, perle noire* organizational pattern of the Old French manuscripts: IX:2, 6, 10 have fabliaux analogues or a fabliau ethos, and IX:4 and 8 are close to fabliaux since they involve tricks, while IX:3 and 5 involve the recurring character Calandrino. The remaining tales of Day IX are of completely divergent thematic material. Not only does this structure resemble the patterns of "fabliaux codices" evoked above, but it once again emphasizes the texts' role as fiction. The stories about Calandrino narrated across these days further highlight the intertextuality and self-reflexivity of these narratives, which essentially concern the creation of a fiction resulting in a trick. As they are based on a recurring character, however, the Calandrino stories are closer to the *branches* of the *Roman de Renart* than the fabliaux.

In general, the structure of *novelle* within the days and the ordering of the days imitate the organizational patterns of many Old French anthologies preserving fabliaux, particularly as they bring together tales from Eastern and Western collections. While this study does not propose specific manuscripts as models for Boccaccio's work, it does suggest that there are extant codices of fabliaux that offer examples of the types of organizational principles employed by Boccaccio. The influence of the fabliaux and of the manuscripts that they helped shape is reflected in the organization of the days. In this way, the structure of the *Decameron* at the intradiegetic and diegetic levels combines the Eastern frame narratives with the Western manuscript anthologies. The impact of the fabliaux on specific *novelle* reveals how Boccaccio combined narrative material and the many ways in which inversions function in the *Decameron*.

4

Boccaccio's Fabliaux

Transmission and Transformation of the Fabliaux to the *Decameron*

> L'una e l'altra [orazione] fu vera.... nella vostra elezione sta di
> torre qual più vi piace delle due.
>
> [Both accounts are correct if there is any truth in a story....
> I therefore leave it to you ... to choose the version you prefer.]
>
> DECAMERON VII:1, 33–34

The previous chapter explored similarities between codices preserving fabliaux and the organizational levels of the *Decameron*, but this relationship was based on two presuppositions: The first is a connection between the Old French literary tradition generally and fabliaux specifically to Boccaccio; this is indisputable.[1] In the fourteenth century when Boccaccio wrote the *Decameron*, the cultural and literary influences of medieval France had already extended to various regions of the Italian peninsula, where popular and courtly ideals continued to be integrated into the nascent vernacular literature. One of the best-known illustrations of this point is in Dante's *Divina Commedia*, Canto V (137) of the *Inferno* where we learn that Paolo and Francesca had been reading about Gallehault. Of course, the subtitle of the *Decameron*, "Prencipe Galeotto," is a reference both to Dante and to the Vulgate Cycle.[2]

Already in the thirteenth century the written vernacular in France had become a firmly established literary tradition that arguably reached its apex in the course of this century. The French literary tradition would also serve as a model for other vernacular literatures. While a vernacular literature developed later and more slowly in most of Italy than in other parts of *Romania*—excluding the north where a Franco-Italian tradition was already well established—the thirteenth century and in particular the court of Frederick II (1222–50) in Sicily marked the beginning of an Italian vernacular literary tradition.[3] Courtly literature from the *langue d'Oïl* region of France and the notion of *courtoisie*, which itself developed under the influence of works written in *langue d'Oc*, were also well known throughout the peninsula and profoundly affected works in the Italian vernacular. These literary ties continued into the following century, during which time relations between France and Italy were strengthened as a function of the political power of the Angevin dynasty. In addition to political connections, there was a continuous influx of French culture into Italy through crusaders, as well as through merchants and *jongleurs/giullari*.

Boccaccio possessed a knowledge of the Old French literary tradition. As Giorgio Padoan explains, Boccaccio studied in Naples where the society "imbevuta di ideali cavallereschi e per di più legata a doppio filo alla Francia, si rivolgeva necessariamente al mondo culturale ed avventuroso dei romanzi di cavalleria, al mondo cortese ed intellettualistico dei fabliaux, noti e diffusi in tutta Italia" [imbued with the ideals of chivalry and also linked to France by a double thread, necessarily turned to the cultural and adventurous world of the romances of chivalry, to the courtly and intellectually bent world of the fabliaux which were renowned and widespread in all of Italy].[4] From this statement, it seems that Padoan considers the fabliaux part of the courtly world, suggesting that with the spread of courtly literature came the fabliaux. Indeed, in addition to the manuscript witnesses of the fabliaux, the diffusion of Old French literature, in general through the courts and popularly through *giullari*, suggests that the fabliaux were widely known in many parts of Italy in the thirteenth and fourteenth centuries.

The second premise linking the codices of fabliaux to the structure of the *Decameron* concerns the transmission of the fabliaux tradition to Boccaccio primarily through written models. While the various points of contact between these cultures present possibilities for both written and oral transmission of literary works, scholars have tended to focus more on the vague possibilities of oral transmission rather than the concrete models of "fabliaux manuscripts." Landau explains that Boccaccio probably heard fabliaux in Naples and that "auch im übrigen Italien konnte man französische Jongleurs und Minstrels finden, die ihre Fabliaux vortrugen" [also in the rest of Italy one could find French *jongleurs* and minstrels performing their fabliaux].[5] In contrast, chapter 2 presented a manuscript with fabliaux that was probably copied in Italy, showing that there were fabliaux available in written form in Italy during the thirteenth and fourteenth centuries. The historical ties between the court of Naples and French courts, especially Anjou and Hainaut, facilitated the transmission of many materials, including literature. Thus, there were a number of ways involving written sources in which Boccaccio could have come into contact with fabliaux. An examination of *Decameron* IX:2 in this chapter will suggest a specific way in which Boccaccio would have come into contact with other French manuscripts while in Naples.[6]

Showing direct literary transmission to the *Decameron* proves difficult in light of Boccaccio's frequent mixture of sources. Additionally, the availability of similar tales in collections such as those mentioned in chapter 3 makes it rare to find a novella in the *Decameron* with a single antecedent or definitive source. Indeed, the notion of literary sources should more properly be replaced by degrees of literary influence, since Boccaccio manipulates the works he uses, often in combination with others, so that the end result is recognizable, but altered. Like the fabliaux, much of Boccaccio's alterations depend on reversals, as this chapter will suggest. Similarly, tales with several antecedents complicate the question of sources because it becomes more difficult to distinguish between textual allusions and common topoi. Even though a number of antecedents for a tale may relate the same theme, actual intertextual connections rely on substantial stylistic, structural, and rhetorical similarities. Some works display a greater degree of influence than others, as measured by the quality and quantity of thematic and linguistic similarities. The occurrence of certain topoi and the use of specific stylistic and lexical forms may correspond. In other words, "qualunque sia la diffusione di un tema—si presenti cioè con frequenza altissima, media o minima—ciascun tema aveva già imposto un lessico particolare, particolari stilemi, entro cui si individuano formule fisse" [whatever the diffusion of a theme—whether it presents itself with high, medium, or minimal frequency—each theme is already stamped with a particular lexicon, particular stylistics, among which some fixed forms may distinguish themselves].[7]

Therefore, this chapter considers select fabliaux in relation to a few stories in the *Decameron*, without necessarily qualifying antecedents as direct and unique sources for Boccaccio unless strong textual, or possibly historical, evidence dictates otherwise. This is not to deny Boccaccio's use of direct sources,[8] but the plurality of sources in the *Decameron* necessitates close reading and comparison of the language of specific examples in order to determine the role of the fabliaux and of reversal.

La Nonete: An Analogue of Novella IX:2

As already noted, the fabliaux supply a high quotient of analogues to the hundred tales in Boccaccio's *Decameron*.[9] Approximately one-fourth of the *novelle* in the collection borrow from the fabliaux tradition. Landau cites several fabliaux in his study of sources for the *Decameron* and Branca mentions about twenty-four fabliaux titles in the notes to his edition of the *Decameron*.[10] Rossi has stated that twenty of the tales in the *Decameron* are demonstrably related to fabliaux sources, but he does not provide a list of these fabliaux or their corresponding *novelle*;[11] the fabliaux's influence arguably surpasses this figure.

Of the tales derived from or inspired by fabliaux, *Decameron* IX:2 is an exceptional case because it takes a single fabliau, *La Nonete* composed by Jean de Condé, as its primary model. Scholars have long agreed that Boccaccio was in some way familiar with *La Nonete*. Branca cites two fabliaux as well-known Old French antecedents of novella IX:2: *La Nonete* and the anonymous *Les Braies au cordelier* (3.211–36).[12] All three of these tales present the popular theme of the *brache del prete* [the priest's breeches], a humorous motif suggesting the lasciviousness of the clergy that was common to a variety of genres in medieval literature.[13] Landau, on the other hand, cites the miraculous tale "L'abbesse qui fu grosse" [The Abbess Who Was Pregnant], which vaguely resembles Boccaccio's story through its mention of hypocrisy among the clergy but makes no use of the *brache del prete* topos.[14] Since the topos is the same, *Decameron* IX:2 may be considered much more closely connected to one of the fabliaux than to the miraculous tale of the abbess.[15] The strongest points of resemblance to *Decameron* IX:2 find the abbess hypocritically blaming her inferiors for her own sin, and the bishop scolding the abbess in front of the chapter, even though she is no longer pregnant at this moment. The miraculous appearance of the Virgin, and the secret delivery and placement of the child with a hermit, liberate the abbess and distinguish this story on a number of levels from Boccaccio's novella.

Not included in the list enumerated by Branca is the thematically similar fabliau, *Les Braies le priestre* (10.11–21), which was also composed by Jean de Condé. Although this fabliau and the anonymous *Les Braies au cordelier* both make use of the theme of the *brache del prete*, they did not necessarily influence Boccaccio's novella.[16] This literary motif usually involves the theft or misplacement of a cleric's pants, with its implications of sexual relations. An example from the *Legenda Aurea* (number 146)—also cited by Branca—gives an anecdote from the life of St. Jerome, whose clothes are stolen by his fellow monks and replaced with women's clothing. When he mistakenly dresses in these clothes, the other monks assume that he has been sleeping with a woman and that he erringly put on her clothing in the dark. There are, however, no breeches in this example of the topos. In *Les Braies au cordelier*, a man, having surprised his wife with a cleric mistakes the cleric's pants for his own the next morning, and his delayed discovery of the mistake is evidence of his wife's infidelity. Despite the similarities of dressing in the dark and mistaken clothing, these two examples in fact present two different types of stories: the former results in cross-dressing, while the latter involves a mere substitution of the cleric's pants for those of another man. The two distinct narratives that emerge from the theme of the *brache del prete* do not alter the implication of sexual (mis)behavior, but they reveal that the anecdote about St. Jerome, which involves an example of cross-dressing, and *Les Braies au cordelier*, which consists of a substitution, belong to two discrete narrative traditions. *Decameron* IX:2 represents a combination of these two traditions, a mixture of cross-dressing and mistaken breeches. Of the possible antecedents for *Decameron* IX:2, only *La Nonete* demonstrates the same combination of the two traditions. Thus, *La Nonete* and *Decameron* IX:2 share more than similar plots and structures; they share the same "textual nucleus" as Rossi calls it.[17] As *La Nonete* offers the highest degree of similarity, it is the most probable source for Boccaccio's novella, which does not seem to combine another narrative with the French analogue.

The basic plots of *Decameron* IX:2 and *La Nonete* share a remarkable number of features. In both stories, a young nun (or novice) is caught with a man. When the other nuns who caught her go to speak with the abbess about her punishment, they interrupt the abbess as she is entertaining a priest. Although the abbess is able to keep the nuns from seeing the priest in her bed, in her rush to dress in the dark, the abbess inadvertently places the priest's breeches on her head. Her mistake goes unnoticed temporarily while she is admonishing the novice for her sinful behavior, but once her own fault is discovered and made known to the other nuns, the abbess recants her position on chastity and henceforth permits the other nuns to do as they wish.

The following discussion will suggest that Boccaccio knew *La Nonete* from a written version and, consequently, that he had access to a manuscript containing works by the *trouvère* Jean de Condé. The possibility that a manuscript containing Jean de Condé's works reached Boccaccio relies on some extensive social networks of the fourteenth century. Determining that Boccaccio used a written model requires establishing precise criteria for examples of written transmission. Both oral performance and written transmission constitute a type of intertextuality inasmuch as one text is dependent on another for its basic structure. Simone Marchesi notes in a discussion of intertextuality in the *Decameron* that "when the target text [here, *Decameron* IX:2] has literal connections with the one we are glossing [*La Nonete*]; [and when] there is a cluster of elements (themes, syntax, and lexicon) that resonates in the text"[18] it is possible to speak of intertextuality or borrowing that demonstrates the use of written sources. Whereas the similarity of the plot structures of the two versions—and the absence of other analogues except for an episode in the contemporary work *Renart le contrefait*[19]—strongly suggests that Boccaccio must have been familiar with *La Nonete*, these similarities on their own are insufficient to prove written transmission. Therefore, in order to make a case for written transmission, the following analysis shows thematic, lexical, and syntactical connections between *Decameron* IX:2 and *La Nonete*.

At the core of both tales is the theme of hypocrisy and its revelation through a single narrative moment that displays the incongruity between appearance and reality. The notion of hypocrisy, made evident in each version by the discrepancy between words and deeds, or public performance and private action, is intimately connected to the character of the abbess. In the fabliau, the narrator informs the audience from the outset that the rules of the convent are not serious because the nuns are all subject to *Amour* (14–21). He also states that the abbess is, herself, not subject to rules. The abbess's reputation is connected to that of the entire convent. Initially the abbess threatens to lock the novice in a cell for a year for defying the rules of the convent and because the abbess wants to prevent the novice from bringing "discredit" to the convent: "l'abbesse . . . mieus voet c'on le mette / Em prison qu'elle s'entremete / De faire a l'abbie diffame. / Et pour *le* jeter hors de blasme / Fu li lassete em prison mise," (44–49, emphasis added) [The abbess preferred that she (the novice) be put in prison rather than bring discredit to the abbey. And in order to free *it/her* from blame, the poor thing was put in prison]. The ambiguity of the feminine singular object pronoun "le" (in italics) in this context means that it can refer either to the abbess or the abbey. While the abbey is syntactically (by proximity) the more plausible referent, the abbess, as the subject of the sentence, is also a possible referent. The ambiguity of the phrase, however, highlights the link between the abbess's public appearance, her reputation, and the abbey's renown. While the issue of "diffame" is presented as her concern, it is later made clear that the abbess's actions are equally likely to cast the convent in a bad light; the abbess's hypocrisy is only later made public. After the abbess has been interrupted in the company of a priest, she comments to the other nuns that the novice should not be freed from prison because her behavior was so "frivolous" ("Tant est sa maniere volage," 125). The abbess's show of moral rigor through her speech openly and publicly contradicts her lascivious, private actions. The priest's breeches dangling from the abbess's head represent the point of contact between her public position of authority in the convent and her private defamatory behavior. From this moment on, the abbess and the convent are exposed.

Boccaccio similarly connects the issue of hypocrisy to the abbess's reputation and to the renown of the convent. The internal narrator, Elissa, presents "un famosissimo monistero di santità et di religione" (IX:2, 5) [a convent, widely renowned for its sanctity and religious fervor, 655] in saintly terms similar to those describing Madonna Usimbalda, a "buona e santa donna secondo la oppinion delle donne monache e di chiunque la conoscea" (IX:2, 7) [whose goodness and piety were a byword among all the nuns and everyone else who knew her, 656]. Boccaccio reverses the exposition in the fabliau by describing both the convent and the abbess as good and holy. In spite of this reversal, Boccaccio preserves the rapport between the appearance of the abbess and the appearance of the convent. Madonna Usimbalda, however, contradicts this opinion through her words of reproach to Isabetta, saying, "la maggior villania che mai a femina fosse detta" (IX:2, 13) [the most terrible scolding that any woman was ever given, 657], while the priest's breeches hang from her head. In this way, the moment of contact between public and private is the same in *Decameron* IX:2 as in *La Nonete*, both punctuated by the abbess's vitriolic speech. Boccaccio reinforces the two parallel levels of hypocrisy that highlight the disparity between appearances and reality in *La Nonete*: first, externally, because the convent has a good reputation, but it is morally liberal on the inside; second, because Madonna Usimbalda projects an image of piety, but privately she is as guilty as Isabetta of sins of the flesh. Nevertheless, discretion ensures that the good reputation of Madonna Usimbalda and of the convent will remain intact.

Another theme common to both versions is the nature of love. Throughout the fabliau, love is presented as a personification in typical courtly terms. *Amour* is the governing agent of the characters in the fabliau. As in other works by Jean de Condé, *Amour* is presented as a power of Nature, which another nun invokes to free the novice: "Li fait faire Amour, bien le sai!" (127) [I know well that Love made her do it].[20] This verse at the midpoint of the fabliau explains, even justifies, the behavior of all three women in the tale (the nun, the novice, and the abbess), for all are subject to the same laws of love. In the story, love is neither base, nor crude, but is instead natural and insists on decorum and discretion, in keeping with the courtly romance tradition. In this way, the narrative shows that love extends beyond the convent laws, which is precisely the women's defense. The poem establishes the mild rules of the convent which the nuns follow: "Li abbesse nel haoit mie, / Car elle avoit souvent sen mie, / Qui de ses maus le garissoit" (19–21) [The abbess did not hate it at all, because she often had her friend with her who cured her of her illness]. Thus, the unspoken practice of the convent is diametrically opposed to the explicit rules; the practice of *Amour* represents an inversion of the law of the convent and consequently sullies its reputation. Not only does the abbess accept these inverted rules of the convent, but the novice takes an *ami* only after witnessing the other nuns with their men (36–39). The novice is simply guilty of following the implicit order of the convent and of *Amour*. The hypocrisy stems from the discrepancy between the written, explicit law of the convent and the unspoken, implicit practice, a discrepancy that reflects a reversal of the traditional order of the convent. Nevertheless, the abbess remains discreet unlike the novice, while the nun's discretion lies somewhere in between that of the abbess and the novice.

Similarly, *Decameron* IX:2 demonstrates the love of the young couple in typical courtly fashion: "Isabetta... d'un bel giovane che con lui era s'innamorò; e esso, lei veggendo bellissima, già il suo disidero avendo con gli occhi concetto, similmente di lei s'accese: e non senza gran pena di ciascuno questo amore un gran tempo senza frutto sostennero" (IX:2, 5) [Isabetta... fell in love with a handsome young man who was with him; and the young man, observing that she was very beautiful, and divining her feelings through the language of the eyes, fell no less passionately in love with her, 655–56]. This description of the couple's love, "con gli occhi concetto," and their long-suffering secrecy reflects tropes of courtly narrative, as described by Andreas Capellanus in the *De Amore*.[21] Although these passages do not share a single line—but the same does not hold for other areas of the novella—the courtly portrayal of love common to *La Nonete* and *Decameron* IX:2 distinguishes these tales from the majority of *novelle* involving fabliaux material where the act of love does not often mingle with the topical discourse of courtly love. Boccaccio borrows the elements of sociogenic reversals and courtly language from *La Nonete*.

In addition to the similar treatments of hypocrisy and courtly love, *La Nonete* and *Decameron* IX:2 also demonstrate lexical similarities at key narrative moments. At the beginning of both tales, the narrators use a similar word to set the scene. In the fabliau, the narrator explains that the rules of the convent are *leger* (16, 18), literally meaning "light": "unne abbie dont li couvens / De dames iert *legiers* com vens, / Car Amour repairoit en l'iestre, / Qui *legieres* les faisoit iestre" (15–18, emphasis added) [an abbey of which the convent of women was light like the wind, for Love, who made them be frivolous, stayed there regularly.] In the *Decameron*, the narrator Elissa informs her audience that the young novice escapes from penalty by speaking "leggiadramente" or "lightly," "gracefully": "Una giovane monaca, aiutandola la fortuna, sé da un soprastante pericolo *leggiadramente* parlando diliberò.... assai sono li quali, essendo stoltissimi, maestri degli altri si fanno e gastigatori, li quali... la fortuna alcuna volta e meritamente vitupera" (IX:2, 3–4, emphasis added) [A young nun who, with the assistance of Fortune, freed herself by means of a timely remark.... A great many people are foolish enough to instruct and condemn their fellow creatures, but from time to time... Fortune deservedly puts them to shame, 655].

The Old French word "leger" and the Italian word "leggiadra" share a common etymology as both are derived from an Old Provençal word from the Latin root, LEVIS, meaning light, without weight. Although employed in different senses, these two words connected by a common etymology support the idea that *Decameron* IX:2 and *La Nonete* partake in the same semantic field. Furthermore, the levity evoked in the fabliau contrasts with the severity of the punishment with which the abbess threatens the novice in the same way that

Isabetta's graceful reply stands in opposition to the "maggior villania" (IX:2, 13) spoken by Madonna Usimbalda. The adverbial nature of the word in Boccaccio's use further emphasizes Isabetta's speech, for it is her wit and quick tongue that extricate her from the situation, not Fortune or pleas on her behalf.

One difference of note between the two versions involves the speech of the novice. In *La Nonete*, the novice is imprisoned when another guilty nun, who petitions the abbess on her friend's behalf, notices the breeches on the abbess's head and makes a remark. In *Decameron* IX:2, however, it is Isabetta, the novice herself, who makes the timely remark about the abbess's headdress. Isabetta's role is a composite of the novice and the nun from the Old French version of the tale. The role of the other nun, who in this novella has been transformed into a group of nuns, is reduced to that of jealous spies, for none of them has a young man: "che di lei avevano invidia . . . che senza amante erano" (IX:2, 19) [the envy of those of her fellow nuns, without lovers, 658]. In spite of this minor difference, the narrative function of these women in both tales is to rush the abbess, which results in her mistake. After the nuns arrive at the abbess's cell, both narrators emphasize the haste with which the abbess dresses:

Puis a *tantost* se plice prise	La badessa . . . temendo non forse le
Et le viesti *delivrement*.	monache per troppa *fretta* o troppo
. . .	volenterose tanto l'uscio sospignessero che
Kant sen cuevrekief cuida prendre	egli s'aprisse, *spacciatamente* si levò suso, e
Laidement au prendre mesprist,	come il meglio seppe si vestì al buio. . . . le
Car <u>les braies a l'abbé prist,</u>	venner <u>tolte le brache del prete</u>; e tanta fu
Et puis <u>les jeta</u> erranment	la *fretta*, che, senza avvedersene, in luogo
<u>Sour son cief</u>, car grant mal talent	del saltero <u>le si gittò in capo</u> e uscì fuori, e
Eut et d'aïr fu alumee.	*prestamente* l'uscio si riserrò dietro.
(138–47, emphasis added)	(IX:2, 9–10, emphasis added)
[Then she took her pelisse right away and put it on hastily. . . . When she thought she was taking her head cover, she was badly mistaken in the taking, for she took the priest's breeches, and threw them rapidly on her head, for she was in a rage and lit by anger.]	[The Abbess . . . fearing lest the nuns, in their due haste and excess of zeal, should burst open the door of her chamber, she leapt out of bed as quick as lightning and dressed as best she could in the dark. . . . She happened to seize hold of the priest's breeches. And she was in such a tearing hurry that without noticing her mistake, she clapped these on to her head instead of her psalter and sallied forth, deftly locking the door behind her, 656–57.]

The same device of repeating words denoting haste (emphasized in italics: *tantost, delivrement, erranment; fretta, spacciatamente, prestamente*) is used in both versions in the same amount of narrative time. In both tales, the abbess:

"took the priest's breeches"
les braies a l'abbé prist   tolte le brache del prete

and "threw them on her head"
les jeta ... sour son cief   le si gittò in capo

The strongest resemblance between the two passages (underlined above) reinforces the turning point of the tale where the abbess makes her crucial mistake, because the phrases are identical in meaning and nearly identical in syntax. Indeed, the second passage, which marks the abbess's fatal mistake, is a direct translation from the Old French, most notable through the identical verb-object pairs "jeta/cief" and "gittò/capo."

Finally, both *La Nonete* and *Decameron* IX:2 point to the abbess's hypocrisy, which is ultimately revealed to the other nuns by a comment from an inferior in the convent hierarchy, a young nun. The moments of revelation of the abbess's hypocrisy display striking similarities in each version. In the fabliau, the narrator says, "la nonne la regarde: / Elle vit *les lanières qui pendaient*" (150–51, emphasis added) [the nun looked at her: She saw the straps that were hanging]. The same revelation in the *Decameron* takes the same form: "veduto ciò che la badessa aveva in capo e *gli usulieri che di qua e di là pendevano*" (IX:2, 14, emphasis added) [she happened to raise her eyes and perceive what the Abbess had on her head, with the braces dangling down on either side, 657]. The imperfect of "to hang" ("pendaient/pendevano") is the same in each passage, but the words "lanières" and "usulieri" meaning "straps" are quite different.[22] The narrator in both versions, however, mentions the same detail of the "hanging straps," rather than simply stating that there was a pair of breeches on her head, and the phrases are once again almost identical.[23]

The similarities of plot and themes such as hypocrisy and the courtly treatment of love suggest that Boccaccio had access to a written form of *La Nonete*, but his version also transforms the fabliau in significant ways. While both stories discuss love, in *La Nonete* the personification of *Amour* serves to exonerate the women; they are not to blame because *Amour* compelled them to act. In the *Decameron*, however, Boccaccio uses *Fortuna* and wit to liberate Isabetta and punish Madonna Usimbalda: "Una giovane monaca, *aiutandola la fortuna*, sé da un soprastante pericolo leggiadramente parlando diliberò"

(IX:2, 3, emphasis added). The characters in the novella make no reference to any outside force of nature as they do in the fabliau, but this absence subtly heightens the role of Fortune in the text, so that when "venne alla giovane alzato il viso e veduto ciò che la badessa aveva in capo," (IX:2, 14) [it happened that the young girl lifted her gaze and saw what the abbess had on her head], the audience appreciates the innocent and favorable turn of events for Isabetta. Whereas the novice of the fabliau indirectly frees herself by blackmailing another nun, Isabetta's own witty remark after noticing the abbot's breeches allows her to escape any penalty. The threats of denunciation in *La Nonete* come to fruition in Boccaccio's version, but are quickly righted and forgiven by the characters themselves. For this reason, the nuns of this story are completely exonerated since there is no need for blackmail as in the fabliau, and the story avoids moralizing. Further evidence of this is the lack of proverb in the novella. The proverb in the fabliau, that one should not blame another if one is himself worthy of blame, is not only absent from the *Decameron* IX:2, but it does not really apply to Boccaccio's tale since the narrative focus shifts to the individual's ability to "bien tourner son afaire" (8) [turn his situation for the better].[24] Aside from this difference, *Fortuna* and *Amour* serve a similar purpose in each text, which reinforces the idea that Boccaccio may have been directly and even deeply familiar with *La Nonete*. Boccaccio's transformation of *Amour* to *Fortuna*, however, places the focus on the individual because it is Isabetta's witty comment enabled by *Fortuna* that frees her from trouble.

Like the fabliau, the novella makes explicit the love of the couple when the narrator states that Isabetta "d'un bel giovane . . . s'innamorò; e esso, lei veggendo bellissima, già il suo disidero avendo con gli occhi concetto, similmente di lei s'accese" (IX:2, 5). An important distinction, however, is the presence of the young man in Boccaccio's version, who not only falls in love with Isabetta, but after being caught has "intenzione di fare un mal giuoco a quante giugner ne potesse, se alla sua giovane novità niuna fosse fatta, e di lei menarne con seco" (IX:2, 12) [(the) intention of making any of them that reached him pay if anything new happened to his young girl, and to take her away with him]. The young man in Boccaccio's version evolves into a character worthy of romance narrative, enriching the courtly appeals to *Amour* from the fabliau.

Another key difference involves the presentation of physical love, specifically in the *scène d'amour*. Isabetta and her friend are caught *in flagrante delicto* by the abbess and the other nuns. While the fabliau merely suggests the act of love, Boccaccio describes the scene where the women "entrate dentro nel letto trovarono i due amanti abbracciati" (IX:2, 11) [found the two lovers, who were lying in bed in one another's arms, 657]. Boccaccio's version of the tale presents a sexual scene between the two lovers whereas the fabliau merely alludes to the same scene. Indeed, as this scene in *Decameron* IX:2 is more physical than that of *La Nonete*, it is more suggestive of other fabliaux than Jean de Condé's tale. At the same time, the novella retains proper, rather courtly language. Boccaccio's use of the physical description in the scene alludes to courtly lovers as it heightens the contrast in discretion between Isabetta and Madonna Usimbalda. The narrator describes how Isabetta was seen with her young man, in his arms, but Madonna Usimbalda is only seen by the audience with the priest's pants, a more subtle sign of her culpability that almost goes unnoticed by the other characters. Boccaccio transforms the reproachful message against hypocrisy in the fabliau into a message of discretion in the novella, a message only hinted at in the fabliau. In this way, Boccaccio seemingly expands features of the original text without necessarily resorting to other sources.

Finally, the noticeable presence of a narrator in the fabliau, evidenced through the first-person singular voice of the introduction, outlines the tale from the beginning with an explanatory proverb. This (faux-)didacticism is completely absent from novella IX:2. Yet when the fabliau narrator states, "j'ai bien oÿ ramentevoir" (14) [I heard mention of], showing that he heard the story as his audience will, it distances the narrator from the story to make both narrator and audience conscious that the fabliau presents a fiction. The frame in the *Decameron* achieves the same effect, because it provides the self-conscious commentary on the tale that the fabliau established through narrator interventions. In this way, Boccaccio's *brigata*, in this case represented by Elissa, resembles the role of the fabliau narrator.

The nexus of both *La Nonete* and novella IX:2 is the inversion of order shown through hypocrisy and the consequent discrepancy between words and deeds. Through his transformation of this cross-dressing topos, Boccaccio replaces the supernatural and exonerating influence of *Amour* with that of *Fortuna*, placing the emphasis of the tale on the individual and her *leggiadri motti*. The use of such a figure, *Amour* or *Fortuna*, is itself specific to these two texts. Boccaccio's characters are both more responsible and more easily forgiven for their actions than the characters of the fabliau, and ultimately triumph, for the emphasis of the Italian text is on language, not hypocrisy. Boccaccio's use of Jean de Condé's words and syntactic structures in the most important episodes of the story suggests that Boccaccio had access to a written form of Jean de Condé's fabliau, a manuscript containing the tale, when composing his own version of the tale.

A Theory of Written Transmission

Accepting that Boccaccio used *La Nonete* as an intertext for *Decameron* IX:2, the question remains: How did Boccaccio become familiar with the text? *La Nonete* is attributed to Jean de Condé. Born between 1275 and 1280 to Baudouin de Condé, himself a poet of great renown, Jean de Condé grew up with a privileged access to the courtly world and to the world of letters. Both father and son were part of an entourage of ecclesiastical and seigneurial families, in the largest sense of the word.[25] Between approximately 1310 and the year of his death in 1345, Jean composed poems of a variety of genres—of which more than seventy are available—mostly for his patrons at the court of Hainaut. *La Nonete* and four other fabliaux have been attributed to the *trouvère* Jean de Condé.[26]

In spite of this prolific production, Jean's works are preserved in only four extant manuscripts:[27]

MS A	Paris, BNF 1446
MS A'	Paris, BNF 24432
MS B	Paris, Arsenal 3524
MS R	Rome, Casanatense 1598
[MS T	Turin, BN 1626][28]

Of the four remaining manuscripts, MSS A and B also preserve the works of Jean's father, Baudouin de Condé. It has even been suggested that the father and son may have overseen the compilation of these two manuscripts themselves.[29] MS A' contains only a half dozen of Jean's poems, while MS R contains the only extant copy of *La Nonete*.

The Casanatense manuscript dates from the first half of the fourteenth century, during Jean de Condé's lifetime.[30] Rediscovered in Rome in 1859 by Adolf Tobler,[31] the codex has been the subject of studies and editions for the *Roman de la Rose*, certain branches of the *Roman de Renart*, and the works of Jean de Condé. According to the description furnished by Langlois, it is parchment, contains 207 ff. with two columns of approximately thirty-eight lines, and measures 257×177 mm.[32] Scholars generally agree that the dialect has Picard traits.[33] Although none of the descriptions discusses the manuscript's origins or scribes, it is seemingly from a northern region of France, a plausible contention given the Picard traits of the dialect. There is no other mention of provenance or discussion of how the manuscript arrived in Rome by the mid-nineteenth century. Tobler describes the manuscript's "gehörige Schrift," which suggests it has a single, consistent hand throughout.[34] The codex may be divided into two parts: *Le Roman de la Rose* (ff. 1–145r), and thirty-seven diverse poems of which all but two are attributed to Jean de Condé (ff. 145r-207v).[35] This manuscript is of particular interest for the works of Jean de Condé since it is the only record of several of his works, including *La Nonete* (ff. 187v–189r).[36]

It is unlikely that *La Nonete* was widely disseminated. Although an argument about a text's dissemination in the Middle Ages may not accurately be based on the number of extant manuscripts, the relatively few copies of this text in conjunction with the lack of analogues aside from an episode in the contemporary *Renart le contrefait* and the *Decameron* strongly suggest that *La Nonete* would not have been as familiar as other fabliaux. The same conclusion may be drawn for all of Jean's fabliaux, which are preserved in only one or at most two manuscripts; this is far fewer than the majority of fabliaux.[37] Jean's works, and in particular his fabliaux, would most likely not have been widely known in the early fourteenth century outside the circle of his courtly patrons. Moreover, by the time Jean composed his works in the first half of the fourteenth century, the fabliaux as a genre were waning in popularity, and Jean is often considered the last *fableor*. The relative paucity of Jean's fabliaux and the decline of the genre more generally suggest that Boccaccio's intimate knowledge of *La Nonete* is quite remarkable.

La Nonete is not, however, the only work by Jean de Condé that bears a relationship with a novella in the *Decameron*. Similarities between other of Jean de Condé's poems and certain *novelle* suggest that Boccaccio may have had a privileged access to the works of the Belgian *trouvère*. Branca cites Jean de Condé's *Le Chevalier a la mance* as an analogue to the fifth story on Day X of the *Decameron*.[38] The theme of both tales was popular in the Middle Ages—serving also as the basis for Chaucer's *Franklin's Tale*—and the thematic, lexical, and syntactical similarities here are few. It is possible that Boccaccio was at least familiar with Jean de Condé's *Le Chevalier a la mance*, which is also preserved in manuscript R, alongside *La Nonete*. *Decameron* VII:6 resembles two of Jean's fabliaux: *Le Clerc qui fu repus derriere l'escrin* (10.57–69) and *Le Pliçon* (10.23–32), although neither Branca nor Landau cited them in connection with the *Decameron*. Both *Decameron* VII:6 and *Le Clerc qui fu repus derriere l'escrin* involve a woman who is entertaining two men when her husband unexpectedly returns home. While these tales do not share the same dénouement, another fabliau by Jean de Condé titled *Le Pliçon* (also preserved in MS R) supplies the deployment of the knife at the moment of the lover's escape used in *Decameron* VII:6. Two factors make it difficult to affirm that Boccaccio's source for *Decameron* VII:6 was Jean's *Le Clerc qui fu repus derriere l'escrin*: the paucity of lexical similarities between the two tales and the popularity of the theme in the Middle Ages in a variety of analogues.[39] Nevertheless, the thematic similarities between the two tales as well as the presence of a similar plot detail in Jean's other fabliau, *Le Pliçon*, suggest that Boccaccio may have been familiar with other works of Jean de Condé. A fourth fabliau composed by Jean, *Le Sentier Batu* (10.21–81), is reminiscent of the overarching theme for the *novelle* on Day VI of the *Decameron* in which "sotto il reggimento d'Elissa, si ragiona di chi con alcuno leggiadro motto, tentato, si riscosse, o con pronta risposta o avvedimento fuggì perdita o pericolo o scorno" (*VI: Intro.*) [under the rule of Elissa, stories are told about those who, on being provoked by some verbal pleasantry, have returned like for like, or who, by a prompt retort or shrewd manoeuvre, have avoided danger, discomfiture or ridicule].[40] In this fabliau, a group of noble ladies and knights seeks entertainment by electing kings and queens to play "roy qui ne ment" [king who does not lie], a situation that cannot fail to evoke the *brigata* of the *Decameron* who elect a king or queen for each day's narration. When the queen disparages the masculinity of one of the knights with a terse comment, the knight avenges himself with his own "mos" [words/joke] to shame the lady by questioning her virtue. In short, there are five of Jean's works that exhibit thematic similarities with the tales in the *Decameron*.

Boccaccio's familiarity with the works of Jean de Condé is so pointed in the *Decameron* that it is credible Boccaccio had a special connection to the works of this *trouvère*. In the case of *La Nonete* specifically, it is likely that Boccaccio had seen a written copy of the work, if not in MS R, at least in a manuscript related to R. As already mentioned, the language of the manuscript has Picard traits, which is the dialect Jean spoke and wrote, and MS R was very probably produced during Jean's lifetime. In order for Boccaccio to have seen it, it must have arrived in Italy before 1351 when the *Decameron* was finished. The most likely place for Boccaccio to have encountered Jean de Condé's work, or any fabliaux for that matter, was in Naples.

Boccaccio went to Naples in 1326 at the age of 13 to work in the Florentine branch of the Bardi bank. He remained there until his return to Florence some time in 1339. The contacts he made there, both literary and human, were of tremendous effect on his life and work. Boccaccio's father worked for the Bardi and by 1328 had become well accepted at the Angevin court. His influence at the court was such that the Florentine seigniory even pressed him to be an intermediary with the king.[41] Through his father, Boccaccio had contact with the court in Naples, where, according to Samantha Kelly, he "participated in the chivalric atmosphere presided over by French princesses of the royal house," namely Marie de Valois and her cousin by marriage, Agnès de Périgord.[42]

In addition to his father's influence, Boccaccio was well connected to the court through many friends. One such friend, Americo Cavalcanti, became a chamberlain of King Robert by 1334, while his friend Paolo da Perugia was a member of the royal household and a man of letters who wrote an encyclopedic work (*Collectanea*), which influenced Boccaccio's *Genealogia Deorum Gentilium*.[43] It was through Paolo that Boccaccio most likely had access to much of the literature that would affect his later works. Although there is no evidence that King Robert knew Boccaccio, it is certain that Boccaccio had access to the courtly world and to literature.[44]

Furthermore, Boccaccio's friend Niccolò Acciaiuoli had an even more intimate connection to the court. By 1334, Niccolò was under the protection of Catherine de Valois-Courtenay, as an advisor and her lover. Catherine was the sister-in-law of Robert through her marriage to his brother Philip of Taranto.[45] She was also the daughter of Charles de Valois. Niccolò Acciaiuoli later became the tutor of Catherine's sons Robert and Louis (see figure 1). In this way, Boccaccio could have gained even greater access to the courtly world. Furthermore, it was through Niccolò that Boccaccio was connected to another French princess at the court, Robert's sister-in-law Agnès de Périgord, mother of Charles of Durazzo. This is not to suggest that members of the Angevin court were Boccaccio's patrons in the traditional sense. In fact, Boccaccio failed to get the patronage of both Catherine de Valois-Courtenay and her nephew Charles of Durazzo before he left Naples in 1339. It is probable, however, that Boccaccio's acceptance into the courtly milieu was an experience that furnished him with texts that found their way into his works; that his writing profited from his having discovered certain literature at the Angevin court.

As Boccaccio probably had opportunities to encounter texts, and in particular French texts at the court in Naples, the question arises how Jean de Condé's work specifically might have arrived there. The following hypothesis claims that Jean's patroness at the court of Hainaut transmitted a manuscript containing the works of her poet to her relatives (specifically her half-sisters and uncles) at the court of Naples.

Jean was a minstrel at the court of Hainaut during the reign of Count William I (1304–37). William had married Jeanne de Valois in 1305. Jeanne was the daughter of Charles de Valois, and thus the half-sister of Catherine de Valois-Courtenay and Marie de Valois, who were both in Naples. By all accounts, Jean de Condé was more attached to Jeanne de Valois; in fact, the records for payments Jean received usually refer to "Medame."[46] Both Susan Groag Bell and June Hall McCash have demonstrated the important role women played in medieval patronage, most notably in the vernacular. McCash highlights the practice of "matrilineal patronage" or the passing from mother to daughter of books and the general practice of patronage. She also demonstrates that books were given from mother to daughter as wedding gifts, since marriage usually meant that a daughter was sent to another country with a different language. While McCash and Bell primarily cite religious texts, bibles, or books of hours in their studies on women patrons, a collection of vernacular works such as MS R would also have been valuable for entertainment.[47]

The role of women in the Italian courts was no less significant. According to Padoan, "erano le donne in particolare . . . il pubblico che leggeva e che quindi anche determinava, influenzandone gli esiti e i motivi, quella letteratura che si era diffusa soprattutto negli ambienti cortigiani e tra l'aristocrazia cittadina" [women in particular were the public who read and therefore who also determined which literature was diffused, especially in the courtly milieu and among the city-dwelling aristocracy, influencing its outcomes and motives].[48] Women were responsible for a large part of the cultural exchange in the Middle Ages. Based on these historical facts of manuscript transmission, it is credible to argue that Jeanne de Valois occasioned a manuscript such as MS R, or a copy, to be sent to her relatives in Naples. In addition to the thirty-five poems by Jean de Condé, MS R contains the exceedingly popular *Roman de la Rose* and the *Pelerinage Renart*.

Jeanne had many family connections to Naples, through both of her parents, including two half sisters and several uncles and cousins. Jeanne's mother Marguerite d'Anjou was the daughter of Charles II d'Anjou, King of Naples until 1309 when his son, Jeanne's uncle, Robert became king. Moreover, two other uncles, Philip I of Taranto and John, Duke of Calabria were also in Naples (see figure 1). Through her father's second and third marriages, Jeanne de Valois also had two half sisters in Naples, Catherine de Valois-Courtenay and Marie de Valois. Furthermore, Philip of Taranto (Jeanne's uncle) and Catherine (Jeanne's half sister) were married in 1313, a date that corresponds to the beginning of Jean de Condé's career. Jeanne's other half sister, Marie de Valois, married Charles, Duke of Calabria (and King Robert's son) in 1324. Given these numerous familial connections, it is probable that Jeanne de Valois sent a manuscript of vernacular poems as a gift to entertain her relatives in Naples and that in doing so, she was responsible for promulgating and disseminating the works of her own minstrel, Jean de Condé. This type of manuscript transmission would have made it possible for Boccaccio to encounter a written copy of the works of Jean de Condé.

Boccaccio's familiarity with Jean de Condé's *La Nonete* is evidenced by the many thematic, lexical, and syntactical similarities between the fabliau and

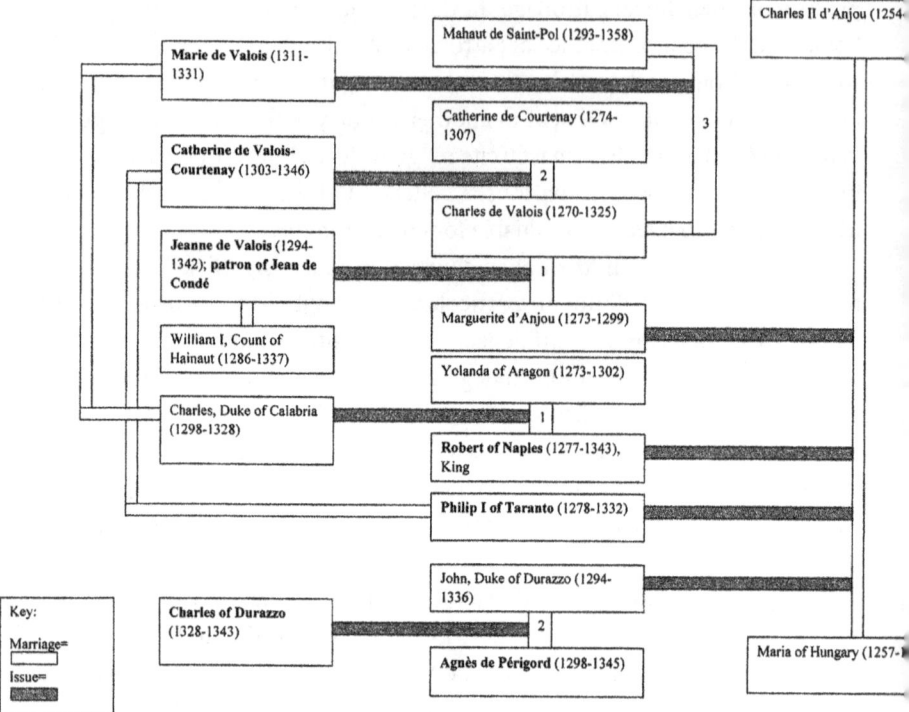

Figure 1. Family tree of the Angevins in Naples. Numbers inside connecting branches indicate order of marriages. From Katherine A. Brown, "Boccaccio Reading Old French: *Decameron* IX:2 and *La Nonete*" *MLN* 125.1 (2010): 69. Reprinted with permission.

Decameron IX:2 that occur at key narrative moments. In conjunction with the familial connections of the patrons at the courts of Hainaut and Naples that might have facilitated the transmission of Old French manuscripts, the similarities between Boccaccio's and Jean de Condé's texts offer the possibility that Boccaccio had access to a written copy of *La Nonete,* and to others among Jean's works.

The influence of *La Nonete* on the *Decameron* surpasses the narrative of IX:2 and includes two intratextual references within the collection. Rossi has shown that Boccaccio refers to novella IX:2 in the *Conclusione dell'Autore* as part of an ironic apology for the work that actually condemns his would-be critics.[49] Specifically, Boccaccio points to the hypocrisy of literal-minded critics in objecting to his use of language, and also claims that the stories were told among young people for entertainment, "in tempo nel quale andar con le brache in capo per iscampo di sé era alli più onesti non disdicevole" (*Conc.* 7) [at a time when even the most respectable people saw nothing unseemly in wearing their breeches over their heads if they thought their lives might be preserved, 799]. While Rossi argues that the reference to the abbess with breeches on her head in *Decameron* IX:2 links her hypocrisy to that of his critics,[50] the immediate context for this passage focuses on a different argument concerning the internal audience and the goal of entertainment. This reference to the abbess in the *Conclusione* highlights not so much the question of hypocrisy as the entertainment and pleasure of fiction. Furthermore, Rossi states that this allusion to novella IX:2 is an attempt by Boccaccio to "give new dignity to erotic stories;"[51] certainly no tale is more fitting for this task than one that Boccaccio knew in its written form, since it validates the subject matter through the authority of writing. The intertext of novella IX:2 also includes a thematically similar tale, namely novella I:4. Novella I:4 reverses the sociogenic elements of IX:2 for the purpose of displaying the multiplicity of interpretation through literary creation.

Structural Inversion: *Decameron* I:4 and Rewriting

Similar to the thematically paired tales on Day III, *novelle* I:4 and IX:2 form a pair that connects thematically "free" Days I and IX through stories of hypocrisy and sociogenic reversal. Moreover, these *novelle* offer gendered inversions of each other. While Branca cites the fabliau *L'Evesque qui beneï le con* as an analogue for I:4, the two versions vary significantly in a number of respects.[52] Only the second half of the fabliau resembles Boccaccio's narrative, since in that part the inferior (the priest) outsmarts and triumphs over his superior (the bishop). Almansi has suggested that I:4 resembles *La Nonete* much more closely than *L'Evesque qui beneï*.[53] Unlike *La Nonete* and *Decameron* IX:2, however, novella I:4 has no cross-dressing or *brache del prete* topos. For this reason, and because the stories deal with male religious, novella I:4 does resemble *L'Evesque qui beneï* to a small degree. There seems to be no connection between the anonymous *L'Evesque qui beneï*, which only appears in MS B, and Jean de Condé's *La Nonete* prior to Boccaccio. As the intra- and intertextual relationships between I:4 and IX:2 will suggest, novella I:4 may be a combination of both fabliaux, *L'Evesque qui beneï* and *La Nonete*, produced in a way to reflect an inversion of narrative details in IX:2.

The story of the monk and the abbot takes place in a monastery in Lunigiana that was formerly renowned for saintliness. In spite of fasting and vigils, a young monk is fresh and full of vitality, so one day when the other monks are asleep, he goes outside to the woods where he encounters a girl. He soon convinces her to go back with him to his cell and the two of them entertain themselves. While they are in the monk's cell, the abbot happens to pass by and hears some noises. After listening quietly at the door for some time, he deduces that the monk has a girl in his cell. The abbot decides to return to his own cell and wait for the young monk to come confess his sin. While the abbot was listening, the monk observed him undetected through a hole in the wall. The monk leaves the girl alone in his cell and goes to the abbot on the pretense of asking him for permission to collect firewood outside, giving the abbot the key to his cell. The abbot soon enters the monk's cell with the intention of talking to the girl, who begins crying when she sees him. Once alone in the cell with the girl, the abbot decides to profit from the situation, but allows the girl the superior position so that she is not crushed by the weight of his person. The monk witnesses this scene through the hole in the wall. Afterwards, the monk finally returns to see the abbot, where the abbot denounces the monk for having a woman in his cell. The monk then responds that the abbot has not yet shown him that women must be endured like fasts and vigils, "ma ora che mostrato me l'avete, vi prometto, se questa mi perdonate, di mai piú in ciò non peccare, anzi farò sempre come io a voi ho veduto fare" (I:4, 21) [but now that you have shown me, I promise you that if you forgive me this, I will not sin in this way again, rather I will always do what I have seen you do].

In both cases the story takes place in a monastery that formerly had a good reputation, and the young protagonists are concerned with freeing themselves from trouble. Both young religious meet their friends outside the monastery walls (although Isabetta is behind the grating), and then bring them to their cells; both couples are found *in flagrante delicto* by their superiors (although the abbot only hears the monk with the girl, he does not see them); both the young religious are reprimanded by their superiors after being caught; and finally, both use a witty remark to call attention to the same sin in the superior. Moreover, both tales prize discretion and end with the implication that the same merriment will continue discreetly. The most remarkable difference between the tales is the gender of the protagonists. Reversing the genders of the protagonists shows that the issues in the tales relate to humankind, not just males or females.

Yet other differences reflect the equivocation of the basic theme common to I:4 and IX:2. As the initial rubrics indicate: "un monaco, caduto in peccato degno di gravissima punizione . . . si *libera* dalla pena" (rubric I:4, emphasis added) [A monk, having committed a sin deserving of very severe punishment, escapes the consequences, 44]; and how the nun found in bed with a man by the abbess "fu *diliberata*" (rubric IX:2, emphasis added). The similarity of the words "libera" and "diliberata" in the rubrics indicates an initial parallel between the stories. The nun of IX:2 is the female counterpart to the vigorous monk of I:4, both using a witty remark in secret reproach of their superior in order to liberate themselves from difficulty. Ironically, the passive construction of the rubric for IX:2 undermines Isabetta's role in avoiding trouble, while the active verb of the rubric in I:4 indicates that the monk alone was responsible for manipulating his situation. The stories seem to suggest an ambiguity between active and passive roles. Both stories evidence a distinction between Fortune and wit, but the rubrics hint that they are two sides of the same coin.[54]

Mario Baratto claims that I:4 places more emphasis on the individual since the story executes a battle of wits between the monk and abbot, while the concern in IX:2 is more about the convent as a whole and its reputation.[55] This reading, though interesting, does not account for the subtext of the chess game in IX:2 that pits Madonna Usimbalda against Isabetta, nor does it treat the difference between the anonymity of the monk, abbot, and girl in I:4 in comparison with the named characters of IX:2. In both stories, the objects of desire—whether the nameless girl of I:4 or the noble-acting young man and priest of IX:2—are hardly mentioned, remaining at the level of object of desire.

Similarly, the issue of hypocrisy is more subtle in the rubric for IX:2, for it is alluded to only by a reference to the priest's pants on the abbess's head, but the hypocrisy in this tale is stressed more throughout the narrative than it is in I:4, particularly as Isabetta makes her comment in the chapter in front of the other nuns. Whereas the rubric for I:4 uses moral terminology (*peccato, colpa, pena*) and stresses the similarity of actions between the monk and abbot, "la medisma colpa," the question of hypocrisy remains discreet, a matter between the two men. While both tales involve observation and public revelation of private acts, the two taken in tandem pose the reader with questions of interpretation: Are these stories to be met with moral or social concern, or with laughter? Are these characters weak, or is the power of the flesh too strong if members of religious communities cannot even abstain? Are religious communities themselves under attack?

If the stories are gendered inversions of each other, only I:4 maximizes the potential of inversion in its deployment of the theme. The girl, object of desire in I:4, functions as the figure of reversal and the "turning point" in this tale, since she repeats the same act with both men, reversing positions the second time so that the reversal is figurative and literal. If both stories relate "la tematica comica e sensuale, rapportata alla satira anticonventuale" [comical and sensual themes related to antifraternal satire],[56] they also demonstrate the sexual appetites of men and women equally. As I:4 precedes the story of Isabetta in the *Decameron*, reinforcing internal inversions in this tale guides the reader toward issues of inversion more generally. Since IX:2 functions as the feminine version, or rather inversion, of I:4, the idea of a similar pair of stories linked by their reversed male/female roles relates to the structure of Day III, where all of the stories form pairs based on similarity of theme and male/female counterparts. In this way, the organization of the macrostructural level of Day III is mimicked in the intertextual pair I:4 and IX:2.

Connecting Days I and IX serves to unify the whole, while also inviting intertextual (and intratextual) readings that point to interpretability. Bringing together Days I and IX highlights the work's structure and suggests that everything in between ought to be read and understood in similar terms, that the *Decameron* itself, not just certain *novelle*, is open to interpretation. Why give two versions of the same theme unless they point to two different ways of understanding the theme? Just as one version of the "Matron of Ephesus" topos in MS K reinforced the antifeminist origins of the theme, the other version comically called attention to storytelling as useful deception. Like the alternate endings for novella VII:1, in which Filomena proposes two different prayers/incantations that rid the woman of her "werewolf," "l'una e l'altra fu vera" (VII:1, 33) [both accounts are correct, 490].[57] As these examples indicate, all stories can be operated to suit a purpose, and by giving the same story in two different versions, Boccaccio makes more apparent this flexibility and interpretability of literature.

The Combination of Opposites in Novella III:10

In the *Decameron*, Dioneo's stories are the most directly related to the frame narrative and to Boccaccio's intention of freeing the ladies that comprise his audience from their *malinconia*. It is through Dioneo's tales that the author's promised "diletto delle sollazzevoli cose" (*Proemio*, 14) [delight in pleasurable things] is fulfilled.[58] In the example of Alibech and Rustico, however, Dioneo's novella addresses the theme of Day III: "di chi alcuna cosa molto disiderata con industria acquistasse o la perduta recuperasse" (II: *Conc.*, 9) [people who by dint of their own efforts have achieved an object they greatly desired, or recovered a thing previously lost, 189]. The theme of the third day conforms to Dioneo's required duty to uplift the ladies. While III:10 is an exception to Dioneo's privilege of exception, it still retains the fabliaux quality of the majority of his tales. Unlike novella IX:2, *Decameron* III:10 draws on and combines a variety of sources. Indeed, perhaps more effectively than any other tale in the collection, III:10 brings together opposites by marrying the fabliaux with religious *exempla*.

Considered among the most scandalous of Boccaccio's tales, III:10 has no obvious analogues as IX:2 does. Although III:10 has been related to various saints' lives and *exempla*, it is arguably equally dependent on the fabliaux tradition.[59] Two fabliaux that relate to the novella, inasmuch as they involve the sexual initiation of a naive young girl, are *Frere Denise* and *Cele qui ne pooit oïr parler de foutre*, and to a lesser extent *La Grue*. Using a young girl's naïveté as a device, these fabliaux transform the description and practice of the sexual act into a metaphor for prayer and worship in *Frere Denise* and a chivalric metaphor in *Cele qui ne pooit*, both of which are found in the tale of Alibech and Rustico.

The two fabliaux in question deploy an innocent female character who is initiated into sexual maturity by a trickster. In *Cele qui ne pooit* a seemingly prudish girl faints or becomes ill at any talk of sex. When a young man arrives to work for her father, he pretends to share the girl's sensibilities in order to seduce her. The seduction scene with the young couple in bed involves an elaborate metaphor of a chivalric quest for the couple's anatomy and eventually the consummation of the seduction.[60] This fabliau inverts details of the chivalric quest in courtly literature in order to parody romance as it shows that sexual discourse can be disguised in seemly yet ridiculous terms.

Frere Denise, which was discussed in chapter 1, exploits cross-dressing, the ambiguous gender of the name "Denise" in Old French, and a euphemism for the sexual act couched in the language of spiritual devotion. A girl named Denise is eager to lead a holy life, but her mother would rather she marry well. When a friar woos Denise from her home with the promise of giving her a rewarding religious life, she dresses as a monk and runs away with him. Once they are together, brother Simon initiates "Frere Denise" to sexual activity by using the guise of prayer and religious life. The ambiguity of the name Denise also reflects her character: innocent, yet willing to join brother Simon in sin. Once again, the sexual language and ideas of the tale are veiled by a metaphor, this time using terminology from religious life.

Dioneo presents novella III:10 as a lesson and begins with a promise to teach the ladies "come il diavolo si rimetta in Inferno" (III:10, 3) [how the devil is put back in Hell, 274]. The story commences in the city of Gafsa, where a fourteen-year-old girl named Alibech, who has heard much about Christianity, decides that she would like to serve God. On hearing that those who best serve God live in the desert, the girl secretly flees to the desert until she finds a holy man ("un santo uomo trovò," III:10, 6). Seeing Alibech's beauty and fearing temptation, the hermit sends her to another "santo uomo" who, like the first hermit, sends her deeper into the desert to another man, Rustico. In spite of his initial desire to test himself against the temptation of the flesh, Rustico succumbs to his carnal appetites and convinces the girl that the best way to serve God is to "rimettere il diavolo in Inferno," a metaphor for the sexual act. After some time together, Alibech remains eager to perform her duty, while Rustico has grown physically weak and lacking in desire. During this time, Alibech's family dies in a fire, leaving her the sole heir of her father's wealth, whereupon a young man from the city, called Neerbale, decides to find and marry her. To Rustico's relief, Neerbale takes Alibech back to Gafsa where she describes to the other women of the city how she and Rustico served God by putting the devil in Hell. As Dioneo explains at the end, the story is so amusing and is retold and passed on so many times, that it becomes a proverb: "vi ridussono in volgar motto che il piú piacevol servigio che a Dio si facesse era rimettere il diavolo in inferno" (III:10, 35) [They coined a proverbial saying there to the effect that the most agreeable way of serving God was to put the devil back in Hell, 279].

The entire tale is a comment on the nature of language and storytelling. In addition to the lewd content, the figurative language of *Decameron* III:10 borrows from the fabliaux tradition. The hagiographic models that Branca cites as antecedents for this novella are the *Legend of St. Alban* and *St. Mary of Egypt*.[61] Alfonso Paolella and Michelangelo Picone both give careful readings of *Decameron* III:10 and its parallels in the Old French *Vie de Sainte Marie l'Egyptienne*, but neither study manages to treat the hagiographic elements in conjunction with the fabliaux elements.[62] H. Wayne Storey and Diane Duyos Vacca discuss the tale as parody of the writings of the Church Fathers, but again without taking into account that the parodic elements stem in large part from the fabliaux tradition, or rather from the combination of pious material with fabliaux elements.[63] The diversity of the sources in the popular tradition of the fabliaux and the learned tradition of hagiography and the Church Fathers are not to be separated in reading the tale of Alibech because these two elements are interdependent. The sacred and the profane as antecedents and as keys to the language of the novella must be read in conjunction with each other in order to understand Boccaccio's intent in placing them together. Moreover, the hagiographic or religious material depends on fabliaux devices for its supposedly parodic intent, while the reversals and figurative language of the fabliaux elements require an opposing tradition and register that permits the verbal interplay. As Almansi notes, the tale is successful because Boccaccio establishes an analogy of sex and religion:

> The first is the precise parallelism set up between erotic ritual and religious ceremony, which is not so much based on a crudely obscene metaphor as on the writer's proposal of an unexpected analogy. Under this

heading one should remember that the analogical connection of sex to religion, the physiological proximity of orgasm and mystic state, and the linguistic similarity of terms describing the genitals and the vocabulary of the Underworld are not, after all, such surprising phenomena to have to deal with in a mediaeval context.[64]

Boccaccio's art of combining narratives is evident from Dioneo's introduction to the tale and from the initial description of Alibech where the text seamlessly alternates between the diction of hagiography and of fabliaux. In addition to the erotic content of the story, the language of the text reveals the presence of the fabliaux and courtly love tropes. The key notions of reversal and the bringing together of opposites, already established as critical features of fabliaux, also indicate *Decameron* III:10's dependence on the Old French tradition. After announcing the theme of his novella, Dioneo explains to the ladies:

> forse ancora ne [udire come il diavolo si rimetta in Inferno] potrete <u>guadagnar l'anima avendolo apparato</u>, e potrete anche *conoscere* che, quantunque **Amore i lieti palagi e le morbide camere** piú volontieri che le povere capanne **abiti**, non è egli per ciò che **alcuna volta esso** fra' folti boschi e fra le rigide alpi e nelle diserte spelunche **non faccia le sue forze sentire**: il perché *comprender* <u>si può alla sua potenza essere ogni cosa subgetta</u>. (III:10, 3; emphasis added)
> [By learning how it is done, there may yet be time perhaps for you to save your souls from perdition, and you will also discover that, even though Love is more inclined to take up his abode in a gay palace and a dainty bedchamber than in a wretched hovel, there is no denying that he sometimes makes his powers felt among pathless woods, on rugged mountains, and in desert caves; nor is this surprising, since all living things are subject to his sway, 274].

The underlined phrases correspond to moral, religious, or hagiographic diction, while the phrases highlighted in bold recall courtly diction. The first underlined phrase, "<u>guadagnar l'anima avendolo apparato</u>," suggests a moral *exemplum* because it mentions the salvation of the soul (guadagnar l'anima) which, as Dioneo posits, can be accomplished through the knowledge his novella has to impart. The past participle "apparato," a form of "imparato" [learned], advocates the didactic function of Dioneo's tale and recalls the didacticism of moral *exempla*. Taken in conjunction with the mention of salvation (guadagnar l'anima), the verb "apparare" ("imparare") makes clear the morally didactic claims of Dioneo's story. Although the word "anima" most obviously evokes moral questions, the verbs underline the notion of didacticism in the text.

The first phrase in bold "**Amore i lieti palagi e le morbide camere** piú volontieri che le povere capanne **abiti**" is a reference to Venus or Eros, the personified figure of love inherited from antiquity that pervades courtly narrative, and was also evoked in *La Nonete*. This reference highlights the fitting locations of *Amore*, the palaces ("i lieti palagi") and bedrooms ("le morbide camere") of the aristocracy. The adjectives "lieti" [happy, gay] and "morbide" (in this case meaning "refined or delicate") emphasize the courtly tenor of the locations and of the phrase. Dioneo associates love with the literary tradition of the *locus amœnus* of courtly love and consequently with a certain class, the aristocracy. In referring metonymically to the aristocracy, Dioneo maps locus onto social class and reduces the notion of courtly love to a physical space; *Amore* dwells ("abita") in the (private) rooms of the aristocracy. There is no association of love with the heart, the mind, or the eyes in Dioneo's description, although these are topical in courtly literature. Through the mention of concrete locations (the "palagi" and "camere"), this phrase announces an emphasis on physical love and simultaneously moves the locus of love to the unknown and unseemly "povere capanne" and later to the natural "folti boschi... rigide alpi... e diserte spelunche." The references to natural settings are opposed to the man-made artifices of the palaces and boudoirs of the aristocracy. Thus, Dioneo creates a series of contrasts between rich (aristocracy) and poor, between an ideological literary tradition and a physical notion of love, and between an artificial, man-made world and the natural world. By introducing his tale as one that shows love in the lower echelons of society and in the wilderness, Dioneo places the story in opposition to the courtly tradition, espousing its opposite, for his novella will demonstrate how the effects of love may be felt anywhere. The systematic reversal of the courtly topics evoked in this introductory passage recalls the reversals of the fabliaux, and specifically the final scene in *Cele qui ne pooit oïr parler de foutre*. Even thematically, Dioneo's novella resembles these fabliaux, which remove the scene describing the physical act of love to a humble setting, with humble (non-noble) characters.

Similarly, the phrase "**alcuna volta esso [Amore] ... non faccia le sue forze sentire**" continues the notion that love may be found anywhere. The verb "sentire" in conjunction with *Amore* reinforces the courtly nature of the phrase, while the idea of love's "forze" [forces, powers], once again evokes a Classical image of the god(dess) of Love. The final underlined phrase, "<u>si può alla sua potenza essere ogni cosa subgetta</u>," refers to the power of love, but the plural "forze" has been transformed into the singular "potenza," signaling a shift from many to one, or rather from pagan to Christian notions of love and supreme power. The past participle "subgetta" not only mimics the first part of the passage, where the past participle "apparato" implied both a moral and didactic function of the novella, but also suggests the Christian idea of being a subject of the Church. The totality implied by "ogni cosa" that is subjected to the powers of love reinforces the Christian notion of God's omnipotence; the proximity of the words "ogni" (derived from the Latin "omni") and "potenza" in this final line spell out the Christian and moral significance of this phrase. By shifting the register of the second half of the passage between Christian and pagan allusions, Dioneo announces the "Christian" theme of his novella while still maintaining the open contrast between the two traditions.

The two italicized verbs in the passage, "*conoscere*" and "*comprender*" indicate and facilitate the transition between the two types of diction because of their double connotations: "conoscere" means "to be familiar with" and "to have sex with," while "comprendere" means "to comprise" and "to understand." These verbs foretell the role the double entendre will play in the story of Alibech, which involves "knowing" and "understanding" Rustico's ruse in more than one way. It is precisely this type of double language that resembles the diction in such fabliaux as *Cele qui ne pooit oïr parler de foutre* and especially *Frere Denise*.

Marilyn Migiel's observations about the language of *Decameron* III:10 complements the reading proposed here of this opening passage by not only revealing the lascivious (fabliaux) elements of the novella as they depend on metaphors, but also by demonstrating how this tale questions the relation between word and deed. As Migiel has observed, Dioneo's tale "far from encouraging seduction and lascivious excess, invites the reader to reflect critically on the role that language plays in the creation of desire—indeed, in [sic] the role that language plays in the construction of all social reality."[65] Migiel highlights the word "dire" in the introductory phrases of the tale in order to reveal the tale's focus on language and on storytelling ("Graziose donne, voi non udiste forse mai *dire* come il diavolo si rimetta in Inferno; e per ciò . . . io il vi vo' *dire*" [III:10, 2–3; Migiel's emphasis]) [Gracious ladies, you have probably never heard tell how the devil is put back in Hell; and for this reason, I will tell you about it].[66] Later, when Dioneo actually begins his narrative, he states "adunque, venendo al *fatto*" (Migiel's emphasis), which, as Migiel explains, means both "deed done" and "fact."[67] The double meaning of the word "fatto" has been set up and stressed by the preceding section with its alternating levels of diction, while the pairing of "fatto" with the verb "dire" draws attention to Dioneo's art or, as Migiel would have it, "representation."[68] Additionally, the verb "dire" is reminiscent of the tale's orality through Dioneo as *novellatore*, recalling also the evident narrators of many fabliaux. This notion of orality is contrasted with the "fatto" of the exemplary or hagiographic register evoked previously, so that, once again, there is a combination of two different levels of diction that produce metaphoric representations. Also of note, as they relate to fabliaux and metaphor, are Migiel's comments on the description of the "rigide alpi" [rigid mountains] and "diserte spelunche" [gaping caverns], which she sees as sexual metaphors, presumably for human anatomy and not for the sexual act itself,[69] metaphors that recall the final scene of *Cele qui ne pooit oïr parler de foutre*. The separation of word from deed provides the theoretical common ground for the fabliaux and *Decameron* III:10.

The combination of different registers of diction is essential to Boccaccio's metaphoric use of language in the novella of Alibech and Rustico. The setting of the story continues to draw from both hagiographic and romance paradigms: "nella *città di Capsa* in Barberia fu già un ricchissimo uomo, il quale tra alcuni altri suoi figliuoli aveva una figlioletta bella e gentilesca, il cui nome fu Alibech" (III:10, 4; emphasis added) [There once lived in the town of Gafsa, in Barbary, a very rich man who had numerous children, among them a lovely and graceful young daughter called Alibech, 275]. The setting in Capsa (Gafsa) is both exotic to a medieval Italian audience and arguably reminiscent of hagiographic material. In a study of Dioneo's novella, Picone has suggested that Alibech's "allontanamento della città e fuga nel deserto per dimenticare i piaceri della carne"[70] [departure from the city and flight to the desert in order to forget the pleasures of the flesh] is the story's first point of intersection with the *Vitae Patrum* and, therefore, with hagiographic literature. Since the desert is the typical locus of conversion in many hagiographic works, the city represents a locus of temptation, the site of the pleasures of the flesh. In this way the city is associated not with romance narrative, but with hagiographic narrative, though in a negative sense. By the end, the novella inverts this hagiographic relationship between city and desert to make the desert the locus of the pleasures of the flesh. Conversely, it was in the presumably Muslim city that Alibech first heard of Christianity: "udendo a molti cristiani che nella vittà erano molto commendare la cristiana fede e il servire dire" (III:10, 5) [having on occasion heard them extol the Christian faith and the service of God, 275]. Nevertheless, the desert remains the site of conversion, that is, of Alibech's metaphorical conversion, which resembles Denise's initiation into prayer. The language of hagiography maps onto the "deed" of the fabliaux-material such that both types of diction are present at the same time.

By contrast with the hagiographic code, the description of Alibech and her father ("un ricchissimo uomo, il quale . . . aveva una figlioletta bella e gentilesca") is a phrase that belongs in courtly narrative. The topical description of a rich (or wise or *courtois*) father is also typical of a number of fabliaux, as is the description of his beautiful daughter. The rest of the narrative continues to mix hagiographic and courtly diction, touching on religious texts with such phrases as: "commendare la cristiana fede," "il servire Dio," "a Dio si potesse servire," and "spirata da Dio" (III:10, 5–7); and suggesting fabliaux themes with the words "ingannato" and "a guisa" (III:10, 10 and 12). These words are not direct translations of *Frere Denise*, yet the device is the same. Alibech's departure, originating in a "fanciullesco appetito" rather than from an "ordinato disidero" (III:10, 6), is reminiscent of a chivalric quest, while the word "appetito," which Branca glosses as "impulso,"[71] is suggestive of a "sexual appetite" and functions as an allusion to fabliaux material. As Migiel has suggested, "the important thing about this impulse or drive ("appetito") is its indeterminacy, which will allow Alibech to be misled."[72] This indeterminacy of character also recalls Denise, whose name and true desires remain ambiguous. Like Denise, Alibech's spiritual hunger will be transformed by Rustico's fiction of putting the devil in Hell into a physical or sexual hunger. Both Denise and Alibech end their religious life only to begin their married life, which has much in common with their former practices of devotion. The alternation of the two registers of hagiography and fabliaux in Dioneo's introductory remarks about his tale is replaced by the intersection of terms in the rest of the novella, such that the lexicon of the text is simultaneously reminiscent of both hagiographic material and courtly or fabliaux antecedents (as well as the Ovidian antecedents that permeate the entire *Decameron*). In the tales of Denise and Alibech, the inversion, or rather perversion, of the referents to sex is mapped onto holy language.

In Paolella's discussion of the tale of Alibech, he cites the similarities between Boccacio's novella and the *Vita S. Mariae Aegyptiacae*.[73] The life of Saint Mary of Egypt was well known in the Middle Ages through various translations—even the poet Rutebeuf composed an Old French version in the late thirteenth century—and, like the story of Alibech, it takes place in the Middle East. In this *Vita*, Mary is a prostitute until an intercession by the Virgin Mary leads to her repentance and conversion. Mary then flees to the desert to lead an ascetic life where she meets Zosima, a hermit, from whom she eventually receives communion. A few years after their second meeting, one where Mary tells the hermit about her life, Zosima finds her corpse and tells others her story. In discussing the *Vita*, Paolella remarks astutely that "l'intreccio del racconto è constituito, in realtà, da due agiografie che si concatenano in modo da inserire la vita della santa in quella dell'anacoreta Zosima" [the plot of the story is in fact composed of two hagiographies that are concatenated in such a way as to insert the life of the female saint into that of the anchorite Zosima].[74] This concatenation of two saints' lives is similar to the combination of different sources characteristic of most *novelle* in the *Decameron*, and it explains the presence of two hermits and saints in a single *vita*. The dual aspect of the St. Mary narrative is a necessary component of Paolella's argument that the *Vita* parallels the novella of Alibech in three important ways: (1) the meeting in the desert serving as a closed episode or "avventura" for Alibech and for Zosima; (2) the sexual element in both narratives: Alibech's sexual initiation with Rustico and Mary's account of her prostitution; and (3) the "allontanamento del personaggio femminile del deserto" [departure of the female character from the desert],[75] by death for Mary and by marriage to Neerbale for Alibech. The first two points and especially the second of these stress the role of narration in these works, for the accounts Alibech and Mary give of their own sexual encounters provide the substance for the stories about them told by the women of Gafsa and Zosima respectively. In order for Paolella's points to correspond in the two narratives, Alibech's role in the novella must replace in part both Zosima's and Mary's roles in the *Vita* because Paolella ascribes the "avventura" in the desert to Alibech and Zosima, rather than to Alibech and Mary. Paolella bases the parallel between Alibech and Zosima on the idea that Mary is recognized as a hermit by Zosima, that she is already saintly, just the way Alibech finds the two "santi uomini" and eventually the hermit Rustico. The similarities between Alibech and Zosima, and also between Mary and Rustico, suggest that *Decameron* III:10 inverts parts of the *Vita*. While Paolella demonstrates the rhetorical similarities between the story of Alibech and the *Vita S. Mariae Aegyptiacae*,[76] his discussion glosses over the mention of the devil, which is an essential part of Boccaccio's reversal.

Using a cycle of tales in the *Vitae Patrum* in which a hermit is tempted by the devil, who has taken the form of a woman, Storey explains how Boccaccio inverts this topos when "Rustico, rather than Alibech, initiate[s] the 'baldoria colloquia' ... and it is he who deceive[s] her 'sotto spezie di servire a Dio.'"[77] This role reversal in the temptation prefigures the ultimate reversal of the tale, Rustico's trick in which serving God by putting the devil in Hell stands for the sexual act. The trick is dependent on another reversal in which the holy man, not the woman, has the form of the devil.[78]

Finally, Vacca offers a patristic antecedent for Boccaccio's novella, citing St. Jerome's Epistle 122 to Rusticus. Obviously Rustico is the vernacular form of the name Rusticus, a similarity that lends credence to this claim. Vacca gives five important parallels between the letter and the novella of Alibech: (1) a commitment to religious devotion by both man and woman; (2) a link of prayer to sexual activity; (3) a fall described using the devil; (4) the women who are "vexed with a devil" in both cases; and (5) the man who is unable to save himself with his "own exertions."[79] Although, as Vacca demonstrates, the language of each text is similar in these examples, the words in Boccaccio's text have a second, sexualized meaning, which comes from both the fabliaux and hagiographic models. Indeed, the hagiographic and erotic fabliaux materials are only combined in this novella because of the sexual elements present in both types of texts. Vacca astutely remarks that the initial pain turned to pleasure in Alibech's sexual experience mimics the ascetic experience of the saintly paradigm.[80] In addition, there is another similarity involving the chivalric quest as it resembles the spiritual quest of these hagiographic models; in both cases an individual departs alone on some type of search, the knight then typically encounters a lady while the saint meets the devil in the form of a woman, and after a series of tests of the person's virtue or devotion, he or she is rewarded with the lady's affection or with salvation. Alibech's quest corresponds to both of these. Thus, Boccaccio combines seemingly opposed literary traditions by exploiting the common elements of quest and sexuality, which necessitates the mixture of various levels of diction while it also maintains the overt oppositions of the original genres.

The mixture of different levels of diction culminates in Rustico's trick, which is dependent on the dissociation of word and deed. It is Rustico, not the narrator, who supplies the metaphoric language for the sexual act, but as Migiel notes, "for Rustico's stratagem to work, Alibech has to imitate his bodily gestures and positions, not his narrativizing or symbolizing."[81] The copying of gestures is also a feature of *Cele qui ne pooit oïr parler de foutre*. Unlike this fabliau, however, the actual significance of the metaphors is nowhere stated explicitly, either by Rustico or by the narrator Dioneo. The figurative language remains throughout and is the same for characters, narrator, and audience. Since this is the case, how does the *brigata* or the reader come to "conoscere" and "comprendere" Rustico's fiction? In the fabliaux tradition, the narrator and even the characters use the correct if not vulgar terms to refer to the anatomy and sexual activity, but Boccaccio's language is less overtly sexual. The dialogue between Alibech and Rustico offers the most evidence to the audience for understanding the metaphor, for Alibech first asks "quella che cosa è che io ti veggio che cosí si pigne in fuori, e non l'ho io?" (III:10, 13) [what is that thing that I see you have which hangs out and that I don't have?]. If Alibech's question, phrased almost as a riddle, were not suggestive enough of the physical reality, Rustico's answer only extends the metaphor: "questo è il diavolo *di che io t'ho parlato*" (III:10, 14, Migiel's emphasis) [that is the devil about which I told you], and again later when he tells Alibech, "tu hai un'altra cosa che non l'ho io, e haila in iscambio di questo . . . hai il ninferno"[82] (III:10, 16, 18) [you have another thing that I don't and you have it in exchange of this . . . you have a Hell]. The use of the verb "dire" reinforces the notion of Rustico's fiction and the idea that he has constructed this metaphorical language to mask the true anatomical names and the sexual act. By exploiting the similarities of the words and the genres, Boccaccio avoids vulgar, noncourtly language as he alludes to seemingly vulgar activities.

After successfully tricking Alibech, Rustico's inability to continue his trick results in a reversal of the initial situation, since Rustico, who was able to convince Alibech to put the devil in Hell, is now unconvinced by Alibech's pleading to continue the activity. The "rigid symmetry of its two halves"[83] is expressed in a chiasmus:

> per che tu farai bene che tu <u>col tuo diavolo</u> **aiuti attutare la rabbia** *al mio ninferno*, com'io *col mio ninferno* **ho aiutato a trarre la superbia** <u>al tuo diavolo</u>. (III:10, 29)
> [Now that I have helped you with my Hell to subdue the pride of your devil, the least you can do is to get your devil to help me tame the fury of my Hell, 278.]

The chiastic structure of this summarizing phrase reinforces the oppositions between devil and Hell, man and woman, that result in the ironic finish of the tale. This circular phrase shows that the trickster has defeated himself, and his own words and desires have been turned against him.

As already noted, Boccaccio is able to combine elements of the fabliaux with hagiography because in these instances the source narratives shared the themes of quest and sex. At the metanarrative level, both types of antecedents lend themselves to combinations. Paolella's remark that the story of Mary and Zosima is a concatenation of two different saints' lives reflects the same types of narrative combinations already seen in the fabliaux. Although seemingly opposed, both fabliaux and *exempla* manage to combine or rather enfold multiple narratives while still retaining their essential character. The fabliaux, however, distinguish themselves from *exempla* because they arguably combine a wider variety of material and use reversals to enact these combinations. In this case, the bringing together of opposites produced a "hagiographic fabliau," which is a subset of the novella. Yet it still remains to determine the value of the story. Does the tale serve to point out the nature of lustiness and the impossibility of resisting the flesh? Or does it rather suggest that narrative, whether didactic or luxurious, can be wildly manipulated and consequently must be interpreted? The dominant force of III:10 is the content and the ways in which registers are combined, not the literal level of the courtly and saintly language. Although Rustico uses language to mask reality, the reader sees that reality in spite of his language. It is only in the story and in the imagination of the reader that one/Alibech may be tricked and that such innocence can be perceived as true.

Multiple Uses of the Fabliau *Le Vilain de Bailleul*

If the previous example indicates how *novelle* merge fabliaux with divergent narrative traditions into a single form, the current example seeks to show how a single fabliau may influence more than one novella. In addition to the pairs of reversed tales on Day III that complement each other, Smarr has noted the relationship between tales of the third and seventh days as part of the patterns of symmetry and balance in the *Decameron*.[84] Without suggesting common sources, Smarr highlights the interrelations among tales on these days: VII:1 and III:4; VII:4 and VII:5 with III:6; VII:3 and III:7; and finally VII:8 with III:3 and III:9.[85] Degani has also noted that III:8 is connected to VII:10 because both *novelle* render ironic the theme of a return from the dead common to *exempla*.[86] This extensive intertextual network involving both "fabliaux Days" reinforces the notions of multiplicity in writing and interpretation suggested in the previous sections. In addition to the connections between Days III and VII, *novelle* related to fabliaux reveal additional thematic relationships to other days in the *Decameron*. Within Day III, novella III:8 offers an intertextual link to IX:3 by the divergent use of a common antecedent: the fabliau *Le Vilain de Bailleul*. This fabliau exerts an influence on these two *novelle* that may be verified through a lexical and thematic analysis, even though the *novelle* do not form a mirrored pair. The objective of this example does not concern showing another combination of stories, but rather showing how Boccaccio "dismembered" a fabliau in order to repurpose its parts in (at least) two tales.

According to both Branca and Landau, the fabliau *Le Vilain de Bailleul* constitutes the clearest antecedent for *Decameron* III:8, yet Boccacccio radically transforms this tale. Landau also noted similarities between this tale and *Decameron* VII:7, which is related to the fabliaux *La Borgoise d'Orliens* (3.337–74) and one part of *Les Trois dames qui troverent l'anel* (2.215–40). Aside from the themes of trickery and of the *mari cocu*, these three fabliaux share few common features.[87] Although rarely cited, *Le Vilain de Bailleul* also lends a number of narrative details to IX:3, which is the penultimate tale in the series about Calandrino.[88]

Le Vilain de Bailleul shares a basic plot with novella III:8. The fabliau begins with Dame Erme, the wife of an ugly laborer (*vilain*), who is dissatisfied with her husband and has arranged a tryst with the priest. While she is preparing for the priest's arrival, her husband unexpectedly returns home, hungry and tired. Dame Erme greets him with calculated comments about his sickly, death-like appearance. Despite the *vilain*'s protestations, his wife insists that he is dying and convinces him to lie down whereupon she closes his eyes and mouth, covers him with a sheet as if dead, and proceeds to find the priest whom she informs of her trick. The priest returns with her and begins to read psalms, while the widow makes an effort to grieve, but the two quickly turn their attention toward each other. When the *vilain* threatens the priest for seducing his wife, the priest reverses the situation through a syllogism, using the scene as proof that the man must be dead, since the priest would not be with the wife if her husband were alive. The final lesson warns that any man who believes his wife more than himself is foolish.

The introduction to the fabliau once again evokes the truth/lies opposition when the narrator states, "Se fabliaus puet veritez estre, / Dont avint il, ce dist mon mestre, / C'uns vilains a Bailluel manoit" (1–3) [If a fabliau can be true, then it happened, so says my master, that there lived a peasant in Bailleul]. Rather than opposing truth and fable, the introduction attempts to equate fabliau with truth and to suggest that the story may be a vehicle of truth. The word "se" establishes the conditional nature of this statement, but the implication for the tale's truthfulness is the same: 'if a fabliau can be true, then this story is true.' What the story recounts, however, is the wife's deception. More pointedly, this story, like the *Decameron* novella that imitates it, presents an impossible scenario as truth; the "true lie" in both tales concerns a living man who believes himself to be dead, even though his senses all indicate that he is alive. Lauretta begins III:8 in similar terms to the fabliau, by stating that she will "raccontare una verità che ha, troppo piú che di quello che ella fu, di menzogna sembianza" (III:8, 3) [narrate a truth that has the semblance of a lie much more than it was]. By presenting her tale as a "false-seeming truth," Lauretta inverts the content of the tale and the abbot's "true-seeming lie," thereby obscuring the distinction between truth and lies much the way the fabliau equates truth and fiction. Although the terms in the novella are "truth" and "lie," as opposed to "truth" and "fabliau," both narrators reveal a similar intention, a similar crux to the story they will tell.

The heart of the narrative also remains close in both the fabliau and novella. Yet the Italian version differs in a number of specifics from the fabliau. The literalization of the figurative use of death is common to both, since the metaphor of sleep for death in the fabliau is enacted in the *Decameron* through the use of the powder the abbot gives Ferondo to convince others he is dead. Nevertheless, Boccaccio's tale is more invested in details of physical appearance than the fabliau, for even the "world of the dead," Ferondo's Purgatory in a subterranean cell normally used as a prison, is physical or rather literal, whereas the other world of the husband's death in *Le Vilain de Bailleul* was created and maintained through language. Indeed, Ferondo's Purgatory reverses the "insupportable torment of Purgatory" in the *exempla* on which it is modeled.[89] Although both the fabliau and III:8 share the theatricality of making the husband believe he is dead, the theatricality of *Decameron* III:8 has two facets: the first is the large-scale deception of the town for which the abbot puts on Ferondo's clothes as his costume in order to maintain the appearance of the widow's virtue; the second is the Purgatory play in Ferondo's cell.

In not narrating the aftermath of the play, "Ce ne vous sai je tesmoingnier / S'il l'enfouirent au matin" (112–13) [I cannot tell you if they buried him the next morning], the fabliau avoids all moral implications in favor of the trick itself. Boccaccio's version, however, seemingly invites moral questions by showing the consequences for adultery, the abbot's illegitimate child, and by introducing Purgatory in the story. This version demonstrates and resolves the aftermath of the deception while still avoiding overt moral implications, since the truth is never made known. Yet the focus in the novella is on the abbot's cleverness and seamless manipulation, not on any moral question of his trickery or adultery. This tale is reminiscent of *Decameron* I:1, in which Panfilo insists that his story is concerned "non il giudicio di Dio ma quel degli uomini" (I:1, 6) [not with the judgment of God, but with that of men, 25]. Ferondo's venture in "Purgatory" has no moral implications, except perhaps to cure Ferondo's jealousy, but rather serves practical purposes for the abbot and Ferondo's wife.

Among the most remarkable differences in Boccaccio's tale is the shift of the central figure from the wife to the abbot. Not only is the abbot solely responsible for devising the trick, but the wife is probably duped herself because the abbot never seems to inform her of his plan. In contradistinction to the fabliau where the wife and eventually the priest deceive her husband, *Decameron* III:8 involves the deception of the husband, the wife, the monastery and the town all by the abbot with the aid of his friend. In this way, Boccaccio transforms a typical *conte à triangle* into an ironic, anticlerical, pseudo-*exemplum*. While both tales playfully exonerate the wife for adultery through perceived widowhood, Boccaccio's version extends her innocence since the abbot alone is culpable. Furthermore, this shift in focus from wife to abbot necessarily alters the scene in which the husband discovers or rather decides he is dead, because it no longer requires the wife to insist he is dying. In the novella, the abbot uses a draft that puts Ferondo into a deep sleep, and then moves his body to a basement room where he is kept and tortured as if in Purgatory. The elaboration of the initial deception and the afterlife that are absent from the fabliau draw from other sources.[90]

Moreover, while Ferondo does not watch his wife *in flagrante delicto* with the abbot, as the *vilain* in the fabliau does, this substantial change to the story signifies the different purposes of each text. Whereas the humor in the fabliau is derived from the irony of having these two worlds exist in the same room, the elaborate separation of the two spectacles in the *Decameron* follows the precept for Day III and highlights the abbot's "industria" in acquiring what he desires. The ghost of Ferondo, or rather the abbot dressed in his clothes, marks the only moment in the text when the two worlds overlap; the outward appearance of Ferondo, as evidenced by his clothes and understood to be a ghost, hides the reality of the abbot's lively nocturnal visits. That Ferondo is dressed in a monk's robes makes physical, or rather literalizes, the idea that the men are changing places. While the fabliau points to the triumph of language over the senses, the novella recalls the dilemma of interpreting the false-saint Ciappelletto in *Decameron* I:1, for at the end of III:8, the abbot's (and possibly Ferondo's) saintliness increases in renown like Ciappelletto's.[91] The episode from the fabliau where the *vilain* observes his wife entertaining the priest has other analogues in the *Decameron*, most notably VIII:1.

The wife's trick in the fabliau also gets repurposed by Boccaccio in novella IX:3. As Dame Erme tries to convince the *vilain* that he is dying, she tells him, "Morez, certes, ce fetes mon! / Jamés plus voir dire n'orrez; / Couchiez vous tost, **quar vous morez**!" (34–36, emphasis added) [You are dying, it is certain! You will never hear anything more true; go to bed right away because you are dying]. The story of Calandrino in IX:3 shows Bruno, Buffalmacco, their friend Nello, and the doctor Simone convincing Calandrino that he is pregnant. The same device used in *Le Vilain de Bailleul* is repeated in IX:3, where all three painters meet Calandrino and comment on how unhealthy he looks, just the way Dame Erme did. The final comments about Calandrino's health, made by Bruno, resemble Dame Erme's speech: "Calandrino, che viso è quello? E' **par che tu sie morto**: che ti senti tu?" (IX:3, 13, emphasis added) [Calandrino, what's wrong? It seems that you're dead: how do you feel?]. Both tricksters tell the man that he is dying, and the results in both cases are similar. In the fabliau, the husband's being convinced that he really is dying constitutes the turning point in the narrative. The *vilain* asks his wife to put him to bed: "Couchiez me donques, bele suer, / Fet il, quant je sui si atains" (50–51) [Put me to bed, kind sister, said he, since I am so ill]. In using the same language as his wife, the *vilain* reinforces his complicity and gullibility. Calandrino is similarly complicit in the trick to convince him that he is pregnant: "disse alla moglie: 'Vieni e **cuoprimi** bene, ché io mi sento un gran male'" (IX:3, 15, emphasis added) [he said to his wife: 'Come and cover me well, because I feel very ill]. The word "coprire" meaning to cover also appears in the fabliau when the wife entertains the priest, since the narrator explains that "Li vilains vit tout le couvine, / Qui du linçuel ert **acouvers**" (vv. 88–89, emphasis added) [The *vilain* who was covered with the sheet, saw the whole meeting place]. Calandrino's use of the word "coprire" when he is put to bed, instead of the more usual expression "mettere a letto," recalls the sheet in the fabliau that covers the *vilain* and serves as the veil of falseness, the literal divide between him and reality.

In similar fashion, both Calandrino and the *vilain* furnish their tricksters with the narrative material for their trick, which in both cases takes the form of a figurative expression transformed into a literal one. As the *vilain*'s wife begins to insist that her husband is ill, the *vilain* at first responds: "Erme, j'ai tel fain que je muir (v. 32)" [Erme, I am so hungry that I am dying]. This figurative expression of "starving to death" will be transformed by the wife into (pretend) literal death in the next sentence. Calandrino also provides Bruno with an expression that will lead to his ultimate problem, his pregnancy, when he sends him to the doctor, telling him "vavvi e sappimi ridire come il fatto sta, ché io mi sento non so che dentro" (IX:3, 18) [go there and let me know what is wrong with me, since I feel I don't know what's inside]. Calandrino will soon be told that his "inside" has a baby, not an unidentified illness. The same device is used in each tale to present an impossible scenario, a dead man who talks in the fabliau and a pregnant man in the novella.

The fabliau *Le Vilain de Bailleul* and novella IX:3 resemble each other in other details, including the part where the trickster, namely the wife or Bruno, runs to an authority (the priest or the doctor), in order to establish collusion and add a sense of veracity to the trick.[92] Similarly, both the fabliau and IX:3 (and most of the Calandrino stories, in fact) involve the preparation of capons: for the priest, Dame Erme "avait le chapon cuit" (17) [Lady Erme cooked the capon], whereas Calandrino pays the doctor and his friends for curing him "buon capponi e grossi" (IX:3, 29) [good and fat capons]. Although not outstanding details in themselves, in conjunction with the other similarities of the narrative, they acquire force. It seems that Boccaccio used *Le Vilain de Bailleul* in two ways in the *Decameron*, by separating the trick into distinct units: a man thinking he is dead and a man being convinced by words that he is ill.[93] Each of these narrative units, combined with other texts, retains the recognizable atmosphere of the fabliau in new narrative contexts. The character of the *vilain* constitutes the thematic thread that links III:8 to IX:3, where Ferondo and Calandrino are both easily duped victims of their so-called friends. Like the *vilain*, Calandrino seems to learn nothing from being tricked.

The fabliau and two *novelle* all question the relationship between seeing and believing, truth and fiction, all revealing the triumph of fiction over fact. In each case, the trick or story prevails over facts and the impossible is made true. Although it is possible to interpret these tales as negative *exempla*, warnings to the reader not to be gullible and mistrustful like these dupes, it is also possible to read the narratives as reflections on the nature of storytelling, where the impossible can be made possible and believed as truth. At the structural level, the two *novelle* that rely on *Le Vilain de Bailleul* suggest that themes are clearly to be manipulated and that stories do not exist as independent, indivisible entities, but rather are part of a complex literary network that is constantly open to new definitions and reevaluation.

These examples have shown that Boccaccio's transformation of the fabliaux deploys fabliaux devices, using reversals on the rhetorical, social, and structural levels in order to bring opposites together. For Boccaccio, these opposites also include literary genres, such as the fabliaux and moral *exempla* or hagiographic works, yet "these reversals are not simply techniques of Boccaccio's art; they are ... the very core of the story."[94] Whereas the fabliaux are a play on language and on the capacity of narrative to involve the audience in making decisions about what is and is not to be believed, the *Decameron* continues to implicate the reader in questions of morality.

Conclusion

In this study I have suggested the ways in which reversal participates in a paradigm shift in reading literature. The closed, didactic system of literature, intended in large part for a community of listeners, cedes its place in the course of the thirteenth and fourteenth centuries to an open literature of choices, whose audience is increasingly private, intimate, and individual: a reading public in the modern sense. As a device, reversal provides a way to situate the Old French fabliaux in relation to other medieval texts, since it is a characteristic of fabliaux that distinguishes them from other short narrative forms. Reversal operates in the language, the literary themes and social norms, as well as the structure of the fabliaux. It also shapes the manuscript collections that preserve the fabliaux. The three types of reversal outlined in this study—chiasmus, narrative or sociogenic reversal, and inversion—reveal the specificity of the fabliaux and the nature of their adaptation in Giovanni Boccaccio's *Decameron*. By evoking the question of readership in his frame narrative and inscribing an audience that also functions as storytellers in the *cornice*, Boccaccio sets forth a model reading public that is fully engaged in understanding the tales they hear and tell. Indeed, the *Decameron*'s frame bridges the gap between writer and reader, producer and consumer, text and imagination, inside and outside that this paradigm shift in reading embodies. The majority of this study has concentrated on the narrative and structural dynamics of texts that produced this shift, in particular the technique of reversal in the fabliaux and the *Decameron* as crucial to influencing the audience's reception of, and involvement with, literature.

The example of *La Grue* has indicated the ways in which the fabliaux can combine Eastern and Western narrative traditions through inversion and narrative reversal in a way that prefigures the joining of these traditions in the *Decameron*. In chapter 2 I have shown that chiasmus in the fabliaux undermines the ostensible lessons in the texts, while this same figure supports the didactic aims of fables. In this way, the fabliaux challenge single interpretations of literature central to didactic texts. Similarly, the use of reversal in the fabliaux influences the interpretation of other texts in Western story collections. Whereas the framed Eastern collections point to one lesson, Western collections are open to multiple interpretations. The anthologies that preserve fabliaux contrast with the didactic frames of Eastern narrative collections because, in the Western compilations, the fabliaux provide not negative *exempla* in relation to the other texts, but rather different interpretive options that are equally valid. Reversal serves to disrupt traditional didactic views of literature in favor of presenting hermeneutic possibilities for the audience of fabliaux, particularly to their public of literary adapters. For this reason, I also considered the ways in which Boccaccio drew from the fabliaux tradition and the "fabliaux manuscripts" for the *Decameron*. Both the fabliaux and Boccaccian *novelle* use reversal to bring together opposites, in particular different narrative discourses. In doing so, they give the various parts new meaning and emphasize multiplicity in the creation and interpretation of stories.

While reversal in the literature of the High Middle Ages is connected to open interpretation for the individual reader, it is a technique that also has validity for other periods in which a shift in reading practices is prevalent. Contemporary ways of reading, which are increasingly dependent on digital texts and open forum discussions, are in many respects staging a reversal of the private, contemplative reading practices that Boccaccio championed. A move away from a specific reader or patron allowed Boccaccio and composers of fabliaux to create open-ended texts for an increasingly open and unknown audience. Today's audience is nearly without limits, as are the possibilities of interpretation, since differences in the geographical, social, and cultural circumstances of individual readers are almost endlessly varied. Yet the immediacy and physical distance of the new forms of reading seem to reduce the sense of intimacy and the space for the reader's imagination.

The introduction to this study began with a series of questions about the relationship of the short narrative form to the collection. Through the device of reversal, the fabliaux show that a frame incongruent with the stories it contains can potentially alter the interpretation of the individual stories, as in the case of the Seven Sages tradition, in which the humor of fabliaux themes had to be downplayed by the internal audience in favor of the antifeminist bent of the frame. It is more common, however, that the stories themselves and their interactions in collections undermined or counteracted the interpretive thrust of the frame, since the Seven Sages tradition actually became less antifeminist once fabliaux themes were introduced. In this respect, the overall effect of the stories usually supersedes the imposed interpretation of the frame when it opposes the messages of the stories. When the frame is removed, however, the meaning of the stories must be supplied by the reader. Without a frame to both justify the tales and orient the reader in a single interpretive direction, the tales are free to have multiple meanings. Yet this question about the relationship between the frame and the contents it encloses still divides scholarship on the *Decameron* because Boccaccio merged the didactic Eastern frame models and stories with open Western collections and stories. Boccaccio exploits oppositions at all levels of the *Decameron*. At the level of the *novelle*, the joining of opposites, namely religious *exempla* and fabliaux, renders null the moral didacticism of *exempla*, as it elevates the literary, secular, and social questions raised by the fabliaux. In regards to the frame, the model behavior of the *brigata* stands in stark contrast to the lasciviousness—and even to the tragedy—of many of the tales.

The influence of the fabliaux manuscripts on the organization of the *Decameron* is most evident at the level of the ten days of narration. The themes for the days function as frames for the minicollections of ten stories. The relationships among these themes parallel those witnessed in anthologies of fabliaux, while Days I and IX, which are not assigned specific themes, more closely resemble the unframed Western collections. Even within each day, the arrangement of stories reflects the influence of anthologies preserving fabliaux. Like these compilations, Boccaccio's *novelle* mix Eastern and Western narrative material. The *novelle* do not always reinforce the frame for the day in which they are included, and they are often rewritten into different frames, suggesting a variability of significations and consequently interpretations. Even when *novelle* conform to the frame for a day of narration, their interconnections with other stories in other frames undermine their adherence to any single theme and expose other interpretive possibilities, just as the fabliaux do. The discussions among the members of the *brigata* reinforce this notion of opening the tales to interpretive possibilities and often forge new connections among *novelle*, since the narrators comment on and make use of each other's stories. The reactions of the *brigata* serve as a model for and mirror of the extradiegetic audience of women suffering in love to whom Boccaccio offers his work and who are in turn a literary representation of the actual, unknown reading public.

Significantly, the fabliaux material in the *Decameron* also reveals highly contrived structures within the work that ultimately do not map onto the whole. As Mazzotta explains, "the *Decameron* aspires to be a whole of parts but, at the same time, declares the impossibility of its being arranged as a total and coherent pattern."[1] The symmetry of the stories narrated on Day III, most of which are derived from the fabliaux, as well as the pairs of inverse tales that borrow from fabliaux, such as I:4 and IX:2, create an image or rather an illusion of order. Furthermore, the tales on Days III and VII, which are both strongly associated with fabliaux, are also told in perfect gardens that are idyllic, protected, and removed from reality. The garden location as frame reflects the metanarrative framing devices that the *Decameron* adapts from other framed story collections as it also recasts these devices, which were often part of an appeal to verisimilitude, as their opposite, since they become deliberately artificial contrivances used to set apart the creation within. That the fabliaux material—perhaps more than any other type of narrative that Boccaccio adapted in the *Decameron*—is associated with structural and natural symmetry is not only because this contrast draws out the play of opposites, but because this association of bawdy fabliaux material and designed perfection emphasizes the myth of order. These ambiguous, mutable tales that are ever changing in the *Decameron* and announce their own mutability can only be fixed by the audience through a clearly artificial structure. This artificial structure mirrors the ideal society of equals removed from the world that the *brigata* creates of and for itself. The *brigata* is at the same time outside the stories it frames and also part of a contrived and perfected society that calls attention to itself as creation. The achieved, fixed symmetry is made up of unfixed fragments which highlight their own artificiality as stories. The *novelle* indebted to fabliaux suggest that the only locus of perfection and order is in the world of narrative, in the imagination, as Mazzotta would have it.[2] Whether this imagination is that of the internal audience that is the *brigata*, or whether it is of the external audience that the members of the *brigata* reflect in a perfected way, depends on the literary or ethical implications the reader chooses. As a closed group of friends, removed from the world, the *brigata* models the new intimacy of private reflection and fulfillment in the internal world of the imagination. This intimacy is losing ground in the public reading forums of contemporary society. Beyond the *brigata* as a model audience, the various inter- and intratextual layers of the *Decameron* also implicate other types of audiences,[3] who in many respects are the opposite of the lovelorn ladies first addressed in the *Proemio*. Boccaccio's friend and contemporary Petrarch constitutes one such reader, a scholar who reimagines and rewrites the last novella in the collection, giving it a strictly exemplary significance.

On the narrative level, this study has shown that Boccaccio used more fabliaux material in his *novelle* than has previously been considered. In chapter 4 I went even further than simply adding some relevant intertext and suggested that traditional views of literary sources are inadequate to understand the influence of the fabliaux, or any type of text, on the *Decameron* because of the variety of ways in which Boccaccio deployed literary themes and devices. Whether a novella is indebted to one source, as is the case with IX:2, to a combination of two diametrically opposed models, as in III:10, which combines saints' lives with fabliaux, or finally whether two *novelle* draw from different parts of a single model text, Boccaccio's stories display seemingly endless possibilities of literary creation through reversal, combination, and dissection of model texts. The fabliaux participated in all of these manipulations.

But what is the purpose of opening stories up to endless variations and readings? As Mazzotta asks, "Is the pleasure the work conveys merely esthetic or is it also a moral good, what in ethics is called a virtue?"[4] Is the ultimate good of both the fabliaux and the *Decameron* the value in making judgments? Indeed, what do these texts imply about the role of literature? In the literary sphere, the opening of narrative combinations and interpretations eliminates finality and suggests that creation is an ongoing, endlessly fruitful process. The writer, who is understood as a reader of other texts that he must adapt, is limited in his creation only by his ability to combine, dismember, and reverse forms. In this way, Boccaccio stands on the threshold between adaptor of stories from previous material for a new audience, and inventor and source of this newly crafted and combined work. The role of the writer must change in relation to that of the audience, who is becoming more of a literate, reading audience. Thus, the implication for the audience of the openness of narrative is responsibility for interpreting the work. If the writer can control only the words in the text, but not how they are understood, then the interpretation of the text can lie only with the audience and more precisely with the individual. Bringing to the fore these questions of open interpretation and endless variation of tales makes explicit that the value of narrative to these individuals is their interpretive work, their interaction with the text, and the awareness that they have a choice. Highlighting open interpretation as the fabliaux do reveals a shift from the controlling, didactic writer who draws on authorities to a creative author who is always already dead; from an audience seeking information to an individual called upon to discern true from false and right from wrong. If this new value to the audience is its being forced to choose and exercise its abilities of discernment, then the reward may be whatever the individual chooses, moral gain or pleasure.

Boccaccio's borrowings of the fabliaux have shaped our understanding of these texts but perhaps have not revealed the full picture. There are other aspects of the fabliaux that Boccaccio did not borrow, but that are equally valid points of entry to understanding the fabliaux. Indeed, the fabliaux that Boccaccio adapted all deploy reversal, but there are other fabliaux that make no use of the techniques of reversal and that still distinguish these tales from other short forms in Old French. For this reason, an examination of the fabliaux and the *Decameron* in relation to Geoffrey Chaucer's *Canterbury Tales* or other French story collections such as *Les Cent Nouvelles nouvelles* and the *Heptaméron*, would likely reveal new aspects of the fabliaux and the *Decameron*. In this way, analyzing the reception of medieval texts by later writers may uncover hidden features of these works and shed more light on the system of medieval literature. As the present study has suggested, comparing the intertexts of the *Decameron* and the fabliaux shows reversal as a crucial technique in the transformation of literature and opens works to new interpretations.

Beyond the world of medieval literature, reversal is a technique that has the potential to illuminate other transformations of genre and shifts in society. The current culture of reading is increasingly moving away from the intimate book culture that Boccaccio's work announced toward a more public and simultaneously less open system. While technological advances have changed and continue to change the ways in which we read, they also herald a shift toward reading and writing as public gestures. The garden of the *brigata* is becoming the World Wide Web where mostly anonymous discussions lack the intimacy and specificity of those that the *brigata* were mirroring and mirrored back to the audience of the *Decameron*. This contemporary reversal of reading practices signals the undoing of the paradigm shift described in this study, a move away from the individual imagination toward the communal. Yet the shift is not a complete reversal and return to didacticism, for modern readers are their own critics and adaptors of literature and they have authorities and would-be authorities at their disposal. The epigraph to the introduction of this book posited the value of interpretive choices in reading fiction as an exercise in individual discernment. The same may not be said of reading literature today, for literature is a commodity that, as it becomes ever-more accessible and ephemeral on the screen, is losing its status as an object that provokes reflection. The exercise of personal discernment seems to enter less into play, or at least has shifted from within the text and the individual to a larger public forum, where the reader can instantaneously search a community of other readers for a satisfying interpretation, the "answer" to understanding the text. In this way, the space of the imagination and interpretation that literature generated for the projected audiences of the fabliaux and the *Decameron* has become a public space that paradoxically plays on opposites to exalt and reduce the role of the individual in the process of interpretation.

APPENDIX

Table 1. List of manuscripts

Abbreviation	Manuscript Name and Number
A	Paris, BNF, fr. 837
B	Bern, Burgerbibl., Codex 354
C	Berlin, Staatsbibl., Hamilton 257
D	Paris, BNF, fr. 19152
E	Paris, BNF, fr. 1593
F	Paris, BNF, fr. 12603
G	Nottingham, Univ. Library, Middleton L.M. 6
H	Paris, BNF, fr. 2168
I	Paris, BNF, fr. 25545
J	Paris, BNF, fr. 1553
K	Paris, BNF, fr. 2173
L	Paris, BNF, fr. 1635
M	London, British Library, Harley 2253
N	Rome, Bibl. Casanatensis, 1598
O	Pavia, Bibl. Univ., Aldini 219
P	Paris, BNF, fr. 24432
Q	Paris, BNF, nouv. acq. fr. 1104
R	Paris, Arsenal, 3524
S	Paris, Arsenal, 3525
T	Chantilly, Condé 475 (1578)
U	Turin, Bibl. Naz., L.V. 32
V	Geneva, Bibl. publ. et univ., fr. 179bis

(*continued*)

(*Continued*)

Abbreviation	Manuscript Name and Number
V^{bis}	Lyons, Bibl. mun., 5495
W	Paris, BNF, fr. 1446
X	Paris, BNF, fr. 12581
Y	London, British Library, Add. 10289
Z	Oxford, Bodleian Library, Digby 86
a	Paris, BNF, fr. 375
b	Paris, BNF, fr. 1588
c	Paris, BNF, fr. 12483
d	Paris, BNF, fr. 14971
e	Paris, Arsenal, 3114
f	Chartres, Bibl. mun., 620
g	Paris, BNF, Rothschild 2800
h	Cambridge, Corpus Christi Coll., 50
i	Clermont-Ferrand, Arch. Du Puy-de-Dôme, F2
j	Paris, BNF, fr. 2188
k	Troyes, Bibl. mun., 1511
l	Cologny-Geneva, Bodmer 113
m	Le Mans, Bibl. mun., 5495
n	Oudenaerde, Décanat 3
o	Oxford, Bodleian Library, Douce 111
p	Paris, Arsenal, 3527
q	Paris, BNF, nouv. acq. fr. 934
r	Turin, Bibl. Naz., 1639 (L II-14)
s	Princeton Univ., Taylor Collection, Phillipps 25970

Table 2. *Decameron* novelle and fabliaux analogues

Decameron Novella	*Fabliaux analogues*	*Manuscripts*
I:4	L'Evesque qui beneï le con	B
II:5	Boivin de Provins	AP
	*Le Segretain moine	BCDEHdp
III:2	Trubert	j
III:4	*Le Prestre qui abevete	EF
III:6	Le Meunier d'Arleux	J
III:8	Le Vilain de Bailleul	ABCF^{1}F^{2}T
III:10	*Frere Denise	AL
	*Cele qui ne pooit oïr parler de foutre	ACE
V:9	Guillaume au faucon	D
V:10	*Le Cuvier	A
VII:1	Le Chevalier qui recovra l'amor de sa dame	B
VII:2	Le Cuvier	A
VII:4	*La Dame qui fist trois tours entor le moustier	AELT
VII:5	Le Chevalier qui fist sa fame confesse	A
VII:6	*Le Clerc qui fu repus derriere l'escrin	RW
VII:7	La Borgoise d'Orliens	ABC
	Un chevalier et sa dame et un clerk	h
VII:8	*Les Tresces	BD
VII:9	Les Trois dames qui troverent l'anel	AC
	La Dame escoillee	CDEFGe
	Le Prestre qui abevete	EF
VIII:1	Le Bouchier d'Abeville	ACHOT
VIII:2	Le Prestre et la dame	D
VIII:4	Le Prestre et Alison	D
VIII:5	Barat et Haimet	ABCD
VIII:6	Barat et Haimet	ABCD
VIII:8	Constant du Hamel	ABDJn
IX:2	La Nonete	N
	Les Braies au cordelier	AD
	*Les Braies le priestre	N

(*continued*)

(*Continued*)

Decameron Novella	*Fabliaux analogues*	*Manuscripts*
IX:3	*Le Vilain de Bailleul	ABCFT
IX:6	Gombert et le deus clers	ABCH
	Le Meunier et les deus clers	BC
IX:10	La Pucele qui voloit voler	BEI

Note: This list of analogues does not take into account their degree of similarity. The list is adapted from Landau and Branca's sourcework. Those marked by an asterisk (*) have not been identified by other scholars.

NOTES

Abbreviations

DEI	*Dizionario Etimologico Italiano*. Edited by Carlo Battisti and Giovanni Alessio.
FEW	*Französisches etymologisches Wörterbuch*. Edited by Walther von Wartburg.
Godefroy	*Dictionnaire de l'ancienne langue française*, edited by Frédéric Godefroy
Lewis and Short	*A Latin Dictionary*, edited by Charlton Lewis and Charles Short
NRCF	*Nouveau recueil complet des fabliaux*
Tobler-Lommatzsch	*Altfranzösisches Wörterbuch*, edited by Adolf Tobler and Erhard Lommatzsch

Introduction

I wish to thank Rick Wright, Simone Marchesi, and Thomas Boeve for their invaluable help with the translation of the epigraph.

1. See, for example, Marius Lange, *Vom Fabliaux zu Boccaccio und Chaucer*, and Philippe Ménard, "Les Sources françaises d'un conte de Boccace." Carter Revard, however, focuses more on the manuscript tradition of the fabliaux in relation to the *Decameron*, in "From French 'Fabliau Manuscripts.'"

2. For example, see Revard, "From French 'Fabliau Manuscripts,'" esp. 269, and Tracy Adams, "The Cunningly Intelligent Characters of BNffr 19152."

3. See Marcus Landau, *Die Quellen des "Dekameron,"* particularly the section on Eastern sources, 4–106, and Michelangelo Picone, "Preistoria della cornice del *Decameron*."

4. In particular, see Mary-Jane Schenck's *The Fabliaux: Tales of Wit and Deception*, as well as Roy J. Pearcy's *Logic and Humour in the Fabliaux*. Giuseppe

Mazzotta frequently mentions reversal in the *Decameron* but does not relate the device to the fabliaux in *The World at Play in Boccaccio's "Decameron."*

5. See Michael Riffaterre's *Semiotics of Poetry* and Graham Allen's summary of these ideas in *Intertextuality*, esp. 119.

6. See Catherine Brown, *Contrary Things*, 13.

7. For the Latin text, see John of Salisbury, *Metalogicon*, ed. J. B. Hall and K.S.B. Keats-Rohan, 61–63, bk. II, ch. 5; for an English translation based on the edition of Clement C. J. Webb, see *The Metalogicon of John of Salisbury*, trans. Daniel D. McGarry, 81–84.

8. Peter Abelard, *Sic et non: A Critical Edition*, ed. Blanche B. Boyer and Richard McKeon.

9. Sarah Kay, *Courtly Contradictions*, 5.

10. For dialectic in the works of Chrétien de Troyes, see Nancy Bradley-Cromey, "Dialectic and Chrétien de Troyes." See also Tony Hunt, "The Dialectic of *Yvain*," and his "Aristotle, Dialectic, and Courtly Literature"; and Alan Robert Press, "Death and Lamentation in Chrétien de Troyes's Romances."

11. See Pearcy, *Logic and Humour*, esp. ch. 2, 34–51.

12. In addition to Pearcy, *Logic and Humour*, see Schenck, *The Fabliaux: Tales of Wit*; Charles Muscatine, *The Old French Fabliaux*; and Thomas D. Cooke and Benjamin L. Honeycutt, eds., *The Humor of the Fabliaux*.

13. John of Salisbury, *Metalogicon*, bk. II, ch. 11.

14. Ibid., ch. 5.

15. For a reading of the fabliaux that highlights intelligence over morality, see Gabrielle Hutton, "La Stratégie dans les fabliaux."

16. For a definition of these terms, see Theo Stemmler, "Miscellany or Anthology?" and Revard, "From French 'Fabliau Manuscripts.'"

17. Stemmler, "Miscellany or Anthology?" 113.

18. Throughout this study, intertextuality refers to the set of relationships among texts, including but not limited to allusions, sources, and citations, whereas intratextuality concerns these relationships among parts of a single work.

19. Mazzotta, *The World at Play*, 67.

20. For the notion of imagination as the value of the *Decameron*, see Mazzotta, *The World at Play*, esp. ch. 9, 241–69.

Chapter 1. Fabliaux Reversals and *La Grue*

1. For a formal definition of chiasmus, see Henri Morier, *Dictionnaire de poétique et de rhétorique*, 194. For an application of chiasmus to Chrétien de Troyes and twelfth-century French literature, see Witt, "Le Chiasme et la poésie courtoise."

2. Heinrich Lausberg, *Handbook of Literary Rhetoric*, trans. Matthew T. Bliss, Annemiek Jansen, and David E. Orton, 354, *Commutatio*, §800. See also §723: "If

the isocolon consists of two cola (cf. §719), the opposition of the cola tends, as regards content, towards antithesis (cf. §787). The antithetic force may be reinforced by the cross arrangement of the corresponding clause elements."

3. *Rhetorica ad Herennium*, 324–27, bk. IV, ch. xxviii, §39. Although not strictly speaking a manual of rhetoric, medieval schools used St. Augustine's writings as rhetorical models. One of the notable features of *De doctrina christiana* is the use of *commutatio* or chiasmus to reinforce ideas. For examples of rhetorical figures in St. Augustine's work, see *De doctrina christiana: Liber quartus*, trans. Sister Thérèse Sullivan, esp. 34.

4. *Rhetorica ad Herennium*, 324 and 325–27, bk. IV, ch. xxviii, §39.

5. See also *Dolopathos*, trans. Gilleland, x–xii, for other examples of chiasmus and for examples of other figures common to Johannes's writing.

6. The manuscript sigla for fabliaux are those given in the *NRCF*. Manuscripts not accounted for by the *NRCF* are listed in the appendix. All references to fabliaux are to this edition; initial text references are to volume then page of this edition, and subsequent references are to line number. All translations of fabliaux are my own unless otherwise noted.

7. This device resembles Johannes de Alta Silva's presentation of *Dolopathos* as history and not fiction, and his references to "gesta," in Alfons Hilka, *Historia Septem Sapientum II*, 3.18 and 31.

8. Pierre Kunstmann explains: "J'entendrai ici l'*annominatio* au sens large, c'est-à-dire incluant la paronomase (qui rapproche des vocables se ressemblant par le son mais différant par le sens) aussi bien que le polyptote (où le mot revient, dans une même phrase, sous une autre forme grammaticale ou sous la forme d'un dérivé)," in "L'*Annominatio* chez Gautier," 101. Also in a study of Gautier de Coinci's *Miracles*, Hunt considers paronomasia a general term for *adnominatio*, which he defines as "the use of one etymological stem which is a homonym or homophone of another etymological stem," in *Miraculous Rhymes*, 38.

9. I would like to thank Sarah Kay for pointing out this second relationship of food and sex in the fabliau.

10. Compare to Eichmann and Duval's translation: "he who plans to shit on someone else / Gets shat on first," in *The French Fabliaux: B.N. MS. 837*, 135.

11. This idea complements Pearcy's definition of the fabliaux as texts whose structure demonstrates the humor in logical fallacies and reveals a "shift in truth-values," in *Logic and Humour*, 34.

12. These stories will be discussed in detail in chapter 4.

13. Both of these fabliaux are rejected from Pearcy's list in his *Logic and Humour* on the grounds that they do not contain any logical fallacies. I would argue that both tales highlight judgment and that *Le Vilain qui conquist paradis par plait* also involves logical argumentation.

14. See Pearcy, "An Instance of Heroic Parody." A few other fabliaux with notable gender reversals include *Sire Hain et Dame Anieuse*, *La Saineresse*, and *Frere*

Denise, which will be discussed in chapter 4. Like *Bérengier*, these last two cases involve cross-dressing.

15. MS D uses the neutral "cheval."

16. For examples of courtly language in the fabliaux, see Per Nykrog, *Les Fabliaux*, esp. ch. III, 72–104. Although I agree with Nykrog's notion of parody or courtly burlesque in some fabliaux, I do not find parody to be the defining feature of the form, nor do I agree with Nykrog on the number of fabliaux with parodic intent.

17. Muscatine summarizes: "As several critics have observed, about two-thirds of the fabliaux either end with an explicit moral in the manner of fables or offer an analogous moral teaching in the course of the narrative. Whatever it means, the phenomenon cannot be dismissed as mere 'vestigial survival' (*Reid*, x), though it may represent a variety of intentions. Some fabliaux offer perfunctory lessons that either have little to do with the story being told or refer to only a trivial aspect of it, and some can be suspected of parody or burlesque. But some are actually called *essemples*," in *The Old French Fabliaux*, 20–21. For a bibliography of this question, see 175, n. 27. Additionally, Schenck, whose views on this issue are compatible with my own, reads the proverbs as practical, not moral lessons that seem to involve some interpretation; see her *The Fabliaux: Tales of Wit and Deception*, esp. 19–36. Dominique Boutet, on the other hand, sees the fabliaux with adequate lessons as a minority and ascribes most lessons to the "game" of the fabliaux writers, in *Les Fabliaux*, 6, 18, and 113–22.

18. Simon Gaunt, *Gender and Genre*, 271–73.

19. Ibid., 272, Gaunt's translation.

20. Ibid.

21. Ibid., 242–48. The question of innocence in the fabliaux, particularly for young female characters, will appear in relation to *Decameron* III:10, discussed in chapter 4.

22. For an example of a final proverb whose application must be inverted and reinterpreted to fit the narrative context, see my "*Bérengier au lonc cul*."

23. Schenck identifies many of these oppositional pairs as functions of her structural analysis of the fabliaux, but she does not emphasize the role of reversal among these pairs; see her list of functions, *The Fabliaux: Tales of Wit and Deception*, 40.

24. Gaunt has spoken of the "startling reversals" in this text, *Gender and Genre*, 262.

25. For a study of this fabliau and various analogues, see Bédier, *Les Fabliaux*, 212–28. Bédier provides an analogue in Marie de France's *Isopet* that differs in a number of particulars from the fabliau.

26. Gaunt, *Gender and Genre*, 262.

27. Thus, it is only in the language of the text that there is actual resolution. For

the idea that dialectic resolves questions relative to itself (in this case of language and not things), see ch. 11 in John of Salisbury's *Metalogicon*.

28. These three stories have been the subject of numerous studies, often in relation to "The Reeve's Tale" in Chaucer's *Canterbury Tales*. See, for example Lange, *Vom Fabliaux zu Boccaccio und Chaucer*; Roger T. Burbridge, "Chaucer's *Reeve's Tale* and the *Fabliau*"; Olson, "The *Reeve's Tale* as a Fabliau"; and especially the text and bibliography of Ménard, "Les Sources françaises d'un conte de Boccace."

29. Of the two traditions of this tale, Nico van den Boogaard explains that "la séparation traditionnelle des deux paraît artificielle si l'on considère . . . qu'on est en présence d'une 'série d'événements qui se déroulent de façon strictement parallèle' et que 'la différence entre *grue* et *héron* est à négliger,'" NRCF, 4.153. While Paul Meyer suggests that the two versions are the result of a tale recorded from an oral tradition in different times and places and that there may have existed other versions, Jean Rychner entertains the possibility that there is a literary or written relation between them; see Meyer's articles "Fragment d'*Aspremont*," and "Le fableau du *Héron*;" and Rychner's *Contribution à l'étude des fabliaux*, 17–18.

30. For the symbolism of animals in the Middle Ages, see Jacques Voisenet, *Bêtes et hommes*, 121–22. In addition to bestiaries, *Inferno* V, 46–48, presents the crane as singing love-song lamentations: "E come i gru van cantando lor lai, / faccendo in aere di sé lunga riga, / così vid' io venir, traendo guai."

31. MSS F and i contain longer rants by the nursemaid about having lost the bird and the girl's virginity. Both of these versions suggest a different interpretation where the nursemaid is the victim in the tale, not the innocent girl in her charge, but neither one contains the same proverb. The editors of the *NRCF* have identified the proverb as part of the nursemaid's speech, which I have followed, but the phrase could also be said by the narrator.

32. Although some critics interpret this reference only in light of its potential historical or social relevance—that fabliaux must have been narrated at markets and locations of monetary exchange—such a reading ignores the term's relevance to the narrative. While it is possible that fabliaux were recited at money tables, I know of no other fabliau that alludes specifically to this idea.

33. MSS D and E give "s'an torna," which reinforces the idea of turning to be played out in the structure of the tale.

34. MSS E and i make no explicit mention of the exchange of the bird.

35. MS B and the critical edition read "se li enbat," while MSS A, D, E, F use "remet" to reinforce the idea of replacement.

36. MS A repeats the line at the end of the first chiastic structure "et la norrice i entra lors," drawing a parallel between the two halves of the fabliau.

37. I have substituted these lines for the ones given in the critical edition. The lessons of all manuscripts except MS B (and therefore of the critical edition of the

NRCF) present: "Se je n'en fusse mescreüe / Je l'achetasse ja de toi," which is the line cited above. The other: "Ainz tele mes ne fu veüe" is less convincing and even rejected in the notes of the *NRCF*, 4.396n. The line reference corresponds to the place in the critical edition where these lines would be.

38. Whether the girl is *that* naive or whether she is pretending is a matter of debate in this and a number of similar fabliaux. As I have already mentioned, her ignorance of the literal meaning of the word *foutre* should not necessarily denote complete ignorance of the act itself. The same type of question appears in *Le Vilain de Bailluel* (to be discussed in chapter 4), where a man's wife convinces him he is dead so that she may entertain the priest under her husband's nose. Can the peasant be so stupid that he does not know he is alive, or is he playing along with the wife's game? There are rarely serious consequences for any actions in the fabliaux; characters usually play along with the outlandish premises. To a degree, it seems the *puceles naïves* of the fabliaux and of the *Decameron* are not an exception, and that they exploit, or rather play on their own naïveté, in order to see and do exactly what they should not.

39. In the story of Filippo Balducci in the Introduction to Day IV in the *Decameron*, the same relationship between sex and food (and birds) is suggested when the son asks to feed the women, referred to as "geese." For a discussion of this story, see chapter 3.

40. Marie de France, *Lais*, ed. Karl Warnke. All references to the *Lais* are to this edition, unless otherwise noted.

41. I would like to express my gratitude to Sarah Kay for pointing out to me that the emir in *Floire et Blancheflor* has several women locked in a tower from whom he chooses a new wife. The idea is the same: to preserve their virginity for the emir, but it is also where Floire and Blancheflor reunite.

42. In MS i, the father does not want his daughter to hear about "druerie," that is, anything to do with sex and love.

43. Indeed, it is the *Chevalier de la Charrette* that most deviates from, if not inverts, the traditional motif because Lancelot, a man, is locked up. In the other examples, women are locked up. Lancelot's tower never becomes the site of a romantic or sexual interlude, as the towers in these other narratives do. Lancelot is even saved by a woman, Méléagant's sister. Is this reversal of the traditional topos intended to show Lancelot's inferiority? Or does it rather highlight Méléagant's pusillanimity? It does not seem to have any traits in common with the towers from the Eastern collections of stories, such as the Seven Sages tradition. I know of no study that looks at the question of prisons and towers in Chrétien's works.

44. Although not common in the fabliaux, there are certainly stories that use marvelous elements, such as the wishes in *Les Quatre souhais St. Martin*, and the magical powers bestowed on the knight in *Le Chevalier qui fist parler les cons*.

45. Although the Eastern story collections will be discussed in more detail in chapter 3, I have briefly mentioned here one relation to fabliaux through

the tower motif. Within the frame of the *Seven Sages* and the *Dolopathos*, the story known as *Inclusa*—which is combined with *Puteus* in *Dolopathos*—also presents a tower that functions similarly to the motif in Western stories. In the Eastern tradition, a jealous husband locks his beautiful wife in a tower, but the wife and her husband's favorite vassal fall in love. The vassal builds a tunnel to the tower in order to enjoy the woman's company, and the two eventually marry under the eyes of the jealous husband. This fabliau-like trick could mean that the Eastern stories are the origin of some fabliaux, or else it could mean that the Eastern stories, as they entered the West, were themselves mixed with Western tales such as the fabliaux. It is not possible to conclude that one type of story engendered the other, particularly as the Eastern story collections rose to popularity around the same time the fabliaux did. The combination of two tales in *Dolopathos* certainly supports the same device in the fabliaux, but it does not display the same level of reversal that seems to pervade the fabliaux more generally. The editors of the *Seven Sages* note the similarity between *Inclusa* and Marie de France's "Guigemar," especially at the end when the couple departs by boat. As *Inclusa* is not found in the Eastern versions of the *Seven Sages*, it is possible that this story actually has Western origins. The Western composition of the *Seven Sages* barely predates the *Lais*, so there is no reason that *Inclusa* must be of Eastern origin.

46. Adams refers to this as a "situational approach," in "The Cunningly Intelligent Characters of BNffr 19152," 911.

47. In discussing the number of fabliaux in a codex, I generally refer to the editors of the *NRCF*. While MS A preserves the largest number of fabliaux according to these editors, providing exact counts of fabliaux in codices undermines the notion of generic fluidity central to this study because the number of fabliaux in a manuscript varies according to the definition of fabliau that is applied. For this reason, I deliberately leave out the exact quantity of fabliaux in a codex, although when necessary I mention relative quantities, whether the manuscript is generally thought to contain—by the agreement of most scholars—several or merely a few fabliaux.

48. Sylvie Lefèvre, "Le Recueil et l'œuvre unique," 208. I would like to thank Sylvie Lefèvre for sending me this article prior to publication. The numbers corresponding to the texts in the manuscript are those assigned by Lefèvre.

49. To my knowledge, there is no edition of this work.

50. For a brief analysis of microcontexts involving fabliaux and a bibliography for MS A, see Keith Busby, *Codex and Context*, 439–43. Busby asserts that the fabliaux serve as "negative moral *exempla*," 441, a claim that my argument disputes.

51. The Rutebeuf section is on ff. 283–332, ending with *La Mort Rustebuef*.

52. See Adams for a description of this manuscript and the notion of *metis* that "frames" it, "The Cunningly Intelligent Characters of BNffr 19152," 898.

53. Noomen and van den Boogaard mention five other fabliaux in addition

to the two in question that are also attributed to an unknown Garin/Guerin, but they explain: "comme il s'agit d'un nom fort répandu, cette rencontre ne permet guère de conclusions s'il n'y a pas d'autres données à l'appui," *NRCF*, 4.155. Busby, on the other hand, has posited the notion that the name Garin might have been a signal indicating to the audience that the story was a fabliau; see his "Courtly Literature and the Fabliaux," esp. 70–71. On the name Garin, see also Luciano Rossi, ed., *Fabliaux érotiques*, 24–26.

54. Adams, "The Cunningly Intelligent Characters of BNffr 19152," 900: "As for collections of works, by the late fourteenth century, they were being composed with framing devices that activated textual interactions. In works like the *Decameron*, the *Canterbury Tales*, *Les Cent Nouvelles nouvelles*, and *L'Heptaméron*, short tales very different in register are deliberately set into relationship with one another by framing sets of narrators who interact through their storytelling, clearly recounting their tales in response to one another, while the individual tales illuminate and throw each others' values into question through the juxtaposition of their themes."

55. Busby, *Codex and Context*, 445–47.

56. Ibid, 446.

57. Ibid.

58. For this reason Pearcy has discarded it from his list of fabliaux in *Logic and Humour*, 233–36. *Les Putains et les lecheors* resembles a *dit* in form and nonnarrative content more closely than it does the fabliaux, yet Nykrog still argued for its inclusion within the corpus of fabliaux, as one of a few supernatural tales "qui se préoccupent surtout de dépeindre des types," *Les Fabliaux*, 56. The other tales in Nykrog's "allegorical group" are: *Le Couvoiteus et l'Envieus, Le Pet au vilain, Saint Pierre et le jongleur*, and finally *Les Sohais*.

59. According to Monique Léonard, the *dit* is conceived of in three ways as "un 'genre' fourre-tout, extrêmement imprécise; ou-un texte littéraire essentiellement porteur d'un enseignement moral ou dogmatique (parfois de forme satirique); ou-un lieu où un locuteur commence à s'exprimer à la première personne," *Le "Dit" et sa technique littéraire*, 12. According to Nykrog, the *dit* lacks action, *Les Fabliaux*, 10.

60. Since there are several foliations for this manuscript, I have chosen the one employed by the editors of the *NRCF*. The edition of *Le Blasme des fames* presented in *Three Medieval Views of Women*, ed. Gloria K. Fiero, Wendy Pfeffer, and Mathé Allain, uses another foliation in which this work begins on f. 153r. All references to *Le Blasme des fames* are to this edition.

61. Ibid., 1–24.

62. Ibid., 122–23, lines 45–48.

63. For a description and discussion of this manuscript, see Richard Trachsler, "Le Recueil Paris, BN fr. 12603."

64. For a description of this manuscript, see Rychner, *Contribution à l'étude*

des fabliaux, 10; Henri Omont, ed., *Catalogue des manuscrits*, 250–51; and Meyer, "Fragment d'*Aspremont*" and "Le fableau du *Héron*"; the second article also preserves a transcription of the marriage poem.

65. Some excellent studies of these manuscripts have been undertaken by the "Swiss School." As representative examples, see Olivier Collet, "Les collections vernaculaires entre diversité et unité"; Wagih Azzam and Olivier Collet, "Le Manuscrit 3142 de la Bibliothèque de l'Arsenal"; and also Yasmina Foehr-Janssens, Olivier Collet, and Wagih Azzam, "Les manuscrits littéraires français."

66. Foehr-Janssens, Collet, and Azzam, "Les manuscrits littéraires français," 660: "Diverses questions s'imposent donc pour l'interprétation des manuscrits qui nous garantissent cet héritage—le fabliau représente-t-il un élément adventice au sein de telles compositions, un composant plus ou moins important parmi d'autres, notamment lorsque le recueil comporte des œuvres d'une certaine ampleur, ou en est-il l'un des éléments fédérateurs? Et le cas échéant, en fonction ou non de son niveau de représentation dans le volume, ou d'autres critères qu'il s'agit de déterminer?"

67. Revard, "From French 'Fabliau Manuscripts,'" 262; and "*Giolte et Johane*: An Interlude in B. L. MS Harley 2253," 122–46. Busby concurs with Revard, arguing that the juxtaposition of texts in these two manuscripts generates humor, "Esprit gaulois," 162.

68. Revard, "From French 'Fabliau Manuscripts,'" 269.

69. Ibid.

70. Alberto Vàrvaro, "Elaboration des textes."

71. Ibid., 18. Vàrvaro also states that this *mouvance* is general for the period and not specific to certain types of genres.

72. Lefèvre, "Le Recueil et l'œuvre unique," 206–7.

73. Ibid., 207: "Sans aller jusqu'à poser une homologie entre manuscrit-recueil et texte hétérogène, certains éléments ou accents du fr. 837 nous invitent à des regroupements d'œuvres et à des commentaires composés."

74. Ibid., 210 and 214.

75. Revard, "From French 'Fabliau Manuscripts,'" 269; and Lefèvre, "Le Recueil et l'œuvre unique," 208.

76. In Busby, *Codex and Context*, see ch. 5, "Readings in Context," particularly subsection III, "The Scandal of the *Fabliaux* Manuscripts," 437–63.

Chapter 2. The Fabliaux in Context

1. All transcriptions and translations of this manuscript are my own unless otherwise noted, including the epigraph to this chapter, *Image du monde*, chapter IV, f. 3v, 225–27. Initial citations include the manuscript folio(s) and relevant edition page numbers, and subsequent references are to lines.

2. The fable collections compiled with fabliaux are those of Marie de France.

For a list of manuscripts containing Marie de France's *Isopet*, see *Les Fables*, ed. Charles Brucker, 20–22.

3. François Avril and Marie-Thérèse Gousset, eds., *Manuscrits enluminés d'origine italienne*, 9–10.

4. See Jaap van Os, "Autour de Guillaume," esp. 187: "[Ce manuscrit] ne trahit d'aucune manière le travail d'un copiste vénitien ou, plus généralement, italien . . . on ne signale nulle part les italienismes habituels aux niveaux graphique et stylistique."

5. The history of French influence on Italian culture in the High Middle Ages is far too vast a topic to be discussed here in any detail. For an examination of the political and personal ties in this period between France and Italy, see the study and bibliography by Jean Dunbabin, *The French in the Kingdom of Sicily*; and Samantha Kelly, *New Solomon: Robert of Naples (1309–1343)*. For the literary ties between France and Italy in the High Middle Ages, see the collection of essays in *"Accessus ad auctores,"* ed. Fabian Alfie and Andrea Dini; Cesare Segre, "La Letteratura franco-veneta"; Fabrizio Cigni, "La ricezione medievale della letteratura francese"; Meyer, "De l'expansion de la langue française en Italie;" and Daniela Delcorno Branca, *Tristano e Lancillotto in Italia*. For the question of Old French manuscripts in Italy, see the study and bibliography by Valeria Bertolucci Pizzorusso, "La réception de la littérature courtoise."

6. Dunbabin, *The French in the Kingdom of Sicily*, 94.

7. Ibid., 95–97.

8. Bertolucci Pizzorusso, "La réception de la littérature courtoise," 5.

9. Dunbabin, *The French in the Kingdom of Sicily*, 22.

10. These measurements are my own, but are similar to those given by E.-D. Grand in "*L'Image du monde*: Poème didactique du XIIIe siècle," 24, and by Avril and Gousset in *Manuscrits enluminés*, 9. Rychner gives a description of some twenty-one manuscripts containing fabliaux, including BNF fr. 2173, at the beginning of his *Contribution à l'étude des fabliaux*, 9–10, and cites a slightly different size for the manuscript: 230×170 mm.

11. See the description by Grand, "*L'Image du monde*: Poème didactique du XIIIe siècle," 24.

12. Avril and Gousset, *Manuscrits enluminés*, 10. Rychner, *Contribution à l'étude des fabliaux*, 9–10, however, gives the date at the beginning of the thirteenth century, but this cannot be correct since the first text, the first redaction of the *Image du monde*, was composed in 1246, and this date is indicated twice in the text itself (III, 17 and 22). See also van Os, *Les Fabliaux du manuscrit Cologny Bodmer 113*, and "Autour de Guillaume."

13. For a description of the images, see Avril and Gousset, *Manuscrits enluminés*, 9–10.

14. See van Os, "Autour de Guillaume," 190 n3. There is little doubt, though, that MS l is a copy of the second part of MS K with a few minor alterations—all

of the images and most of the lacunae are identical—and that it dates from the fifteenth century. For a study of MS l, see van Os, *Les Fabliaux du manuscrit Cologny Bodmer 113*.

15. For a summary of the Latin folio and an argument in favor of its textual integration among the fabliaux, see Barbara Nolan's article "Turning over the Leaves of Medieval Fabliau-Anthologies." I would like to express my deep gratitude to Janet Martin and Angeline C. Chiu for their help in deciphering and transcribing this Latin insert, as well as for discussing the above-outlined theories about its inclusion in this codex.

16. See Chantal Connochie-Bourgne, *L'Image du monde*, 43.

17. On fables, see Harold John Blackham, *The Fable as Literature*, xii–xiii. Blackham argues that fables are not moral per se; instead they can be said to illustrate a truth in a fictitious way.

18. According to Bédier, both *fable* and *fabliau* are derived from the Latin noun FABULA>fable to which the diminutive suffix -ELLUM was added, forming: FABLELLUM>*fableau*. It should be noted that the fabliaux are primarily of Picard origin, a region where the development of the ending -ELLUM became "-*iau*," hence the word *fabliau*, in Bédier, *Les Fabliaux*, 25. The modern form *fabliau* was also much debated by scholars in the nineteenth century, some, including Gaston Paris, preferring the form *fableau*, until Bédier's study standardized the Picard form *fabliau*. Nykrog, on the other hand, claims that the word is purely French, derived from the word *fable*, and that the suffix must not have been -ELLUM, but -els or -el because the form FABLELLUM, he maintains, is a pseudo-Latin construct, while for the form FABELLUS, the Latin intervocalic -b- regularly became -v-, which would have given the form *favelle*, in Nykrog, *Les Fabliaux*, 3. The most common Old French forms of the word have the spelling *fablel(s)* or *fabliau(x)*. More recently, Rossi has asserted that the origin of the word *flabel*, another variant of *fabliau*, is derived from the Latin FLABELLUM meaning "bellows, puff of wind" and then by extension the more figurative meaning "tall tale." Rossi establishes a parallel between this word and the Old French word "soufflet" ("puff of wind"), which he relates to the art of the *jongleur*. He classifies "flabellum" in the same semantic field as vernacular words derived from the Latin FOLLIS and BUFO, meaning respectively "folly" and "joke," and explains that "dans les langues romanes tous ces mots renvoient de manière allusive au halètement presque aphasique du fou, qui provoquait le rire à cause de son inadéquation verbale," in "Observations sur l'origine et la signification du mot *flabel*," 343. Rossi does not take into account that the intervocalic -b- of FLABELLUM would have been subject to the same morphological changes as the one in FABELLUM, resulting in the unknown form "*flavelle*." Although Rossi's etymon accounts for both the humor and *gab* of the fabliaux, it neglects the vast majority of occurrences of the word in the forms *fablel* and *fabliau* and ignores the genre's relation to the fable. Nykrog explains that the rare forms *flabiau*, *flabel*, *flablel*, and *fabel* are all

the result of difficulties of pronunciation encountered with the two l's of the form *fablel*, in *Les Fabliaux*, 3. I believe, however, that a copyist's error is a more likely explanation for this repetition. While Nykrog's contention is justifiable, it is also plausible that these forms are the result of a conflation with the etymon supplied by Rossi. It is perhaps this confusion, or rather joining of etymologies, that explains both the (pseudo-)didactic nature of the fabliaux and their exaggerated, playful, anecdotal quality.

19. The numbers in parentheses after fable titles refer to the order of the fables in Warnke's edition, *Die Fabeln*, but the titles are from Pearcy's fabliau inventory, *Logic and Humour*, 233–36.

20. Pearcy, *Logic and Humour*, 133.

21. The first verse corresponds to the beginning of the text, not the first line of the folio; see also Warnke, *Die Fabeln*, 95, and Brucker, ed., *Les Fables*, 350.

22. Pearcy, *Logic and Humour*, 134.

23. FEW, and Lewis and Short.

24. The lesson given by the manuscript for line 47 reads: "Car en l'eve n'est pas alee" [since she did not go in the water], but this makes no sense in the context for it is clear from the remainder of the text that the wife did enter the water upstream. I have corrected this with Warnke's edition, *Die Fabeln*. The contrary nature of the wife, however, is clear in both versions.

25. Inherited from the Classical tradition, the use of *adynata* in the Middle Ages is known primarily through Vergil. A series of impossibilities engenders "the world upside-down" topos. See Alex Preminger, ed., *Princeton Encyclopedia of Poetry and Poetics*, 5, and also Ernst Robert Curtius, *European Literature*, 94–98, for the *mundus inversus*.

26. Mary Lou Martin's English translation of this fable puts these last verbs in the past tense, so that the men looked and found the wife upstream, thus making the husband's words true, in *The Fables of Marie de France*, trans. Mary Lou Martin, 239. In MS K, the image of the scene at the top of fol. 78r (a) shows water flowing down between the two columns and a woman leaning over with two men reaching for her while a third man reaches in the opposite direction. The image singles out the husband, who is heading in the opposite direction in order to emphasize his wife's contrariness. Unfortunately, the top of this folio has been cut off, so the men's heads are only partially visible.

27. About the final lesson of the fable corresponding to the narrative, see Blackham, *The Fable as Literature*, xix.

28. Pearcy, *Logic and Humour*, 159. Pearcy calls the ending of MS B "inconclusive," whereas I think it draws attention more to the humor in language than to the quid pro quo between husband and wife.

29. Ibid. Pearcy also notes a similarity between this tale and *Cele qui se fist foutre*, the fabliau title of the "Matron of Ephesus" theme discussed in this chapter.

30. See ch. 1 for different interpretations of proverbs.

31. I thank Sarah Kay for pointing out that these words would rhyme in Anglo-Norman. The editors of the *NRCF* believe that the version in MS K exhibits traits of a western dialect, *NRCF*, 6.128.

32. Nolan, "Turning over the Leaves of Medieval Fabliau-Anthologies," 17, original emphasis.

33. Ibid, 18.

34. For Pearcy, this is the logical trick in the text, *Logic and Humour*, 159–60.

35. Francisco Rodriguez Adrado, *History of the Græco-Latin Fable*, 39.

36. For a brief discussion of the literal child and figurative language in this fabliau, see Norris J. Lacy, *Reading Fabliaux*, 84n and 125.

37. Pearcy, *Logic and Humour*, 35–36.

38. The lesson for line 18 in *Die Fabeln*, Warnke's edition reads: "par engresté me vols ateindre," referring to the husband himself as opposed to his "parole."

39. For a discussion of the transition from fable to fabliau, see Pearcy, *Logic and Humour*, esp. ch. 1: "Origins: Fable to Fabliau: *Cele qui se Fist Foutre sur la Fosse de son Mari*," 11–33.

40. Ibid., 35, for *aequivocatio* in fables and fabliaux.

41. Jürgen Beyer, "The Morality of the Amoral," 25.

42. This lesson in MS K differs from the other manuscripts because here the wife very strongly insinuates that her husband is impotent, whereas in the other versions there is no question of conception.

43. This verse is specific to MS K; other manuscripts provide the variant: "La verité vos ai contee."

44. Pearcy, *Logic and Humour*, 12 and 77; for a summary of the differences, see ch. 2, 34–51.

45. Lacy notes a dozen medieval French versions of this story, including the *fableor* Gautier le Leu's text, *La Veuve*. For a comparison of *Cele qui se fist foutre sur la fosse de son mari* with *La Veuve*, see *Reading Fabliaux*, 1–34. Lacy also discusses this text in "Courtliness and Townspeople." Of the many Classical versions, Marie's model was most likely the *Romulus Nilantii*, but John of Salisbury also mentions the theme in his *Policraticus*. Pearcy's analysis of the theme is most compelling, *Logic and Humour*, 34–51.

46. Pearcy, *Logic and Humour*, 34–51.

47. Lacy, *Reading Fabliaux*, 11.

48. Ibid., 1–17. Lacy argues the opposite view and claims that the fabliau follows through on the moralizing claims against the inconstancy of women. I think it is still possible to interpret this fabliau in an antifeminist way, but the text also lends itself to the interpretation proposed above.

49. In MSS B and C, line 2 reads "de *fabliaus* dire," instead of "fables" as in MSS A, E, K, and l. The first possibility establishes a parallel between "fabliaus"

and "fable" through the chiasmus of lines 2–3: *fabliaus/dire//dirai/fable*, in which *fabliaus/fable* are synonymous and opposed to "voir." This example confirms the fluid nature of these terms and demonstrates the risks associated in drawing too fine a distinction between the terms and then applying them to texts. These ambiguous occurrences of the word "fable" support the notion that a genre cannot simply be classified by the designation(s) ascribed to it by a narrator or copied by a scribe.

50. For the mixture of courtly and common diction, see Lacy, *Reading Fabliaux*, 7. The phrase "en fotant" appears in the critical edition (88), but it does not appear in MS K, which retains the word "foutre" in other phrases.

51. The manuscript contains a *vers orphelin* at line 113.

52. Pearcy, *Logic and Humour*, 39–41.

53. As Nykrog explains about this fable and fabliau in *Les Fabliaux*, 146: "Il ne reste du modèle que l'idée fondamentale: la veuve séduite. A part cela, tout est changé. . . . La substitution répugnante des cadavres a disparu. Pour les protagonistes de la nouvelle version, le tout est une amusette; ils n'y attachent aucune importance. . . . Dans les versions antérieures on abuse froidement d'elle [la veuve]; la veuve du fabliau n'aura pas à se plaindre après: on ne l'a pas séduite; c'est elle qui a demandé de l'être."

54. Chrétien de Troyes, *Le Chevalier au lion/Yvain*, ed. D. Hult, emphasis added. English translation of *Yvain* in *Arthurian Romances*, trans. William W. Kibler, 309. Others who have noted the similarity of these scenes include Pearcy, *Logic and Humour*, 38; and especially Busby in "Courtly Literature and the Fabliaux." For the relationship between this fabliau and Chrétien's *Perceval*, see Pearcy, "Intertextuality and *La Damoiselle qui n'ot parler*." Lacy discusses the tale extensively, *Reading Fabliaux*, esp. 1–16.

55. For example, Didon faints when Enéas leaves, and Perceval's mother faints when she hears anything about *chevalerie*.

56. These substitutions also correspond to Nykrog's definition of courtly burlesque, *Les Fabliaux*, esp. 72–91.

57. Richard Spencer, "Le *Courtois-Vilain* Nexus in *La Male Honte*," 272. I have changed Spencer's translation of "*male*" from "bag" to the more accurate "trunk." The image in this codex (f. 93v) clearly depicts a trunk.

58. Pearcy, *Logic and Humour*, 36–37. Pearcy uses this example to relate this type of *aequivocatio* to medieval treatises on logic, giving an example of the pun āra (altar) and ăra (pigsty) from Peter of Spain, which is ultimately from Aristotle's *Sophistici elenchi*, in *Logic and Humour*, 3.

59. Spencer, "Le *Courtois-Vilain* Nexus in *La Male Honte*," 290.

60. Ibid., 291.

61. The *vilain*'s explanation, however, occurs only after he is invited to explain himself by a nobleman (*un comte*) of the king's court, an invitation that

is perhaps a reference to aristocratic patronage and is reminiscent of Marie de France's reference in the epilogue to a certain "conte Guillaume" for whom she translated the *Isopet*. Other references to *clergie* and *clercs* in the codex include Marie de France's epilogue to the fables, where she names herself as the writer "por remembrance" (3) so that no other *clercs* may take credit for her work. Coincidentally, this version of *La Male Honte* also cites the name of an author at the end, "ce dist Guillaumes en son conte" (149). Although the version in MS A mentions Huon de Cambrai as the author at the beginning of the fabliau, there is no reason to assume that Guillaume is not the author of this version. He, not Huon, is mentioned in other manuscripts as well. The compiler of MS K most likely only knew of this version, which is attributed to Guillaume. The emphasis on *clergie* in *La Male Honte* also links this text thematically to the beginning of the *Image du monde*, which highlights the role of the *clerc* in the transfer of knowledge (part I, chapters 5–6). Although linked thematically by *clergie* to the *Image du monde* and the *Isopet*, *clergie* in the fabliau relates characters to the narrator in the creation of stories for a mise-en-abyme effect.

62. Pearcy, *Logic and Humour*, 40–41.
63. *Three Medieval Views of Women*, ed. Fiero, Pfeffer, and Allain, 8 and 12.
64. Nykrog, *Les Fabliaux*, 60–63.
65. Ibid., 62.
66. Pearcy, *Logic and Humour*, 204.
67. For this argument, see Nykrog, *Les Fabliaux*, 27. The introduction to the fabliau *Le Chevalier qui fist parler les cons* draws the same parallel between telling/reciting fabliaux and a financial transaction: "Fablel sont or mout encorsé: / Maint denier en ont enborsé / Cil qui les content et les portent, / Quar grant confortement raportent / As enovrez et as oiseus," (1–6).
68. I am indebted to a conversation with Maria Luisa Meneghetti for this suggestion about the codex. Additionally, the concept of macrocosm and microcosm may explain the relatively frequent occurrences of the *Image du monde* in other manuscripts with fabliaux and animal stories or bestiaries.
69. Although Peter Dronke studied "Latin fabliaux," the majority of fabliaux have not been attributed to Latin sources. See his "The Rise of the Medieval Fabliau."

Chapter 3. Medieval Story Collections and Framing Devices

1. M. Léonard discusses similar relationships between the *dit* and other thirteenth-century short narrative works, although without mentioning reversal. In relation to the fabliaux, see *Le "Dit" et sa technique littéraire*, 10, 14–20, 120–22, and 279–96.
2. All references are to Giovanni Boccaccio, *Decameron*, ed. Vittore Branca and are cited in the text by day in Roman numerals, followed by story and sen-

tence in Arabic numerals. All English translations from *The Decameron*, trans. G. H. McWilliam, are cited by page number in the text.

3. In "Studi sugli *exempla* e il *Decameron*," Chiara Degani and Vittore Branca draw parallels between the *Decameron* and "casual and inorganic agglomerations" (my translation) like the fabliaux, the *Novellino*, the *Pantchatantra*, and the oldest *exempla* anthologies of the twelfth century, yet claim the ideological unity in Boccaccio's text resembles the *exempla* "sillogi," 181. In this study, Degani and Branca also claim that Boccaccio addresses the same audience as collections of *exempla*, namely ladies, 182. For a study of *exempla* and a list of manuscript collections, see Jean-Thiébaut Welter, *L'exemplum dans la littérature*. For the relationship of *exempla* to the *Decameron*, see also Carlo Delcorno, "Studi sugli *exempla* e il *Decameron*, II," and Hans-Jörg Neuschäfer, *Boccaccio und der Beginn der Novelle*. Finally, Millicent Marcus, among others, argues that the *Decameron* subverts the utility of the *exemplum* as a valid literary form and that the two stories that frame the *Decameron*, I:1 (Ser Cepparello) and X:10 (Griselda), reflect the "undoing" of the *exemplum*, in *An Allegory of Form*, 93–109, esp. 101.

4. Degani and Branca, "Studi sugli *exempla* e il *Decameron*," 181. For information on origins, see the introduction and bibliography of Mary B. Speer, ed., *Roman des Sept Sages de Rome*, 13–17 and 98–111. For information about sources for the *Decameron*, see also Landau, *Die Quellen des "Dekameron*," and the notes for the individual stories in Branca, ed., *Decameron*.

5. Other distinctions that ideally could inform Boccaccio's literary combinations might include the manner(s) in which Boccaccio knew of his sources, whether in Latin or a vernacular language, or whether as written pieces or oral accounts, whether in Naples or Florence, and so forth. Marga Cottino-Jones has convincingly shown that Boccaccio made distinctions between East and West in his tales, esp. II:9, but this issue of origins is not necessarily related to questions of structure, see *Order from Chaos*, 58.

6. Fable collections arrived in Europe long before the frame narrative collections under consideration here. In his introduction to Petrus Alfonsi's *Disciplina Clericalis*, editor Cristiano Leone makes the distinction between a *cornice* properly speaking and a *filo conduttore*, where the stories are told as part of the dialogue between father and son; a *cornice*, on the other hand, creates a separate narrative space for storytelling, XXIX.

7. The title is authentic to the text and found in the work; Leone, ed., *Disciplina Clericalis*, 5.

8. *Le Chastoiement d'un père à son fils*, ed. Edward D. Montgomery Jr., 16. For editions and comparative studies of the *Disciplina Clericalis* and its Old French translations, including *Le Chastoiement d'un père à son fils*, see the *Étude et édition . . . de la "Disciplina Clericalis"*: http://www.unige.ch/lettres/mela/recherche/disciplina.html.

9. Although Landau makes the same point that Boccaccio could have known the *Disciplina Clericalis* through an Old French source or the Latin version, his analyses of these tales with analogous *novelle* show that the Old French *Chastoiement d'un père à son fils* has more in common with the *Decameron* than the Latin version, in *Die Quellen des "Dekameron,"* 258–68, esp. 262. Landau's study of Boccaccio's sources remains one of the most comprehensive for both the macrostructure of the frame narrative and the individual *novelle* and includes references to the following collections of tales: *1001 Nights, Pantschatantra, Çukasaptati, Vetâlapantschavinçati, Ardschi Bordschi, Somadeva, Dasakumâra Tscharitra, Saadi, Hitopadesa, Kathasaritsagara, Calila et Dimna, Septem Sapientum, Sindibad, Dolopathos, Barlaam e Josaphat, Gesta Romanorum, Disciplina Clericalis, Libro de los engaños, Libro de buen amor, Novellino*. This list accounts for analogues more frequently than actual sources.

10. Leone, ed., *Disciplina Clericalis*, XLVI. Leone summarizes the differences between the *Disciplina Clericalis* and these adaptations, XLVI–LI.

11. Ibid., LIX. In contrast to Welter, Leone refers to these as "proto-*exempla*" and also mentions Humbert de Romans as a disseminator. Rewritings of the *Disciplina Clericals* as *exempla* appeared in the late thirteenth- or early fourteenth-century *Gesta Romanorum*, according to Leone, LXI. See also Bédier, *Les Fabliaux*, 134, for a list of stories from the *Disciplina Clericalis* circulating independently from Petrus's collection.

12. For an example, compare *exemplum* 8 in Montgomery's edition of *Le Chastoiement d'un père à son fils*, 82–84, with *exemplum* 10 in the *Disciplina Clericalis*, ed. Leone, 45, to see the increase in narrative and decrease in didacticism. Montgomery also notes that *Le Chastoiement* is less didactic than the Latin *Disciplina Clericalis*. Roy Pearcy and Ian Short, eds., *Eighteen Anglo-Norman fabliaux*, 1–5, consider this and other tales to be "fabliaux avant la lettre," along with several other *exempla* from the *Disciplina Clericalis*. They also include some of Marie's fables in their collection of Anglo-Norman fabliaux, see stories 1–4. Leone comments: "molti altri racconti dello *Chastoiement* come anche delle *Fables*, potrebbero essere considerati *fabliaux*," [many other stories of the *Chastoiement* and also from the *Fables* could be considered *fabliaux*], *Disciplina Clericalis*, LI. Leone also posits that the merchant class in *Le Chastoiement* is related to fabliaux culture, but that the "destinataire" in vernacular adaptations changes from the *clericus* to the common man or aspiring philosopher in Old French versions, XLIX.

13. Montgomery, ed., *Le Chastoiement d'un père à son fils*, 23, n. 34.

14. See lines 247–48 of *Le Chevalier qui recovra l'amor de sa dame*. See also Branca's notes to *Decameron* VII:1. Bédier cited the *Disciplina Clericalis* as a source for some other fabliaux, *Les Fabliaux*, 133–34.

15. Leone, ed., *Disciplina Clericalis*, L and n. 11. Leone argues that the influence of vernacular literature on translations of the *Disciplina Clericalis* may also be seen in the *Fables Pierre Aufors*, which includes elements of the *Roman de Renart*, XLVII.

16. For a complete list of the manuscripts of *Le Chastoiement* and *Les Fables Pierre Aufors*, see http://www.unige.ch/lettres/mela/recherche/disciplina.html. The editors of the *NRCF* do not cite MS London, British Library, Harley 527 in their list of manuscripts containing fabliaux. For the observation on the substitution of *Le Cuvier* for the tenth *exemplum*, see also *Petri Alfonsi Disciplina clericalis I*, Alfons Hilka and Werner Söderhjelm, eds. Unfortunately, I was unable to verify this information directly.

17. See Landau, *Die Quellen des "Dekameron,"* 258–68. See also Montgomery, ed., *Le Chastoiement d'un père à son fils*, 19–20, for the *Disciplina Clericalis* sources for *Decameron* VII:4 and 6, VIII:10, and X:8.

18. Leone mentions the metaphor of a string of pearls for this type of composition, where the string represents the dialogue that holds together the pearls, here the stories and moral *sententiae*, in the *Disciplina Clericalis*, XXIX.

19. Ibid., XXXVI.

20. Speer, ed., *Roman des Sept Sages de Rome*, 14. For other titles and different versions, see Antonella Feola-Baladier, *Le Merveilleux dans le cycle des Sept sages de Rome*, esp. 69–70.

21. Speer, ed., *Roman des Sept Sages de Rome*, 13.

22. See the individual titles in Landau, *Die Quellen des "Dekameron,"* for the relationships of each version to the *Decameron*.

23. Speer, ed., *Roman des Sept Sages de Rome*, 13. For a discussion of origins and transmission, see the introduction to Speer's edition, 13–17. According to Speer, Hans Runte puts the dates of composition between the tenth century and the middle of the twelfth century, but the two surviving manuscripts are from the late thirteenth century, as cited in Speer, 67 and 95, n. 110. For a discussion of the manuscripts, see Speer's introduction, 17–74.

24. See Jean Misrahi, ed., *Le Roman des Sept Sages*, xi. Feola-Baladier notes the same route of transmission, *Le Merveilleux dans le cycle des "Sept Sages de Rome,"* 7. Leone posits that the *Sindbad/Seven Sages* was a source for some of the stories in the *Disciplina Clericalis*, XXXVI. See also the arguments in chapters 2 and 4 on the relationship between France and Italy.

25. See Feola-Baladier for a list of Italian and French redactions of the Seven Sages tradition, *Le Merveilleux dans le cycle des "Sept Sages de Rome,"* 6–7. The first half of her study explores the thematic differences of these versions and provides information on the manuscripts.

26. Ibid., 6.

27. Both Speer and Misrahi present this manuscript witness.

28. In Misrahi's edition, *Le Roman des Sept Sages*, references to the "Renart" (cunning) that the wife knows are found at lines 2250 and 2456. See also Armand Strubel, ed., *Le Roman de Renart*; and especially for the manuscript tradition, see Naoyuki Fukumoto, Noboru Harano, and Satoru Suzuki, eds., trans. Gabriel Bianciotto, *Le Roman de Renart*.

29. See Feola-Baladier, *Le Merveilleux dans le cycle des "Sept Sages de Rome,"* 69–70, for a chart of the tales by version of the *Seven Sages* in the West.

30. Even if Ephesus was considered Eastern, the "Matron of Ephesus" topos was long familiar in the West and had been adapted in many Latin and vernacular versions. See the discussion of this topos in chapter 2 and Pearcy's analysis of the history of this tale in *Logic and Humour*, 11–33. See also Misrahi, ed., *Le Roman des Sept Sages*, lines 3709–36, for resemblances to the fabliau *Cele qui se fist foutre sur la fosse de son mari*, and lines 3807–60 for similarities to Marie de France's fable. Most of the tales in *Le Roman des Sept Sages* do not promote antifeminism as much as they call on the king to make good decisions. Similarly, the queen's stories malign both the son and the sages.

31. For the dates of the Latin *Dolopathos*, see *Dolopathos*, trans. Gilleland, vii.

32. According to Speer, ed., *Roman des Sept Sages de Rome*, 17. She also notes that *Dolopathos* has only *Canis* in common with the Eastern *Sindbād*. See also Feola-Baladier, *Le Merveilleux dans le cycle des "Sept Sages de Rome,"* 12, who gives the translation date as 1220. For the dates 1207–12, see Misrahi, ed., *Le Roman des Sept Sages*, xvi.

33. For manuscript information, see Herbert, *Le Roman de Dolopathos*, ed. Jean-Luc Leclanche, 7–48.

34. See *Dolopathos*, trans. Gilleland, 79; in Latin "Et ecce maiorem hac in muliere uideo maliciam," in Hilka, *Historia Septem Sapientum II*, 90.

35. See Bédier, *Les Fabliaux*, 134; Landau, *Die Quellen des "Dekameron,"* 28–89; and the notes in Branca, ed., *Decameron*.

36. See Feola-Baladier, *Le Merveilleux dans le cycle des "Sept Sages de Rome,"* 74–91. The creation of a cycle resembles the pattern of romance cycles in the thirteenth century, such as the Vulgate cycle. Here, Western narrative has accepted and adapted the Eastern collection.

37. Ibid., 45–48.

38. Leonard R. Mills, ed., *L'Histoire de Barlaam et Josaphat*, 7.

39. Ibid.

40. See Landau, *Die Quellen des "Dekameron,"* and Branca, ed., *Decameron*, under the individual titles for the precise sources for the story of Filippo Balducci, as well as for the influence of *Barlaam et Josaphat* on the *Decameron*.

41. Bédier briefly mentions some tales from *Barlaam et Josaphat* used by Jacques de Vitry, but does not suggest any relationship to fabliaux, *Les Fabliaux*, 139.

42. Marie de France, *Lais*, ed. Warnke. See also Fukumoto, Harano, and Suzuki, eds., trans. Bianciotto, *Le Roman de Renart*.

43. I wish to thank Sarah Kay for pointing out this similarity.

44. This list in no way purports to be exhaustive. Not only are there other *Isopet* and miracle story collections, but such works as the *Vie des pères* and the *Legenda Aurea* offer examples of other types of pious collections. Another important collection for studying the *Decameron* is the *Gesta Romanorum*, compiled

in the late thirteenth or early fourteenth century; see Landau for its use in the *Decameron, Die Quellen des "Dekameron,"* 274–80. The *Roman de Renart* is not technically a collection, although many *branches* of the Renart cycle are often compiled together in manuscripts. For editions of the *branches*, see Strubel, ed. *Le Roman de Renart*; and especially for the manuscript tradition, see Fukumoto, Harano, and Suzuki, eds., trans. Bianciotto, *Le Roman de Renart*. In relation to the *Decameron*, the *Renart* tales have more in common with the series of *novelle* about Calandrino (VIII:3 and 6, IX:3 and 5), because they achieve unity through a set of characters and tricks, but have different narrators. Landau also discusses Classical collections, such as Ovid's *Metamorphoses* in relation to the *Decameron*, *Die Quellen des "Dekameron,"* 288–316.

45. Gautier de Coinci, *Les Miracles de Nostre Dame*, lines 8–9.

46. For Vincent de Beauvais *ordinatio* was related to the *mise-en-page*; see Alastair J. Minnis, "Late-Medieval Discussions of *Compilatio*," 391–92. Malcolm B. Parkes discusses how *ordinatio* functions on two levels: as structure to incorporate materials and as a "critical procedure by which diverse *auctoritates* can be divided up and redeployed according to the nature of the subject matter" in "The Influence of the Concepts of *Ordinatio* and *Compilatio*," 128.

47. Minnis, "Late-Medieval Discussions of *Compilatio*," 390.

48. Ibid., 397.

49. Ibid., 416–17. Also Parkes, "The Influence of the Concepts of *Ordinatio* and *Compilatio*," 123–24.

50. Parkes, "The Influence of the Concepts of *Ordinatio* and *Compilatio*," 128.

51. Ibid., 130. Stephen G. Nichols has also posited a parallel relationship between the order of the *mise-en-page* and textual order in a manuscript of *chansonnier* miscellanies of the late thirteenth century. He argues that "the conception of an aesthetic for the manuscript page . . . participated in and contributed to a conception of a structure for the work as a whole—both an aesthetic structure and an intellectual one," in "'Art' and 'Nature,'" 85. Similarly, Vàrvaro has suggested that the scholastic model of reading was not linear and consequently required formal organization, such as breaks and rubrication, as well as alphabetization of texts or authors as a means to sort the material, "Elaboration des textes," 44. Delcorno argues that summas of *exempla* were organized in alphabetical order at times with rubrics and other breaks and markers, which allowed for "diversi percorsi di lettura," in "Studi sugli *exempla* e il *Decameron*, II," 193.

52. Welter, *L'Exemplum dans la littérature*, 84, 99, and 102.

53. Ibid., 106–7. Welter identifies these subtypes. The fabliaux-related *exempla* tend to be classified as *"exempla*-contes."

54. Ibid., 211.

55. Ibid., 108 and 212. These collections have "chacun une physionomie propre provenant, malgré une parenté de fond et de forme, soit de la préférence donnée à certains types d'*exempla*, soit de l'emploi d'un dispositif spécial comme cadre

des récits," 211. Welter describes several collections of the thirteenth century and explains that they often favor one subtype over another, but still present a range of the genre, 214-60. A list of manuscripts containing *exempla* collections may be found beginning on page 477; the catalogue listings for those manuscripts in Paris at the BNF do not suggest that the *exempla* were compiled with vernacular narratives.

56. Ibid., 63 and 75.

57. Degani and Branca, "Studi sugli *exempla* e il *Decameron*," 181.

58. For the influence of the *Novellino* on the *Decameron*, see Landau, *Die Quellen des "Dekameron*," 164-74, as well as the notes to individual stories in Branca, ed., *Decameron*.

59. MS H in the fabliaux tradition preserves at least five fabliaux and three of Marie's *lais* in a sequence, which is an implied collection. MS P contains only one fabliau (*Boivin de Provins*) and one of Marie's *lais* (*Yonec*). Indeed, whether Marie's *lais* actually were a collection has been debated by scholars, since only one manuscript contains all *lais* attributed to Marie as well as her fables: London, British Library, Harley 978. On this manuscript and Marie's texts, see Andrew Taylor, *Textual Situations*, 76-136. See also Glyn S. Burgess, *Marie de France: An Analytical Bibliography*.

60. For a list of manuscripts for Gautier de Coinci's *Les Miracles de Nostre Dame*, see V. Frédéric Koenig, ed., xxxiv-xxxviii.

61. For taxonomy in manuscripts, see Foehr-Janssens, Collet, and Azzam, "Les Manuscrits littéraires français."

62. For a brief description, see Rychner, *Contribution à l'étude des fabliaux*, 9.

63. Sylvia Huot, *From Song to Book*, 38.

64. Although this is a modern designation, scholars frequently refer to this and other codices as "fabliaux manuscripts" as in Revard's article "From French 'Fabliau Manuscripts.'" Several manuscripts besides MS J that contain a few fabliaux are often identified as "fabliaux collections," even though they preserve a variety of texts, many of which are more substantial in length and influence than the fabliaux. Even the BNF manuscript catalogues describe these manuscripts as "recueil de fabliaux" first. Busby refers to the "The Scandal of the *Fabliaux* Manuscripts," in *Codex and Context*, 437-63. Print editions of stories from medieval manuscripts from the eighteenth century also favored the fabliaux over other types of "contes," for example in Étienne Barbazan and Dominique-Martin Méon, eds., *Fabliaux et contes des poètes françois*. Medieval designations cannot be known. Though outside the scope of this study, tracing the early ownership of each manuscript could prove helpful in identifying how these manuscripts were designated in the late-medieval and early modern periods.

65. The MSS of *Dolopathos* are: BNF fr. 1450, 24301, nouv. acq. 934, Montpellier, H 436; see Leclanche, ed., *Le Roman de Dolopathos*, t. 1: 7-14. See Mont-

gomery, ed., *Le Chastoiement d'un père à son fils*, 12: MS British Museum MS additional 10289 (ff. 133–72), which is MS Y in the fabliaux tradition.

66. Leone, ed., *Disciplina Clericalis*, L; Short and Pearcy's edition and translation of fabliaux cites seven "fabliaux" from the Old French version of the *Disciplina Clericalis, Le Chastoiement d'un père à son fils* of MS Z, see stories #5–11 in *Eighteen Anglo-Norman Fabliaux*. Nykrog also included stories from these collections in his list of fabliaux in *Les Fabliaux*, 311–24, in spite of his declaration that the fabliaux owe nothing to these collections, xxxi. While I am using the manuscript information furnished by the editors of the *NRCF*, their list giving the number of fabliaux in a codex can be misleading because of the fluid definition of a fabliau, especially for some of the manuscripts with few fabliaux.

67. Busby, *Codex and Context*, 212, for MSS of Marie de France's *Fables* with fabliaux: BNF fr. 1593, 2168, 19152, 25545, Arsenal 3142. MS K is one of six illustrated manuscripts of *Isopet*.

68. Guido Almansi, *The Writer as Liar*.

69. Marcus, *An Allegory of Form*, 10. The history of *Decameron* scholarship is immense, and the question of the work's meaning much debated, as this study has suggested. For a seminal work on the *Decameron* as an aesthetic text, see Almansi, *The Writer as Liar*. See also the bibliography for specific references to *Decameron* studies.

70. Picone, "Preistoria della cornice del *Decameron*," 91–92. An example of such a story would be Alatiel's explanation to her father in II:7 or Cepperello's fiction of his virtuous life in I:1.

71. Joy Hambuechen Potter, *Five Frames for the "Decameron*," 121; see particularly chapter 5, "The Function of Framing in the *Decameron*," 120–51.

72. Ibid., 127–28.

73. Picone, "Preistoria della cornice del *Decameron*," 92.

74. Robert Hollander, *Boccaccio's Dante*, 56, n. 6.

75. Ibid., 96.

76. The *De Amore* is also indebted to Ovid. While there are probably more allusions in this passage to courtly literature, these two seminal examples suffice to place the *Decameron*'s outer frame in a courtly tradition. For the *De Amore*, see John Jay Perry, trans., *The Art of Courtly Love*; Alfred Karnein, "*De amore*" in *volkssprachlicher Literatur*; and Don A. Monson, *Andreas Capellanus*.

77. Potter, *Five Frames for the "Decameron*," 71. For Potter's definition of the word "code," see 188–89 and n.7. This discussion is in no way intended to be exhaustive of the literary allusions in the *Proemio*. For other discussions of the *Proemio*, see Potter, *Five Frames for the "Decameron*," esp. 33, and Hollander, *Boccaccio's Dante*, 91, and especially "The Proem of the *Decameron*," 104–7.

78. Potter argues that the references to God in the *Proemio* are "clearly serious enough to suggest that Boccaccio had not planned a mere 'human comedy,'" in comparison to Dante, *Five Frames for the "Decameron*," 33. Potter has also

noted (105) that the *Proemio* begins with a syntactic inversion that emphasizes the grammatical subject. While it is tempting to say that this inversion announces other inversions in the text related to the fabliaux, the grammatical structure more properly evokes a high Latin style (*genus grave*), as Potter explains. Marcus sees the *Decameron* as a rejection of Dante's model, in favor of a Boethian model in the epilogue to *An Allegory of Form*, 110–25.

79. Branca, ed., *Decameron*, 9, n.1, my translation.

80. Pamela D. Stewart, *Retorica e mimica nel "Decameron,"* 14. Stewart's examination of the *Proemio* focuses on Quintilian as the model for Boccaccio's rhetorical terminology. For another discussion of Boccaccio's use of rhetoric in the *Proemio*, see Amalia Cecere, "Usi retorici boccacciani."

81. See Stewart, *Retorica e mimica nel "Decameron,"* 8–9, for examples of the use of *favole* and *istorie* in specific tales.

82. Potter, *Five Frames for the "Decameron,"* 83.

83. Ibid., and Curtius, *European Literature*, 83–85.

84. For a list of allusions and bibliography for this passage, see Simone Marchesi, "'Sic me formabat puerum,'" 10–11 and notes.

85. Potter explains that the story of Filippo Balducci "performs a further telescoping function between frames one and five," *Five Frames for the "Decameron,"* 128.

86. See Branca, ed., *Decameron*, 462, n.5. According to Giancarlo Mazzacurati, it is unlikely that the analogue in the *Novellino* served as Boccaccio's direct source; see "Rappresentazione," 293 and notes.

87. The Italian word "ingegno" and the Old French "engin" are both derived from the Latin INGENIUM, meaning "innate or natural quality." As Marchesi states, the semantic field of the word is vast, but in the context of the fabliaux it often refers to the trickster's wit, "'Sic me formabat puerum,'" 22n. For this reason, it is tempting to associate Balducci's "ingegno" with that of a fabliau trickster who receives his comeuppance, not from his wife, but from the goddess *Natura*.

88. Marcus, *An Allegory of Form*, 50.

89. Ibid., 51.

90. Scholars often view this story as confirmation of Boccaccio's "naturalism," and Mazzotta reads the text as "the failure of the artifice (of Filippo Balducci) to contain within its bounds Nature's wondrous powers," *The World at Play*, 133.

91. Branca, ed., *Decameron*, 462, n. 5.

92. For a discussion and bibliography of the tale of Filippo Balducci as the defeat of the moral *exemplum*, see Ernesto Virgulti, "Lies My Father Told Me."

93. Potter, *Five Frames for the "Decameron,"* 39.

94. Marchesi explains that "it is on the basis of Boccaccio's implied traditions [Dantean and Horatian] that the story of Filippo Balducci and his son is in the end more concerned with commenting on different teaching strategies than with the subject matter of instruction *per se*. The point of the text is not to advance a

new morality, but to comment on methods of instruction," in "'Sic me formabat puerum,'" 20.

95. Branca notes that this conclusion "è dunque in parte un'integrazione, o meglio un aggiornamento, della difesa sviluppata piú vigorosamente e programmaticamente nella introduzione alla IV giornata," *Decameron*, 1254, n.7. Most scholars also observe symmetry between the *Proemio* and the *Conclusione dell'Autore*.

96. Branca, ed., *Decameron*, 1255, n. 1; and Potter, *Five Frames for the "Decameron,"* 88.

97. Potter, *Five Frames for the "Decameron,"* 88–89.

98. For the influence of Humanism and leaving stories "open," see Susanna Barsella, "Boccaccio and Humanism," 64.

99. Some critics object to the use of the terms *cornice* and frame to refer to the outermost levels of narration in the *Decameron*, on the grounds that a frame is by definition outside of the narrative, while the *cornice* of the *Decameron* is fully integrated into the narrative. Almansi, on the other hand, argues that the frame must be outside in order to highlight its contents as art, *The Writer as Liar*, 14. I use the term *cornice* to refer to the parts of the *Decameron* that are not strictly part of the hundred *novelle*, but with the understanding that it may include narrative or intertextual dimensions.

100. See Picone's "Tre tipi di cornice novellistica," his "Preistoria della cornice del *Decameron*," and finally "Il *Decamerone* come macrotesto."

101. I am inclined to think the Seven Sages tradition "proves a point" in addition to delaying action, because the sages must argue that the queen is evil in order to put off the prince's execution. In this way, the *Seven Sages* may already represent a combination of different framing functions.

102. Picone, "Preistoria della cornice del *Decameron*," 11–12.

103. Picone, "Il *Decamerone* come macrotesto," 16. His arguments in favor of these three frames found in the *Introduzione* are less convincing.

104. For a discussion of the *brigata* and the restoration of civic order the *cornice* enables, see Joseph Gibaldi, "The *Decameron* Cornice," esp. 352; see also Potter, *Five Frames for the "Decameron,"* esp. ch. 1, 11-40.

105. Branca, ed., *Decameron*, 14, n.5. See also Marchesi, *Stratigrafie decameroniane*, XIV–XV.

106. Cited in Marchesi, *Stratigrafie decameroniane*, XV–XVI. See also Giovanni Getto, *Vita di forme e forme di vita nel "Decameron."*

107. Gibaldi, "The *Decameron* Cornice," 351.

108. See Branca's notes to individual stories for sources in *Decameron*, ed. Branca.

109. Almansi, *The Writer as Liar*, 12–13.

110. Hollander, *Boccaccio's Dante*, 40; Marcus, *An Allegory of Form*, 35.

111. Almansi, *The Writer as Liar*, 51. For a study of the implicit themes of Days I and IX, and for an overview of the organization of the *Decameron* as divided in two halves, see Cottino-Jones, *Order from Chaos*.

112. Marcus, *An Allegory of Form*, 62.
113. Victoria Kirkham, "Love's Labors Rewarded," 84.
114. Ibid., 88.
115. Marcus, *An Allegory of Form*, 65.
116. Hollander, *Boccaccio's Dante*, 40 and 41, n. 50.
117. Janet Levarie Smarr, "Symmetry and Balance in the *Decameron*," esp. 160.
118. Ibid., 162–65 and 172.
119. Robert Hollander and Courtney Cahill, "Day Ten of the *Decameron*: The Myth of Order."
120. Ibid., 113.
121. Ibid., 142.
122. Picone, "Il *Decamerone* come macrotesto," 23.
123. Picone presents a chart of the narrators, principal characters, themes, primary sources, etc. of all of the stories narrated on the first day in "Il Principio del novellare," 62.
124. Ibid., 58 and notes for bibliography.
125. Timothy Kircher, "The Modality of Moral Communication in the *Decameron*'s First Day," 1047.
126. Picone, "Il Principio del novellare," 59.
127. See Getto, *Vita di forme*, ch. 2, 34–77.
128. Cottino-Jones, "Desire and the Fantastic," 3.
129. Marina Scordilis Brownlee, "Wolves and Sheep," 263.
130. Ibid., 264.
131. Ibid., 265; Edith Kern, "The Gardens in the *Decameron Cornice*." For the story of Ferondo (III:8), see also chapter 4.

Chapter 4. Boccaccio's Fabliaux

1. For a list of the fabliaux and their corresponding *novelle* in the *Decameron*, see the appendix.
2. Hollander, *Boccaccio's Dante*, esp. ch. 4. See also the discussion of French influence in Italy in chapter 2.
3. In addition to the references in chapter 2, see Kelly, *The New Solomon: Robert of Naples (1309–1343)*.
4. Giorgio Padoan, "Mondo aristocratico," 90.
5. Landau, *Die Quellen des "Dekameron*," 120.
6. Ibid. Landau also mentions that Boccaccio did not come into contact with fabliaux directly in Paris; "er die Fabliaux nicht lesen konnte, weil er dazu in Paris keine Zeit hatte . . . denn wenn er sie auch in Paris nicht kennen lernte, so hatte er doch in Neapel, wo er sich längere Zeit aufhielt, die beste Gelegenheit dazu," 120. I agree with Landau's assertion that Boccaccio's most profound contact with these tales, particularly in written form, probably occurred in Naples.

7. Maria Picchio Simonelli, "Il 'grande canto cortese,'" 204. While this reference is to *troubadour* influence on the poets of Frederick II's court, it is arguably as valid for narrative forms and consequently merits consideration in the following analyses.

8. I agree with Ménard's view that the word *source* "ne signifie nullement que l'œuvre étudiée se contente de reproduire le texte dont elle s'inspire sans en changer la forme et le sens. Il marque simplement qu'aucune création ne se fait *ex nihilo*, qu'on hérite d'une tradition écrite ou orale et qu'on la modifie. . . . Il peut y avoir, au demeurant, pluralité de sources, et dès lors le critique moderne doit chercher à distinguer et à préciser les emprunts, à les soupeser sur de fines balances, aussi sensibles que celles d'un orfèvre, pour apprécier les influences, si elles apparaissent clairement," in Ménard, "Les Sources françaises d'un conte de Boccace," 113–14.

9. A version of this section ("*La Nonete*: An Analogue of Novella IX:2") and the following section ("A Theory of Written Transmission") was published as "Boccaccio Reading Old French." All translations in these sections are mine unless indicated otherwise.

10. In addition to the appendix, see the notes for individual *novelle* in Landau, *Die Quellen des "Dekameron,"* and Branca, ed., *Decameron*.

11. Rossi, "In luogo di sollazzo," esp. 13–14.

12. See Branca, ed., *Decameron*, 1042, n.3.

13. For a discussion of this topos in medieval literature, see Curtius, *European Literature*, 433–35.

14. Landau, *Die Quellen des "Dekameron,"* 247.

15. The only edition of the text of which I am aware is in Méon's *Nouveau recueil de fabliaux*, vol. 2, 314–30.

16. For a comparison of these two fabliaux, see Christopher Pinet, "From Fabliau to Farce."

17. Rossi, "In luogo di sollazzo," 13.

18. I am much indebted to Simone Marchesi for sharing these ideas before the publication of his article, "Boccaccio's Vernacular Classicism," 31.

19. See Rossi, "In luogo di sollazzo," 18–22. While Rossi admits that *La Nonete* is a source for *Decameron* IX:2, he also argues that the climactic scene in the Italian novella more closely resembles an analogous episode in the anonymous *Renart le contrefait* than *La Nonete*. Even though his evidence is compelling, I maintain that *La Nonete* is closer to *Decameron* IX:2 at this key moment.

20. For a study of *Amour* in the works of Jean de Condé, see Jacques Ribard, *Un Ménestrel du XIVe siècle*.

21. See Perry, trans., *The Art of Courtly Love*; Karnein, "*De amore*" *in volkssprachlicher Literatur*; and Don A. Monson, *Andreas Capellanus*.

22. The word "usulieri" seems to be derived from "uosa" meaning "legging." The appearance of "uosa" in Italian dates to the thirteenth century when it had the meaning "boot," but the appearance of the form "usulieri" is not attested

elsewhere, suggesting that Boccaccio introduced this form to the written language (DEI). The origin of "usulieri" is ultimately the Old High German word "hosa" signifying "gaiter, boot, legging," which was borrowed into Late Latin as HOSA(M). The Late Latin HOSA(M) gave derivatives in nearly all the vernaculars. In Old French, the form "huese" is attested in the eleventh century, and later "heuse"; the meaning had developed to refer exclusively to boots, particularly in northern regions such as Picardy where "heuse" signifies "little boot" (FEW XVI, 228). The Old French word "lanières" is a mixture by consonance of the Germanic "nasle" meaning "cord, lace" and the Old French "lacet" also meaning "lace" (FEW XVI, 598). Godefroy, vol. 4, furnishes an example from the thirteenth century, *Proverbes ruraux et vulgaux,* with both "heuse" and "lanieres": "A courtes hoeses longues lanieres" [With short boots, long straps]. It is possible that Boccaccio's form "usulieri" came to be a diminutive of "uosa" that signified the cord that attached the leg coverings, whereas the Old French "heuse" retained the meaning "boot."

23. Rossi argues that the moment of revelation in *Decameron* IX:2 more closely resembles the episode in *Renart le contrefait* than *La Nonete,* since in the *Renart* and the *Decameron,* the novice uses a metaphor about what is hanging from the abbess's head to point out her error, whereas the nun in *La Nonete* explicitly mentions the straps, "In luogo di sollazzo," 22. While this is a valid distinction for the direct discourse among the characters, the citation above shows the similarity of speech between the narrators in *La Nonete* and *Decameron* IX:2.

24. The fabliau begins:

On ne doit mies trop reprendre
Aucun fol, s'on li voit emprendre
Par ynnorance aucunne cose:
Il avient que teils hons encose
Sour qui il a bien a koser.
Pour çou vous di ge bien qu'oser
Ne doit nuls hons tel cose faire
Mais a bien tourner son afaire,
La doit cascuns mettre s'entente. (1–9)

25. For a discussion of Jean de Condé's life and that of his father, Baudouin, see Ribard, *Un Ménestrel du XIVe siècle,* 69–95.

26. The attribution of *La Nonete* to Jean is relatively certain since the only extant manuscript in which it is preserved contains a section of more than thirty poems, many of which are inscribed with Jean's name in the final lines. For an in-depth consideration of attribution of the fabliau to Jean de Condé, see Ribard, *Un Ménestrel du XIVe siècle,* 45–46.

27. All manuscript abbreviations are those of Ribard, *Un Ménestrel du XIVe siècle,* 19–38.

28. The Turin manuscript, lost in the fire of 1904, contained two of Jean's most famous poems: "Li lais dou blanc chevalier" and "Li dis dou chevalier a le mance." For a description of this and the other manuscripts, see Ribard, *Un Ménestrel du XIVe siècle*, 20–27.

29. Ribard, *Un Ménestrel du XIVe siècle*, 22.

30. This manuscript has been described in part, or in its entirety, by several scholars, including Adolf Tobler, "Le Dit du Magnificat," Mario Eusebi, "*Il Pelerinage Renart* del ms 1598," and finally by Simonetta Mazzoni Peruzzi, *I manoscritti d'Italia*. For a bibliography of studies, see Ribard, *Un Ménestrel du XIVe siècle*, 25. For a discussion of the *Roman de Renart* in the manuscript, see Eusebi. For a description of the two Italian manuscripts preserving Jean de Condé's works and a complete bibliography until 1990, see Peruzzi.

31. Ribard, *Un Ménestrel du XIVe siècle*, 52. See also Mazzoni Peruzzi, *I manoscritti d'Italia*, 23–24, and Tobler, "Le Dit du Magnificat."

32. See under the former name for the manuscript: Minerva B, III, 18, Ernest Langlois, *Notices et extraits*, vol. 33, part 2, 301.

33. Ribard, *Un Ménestrel du XIVe siècle*, 44. For a discussion of the graphico-phonetic particularities of this manuscript, see also Mazzoni Peruzzi, *I manoscritti d'Italia*, 47–52.

34. Tobler, "Le Dit du Magnificat," 82.

35. Mazzoni Peruzzi, *I manoscritti d'Italia*, 24–25; Langlois, *Notices et extraits*, 301–2; Ribard, *Un Ménestrel du XIVe siècle*, 25–26.

36. Ribard, *Un Ménestrel du XIVe siècle*, 26.

37. The most popular examples of the fabliaux, such as *Auberee* and *Le Sacristain*, are found in as many as seven or eight extant manuscripts. By way of comparison, this is about as many manuscripts as Chrétien de Troyes' *Chevalier de la Charrette/Lancelot*. *La Grue*, studied in chapter 1, is preserved in six manuscripts. See the appendix for a complete list of manuscripts preserving fabliaux.

38. Branca, ed., *Decameron*, 1148, n.1.

39. See Landau, *Die Quellen des "Dekameron,"* 83.

40. McWilliam, Rubric for Day VI.

41. For biographical information on Boccaccio, especially for the period in Naples, see Branca, *Boccaccio medievale*, and *Boccaccio: The Man and His Works*, trans. Richard Monges, 11–12; and E.-G. Léonard, *Boccace et Naples*.

42. Kelly, *New Solomon*, 43.

43. Ibid., 42.

44. Ibid., 44.

45. Branca, *Boccaccio: The Man and His Works*, 24.

46. See Ribard, *Un Ménestrel du XIVe siècle*, 82: "il semble ressortir de l'examen des comptes qu'il [Jean de Condé] était plus particulièrement attaché à la suite de Jeanne de Valois."

47. See Susan Groag Bell, "Medieval Women Book Owners"; and June Hall

McCash's introductory remarks to *The Cultural Patronage of Medieval Women*, 1–49.

48. Padoan, "Mondo aristocratico," 91.

49. Rossi, "In luogo di sollazzo," 14.

50. Ibid., 17.

51. Ibid., 22. Rossi argues that this passage is "an homage to the *giullari*." While this is a possibility, it is not clear why Boccaccio chose *Decameron* IX:2 as his reference over similar stories with examples of hypocrisy that were indebted to the *giullari*, such as the story of the abbot in *Decameron* I:4.

52. The fabliau *L'Evesque qui beneï* is divided into two parts: in the first part, the bishop prohibits the priest from partaking in three activities (drinking wine, eating a goose, and sleeping in a bed) until the priest gets rid of his "wife," but the woman interprets the bishop's interdictions in such a way as to avoid the letter of the prohibitions; the second part of the narrative involves the bishop's *borgoise* asking him to bless her *con*, with the priest watching from behind a curtain. Right after the blessing, the priest surprises his bishop and the two reach an understanding.

53. Almansi, *The Writer as Liar*, 65. Almansi rejects the analogue in the *Novellino* (54) as being too thin a narrative to constitute the source. See also A. Collingwood Lee, *The "Decameron": Its Sources and Analogues*, 14–17. Although not mentioned by these critics, novella I:4 also resembles *Le Prestre qui abevete* when the monk spies on the abbot through a hole in the wall.

54. See Marcus on characters who take advantage of their fortune, as opposed to those who remain "victims" of their circumstances, *An Allegory of Form*, chapter 2, esp. 35.

55. Mario Baratto, *Realtà e stile nel "Decameron,"* 249.

56. Ibid., 88.

57. See chapter 3. See also Marcus on the alternate endings of VII:1, *An Allegory of Form*, 104.

58. The translation in this sentence is mine. In Day IV under the rule of Filostrato, Dioneo deliberately avoids the theme of love that ended unhappily: "di coloro li cui amori ebbero infelice fine" and narrates a story that is "piú lieta et migliore" (IV:10, 3).

59. Landau, *Die Quellen des "Dekameron,"* 162.

60. For the conclusion in the second version of the fabliau, see *NRCF* 4.88, lines 167–87. For a discussion of the relationship of this tale to romance, see Pearcy, "Intertextuality and *La Damoiselle qui n'ot parler*." See also the bibliography in my "Inversion and Parody."

61. Branca, ed., *Decameron*, 443, n. 1.

62. See Alfonso Paolella, "I Livelli narrativi"; and Picone, "La Vergine e l'eremita."

63. Harry Wayne Storey, "Parodic Structure in 'Alibech and Rustico'"; and Diane Duyos Vacca, "Converting Alibech."

64. Almansi, *The Writer as Liar*, 84.
65. Marilyn Migiel, "Beyond Seduction," 164.
66. Cited by Migiel, "Beyond Seduction," 165. The English translations of passages cited by Migiel are mine unless otherwise indicated.
67. Ibid.
68. Ibid.
69. Ibid.; translations in brackets are those of Migiel.
70. Picone, "La Vergine e l'eremita," 86.
71. Branca, ed., *Decameron*, 444, n. 9.
72. Migiel, "Beyond Seduction," 166.
73. Paolella, "I Livelli narrativi," 189.
74. Ibid., 190. For the parallels between the main episodes of Zosima's *vita* and *Decameron* III:10, see also 191.
75. Ibid., 194.
76. Ibid., 196–204, and for comparisons of passages.
77. Storey, "Parodic Structure in 'Alibech and Rustico,'" 167.
78. Migiel, "Beyond Seduction," 171.
79. Vacca, "Converting Alibech," 211–12.
80. Ibid., 216.
81. Migiel, "Beyond Seduction," 168.
82. Ibid.
83. Almansi, *The Writer as Liar*, 85.
84. See Smarr, "Symmetry and Balance in the *Decameron*."
85. Ibid., 166.
86. Degani and Branca, "Studi sugli *exempla* e il *Decameron*," 203. Both tales also show interventions of the "aldilà," 187.
87. Lee, *The "Decameron": Its Sources and Analogues*, 91–101. Neither Branca nor Landau considers *La Borgoise d'Orliens* or *Les Trois dames qui troverent l'anel* to be direct antecedents for *Decameron* III:8, but rather just thematically similar in parts.
88. The other tales of Calandrino, Bruno, and Buffalmacco are: VIII:3, 6, 9 and IX:5.
89. See Delcorno, "Studi sugli *exempla* e il *Decameron*," 209, on the relationship between *exempla* and *Decameron* III:8.
90. For drugging the husband and bringing him to the monastery as he sleeps, see an antecedent in part of the fabliau *Les Trois dames qui troverent l'anel*. Ferondo's experience of Purgatory seems to be a reference to Dante's *Commedia*, Hollander, *Boccaccio's Dante*, 4. Ferondo's ultimate resurrection may also be indebted to religious *exempla* or saints' lives. See Delcorno "Studi sugli *exempla* e il *Decameron*," esp. 205–11. For ambiguity in the story of Ferondo, see Migiel, "Some Restrictions Apply: Testing the Reader in *Decameron* III:8."
91. For this tale as metanarrative, see Mazzotta, *The World at Play*, 58–63.

92. There is nothing remarkable about the language of this detail in the texts. The fabliau says the wife "de son vilain tout li acointe / Et entendre fet la folie" (68–69), while the narrator of IX:3 explains that "Bruno, andatose al maestro Simone, vi fu prima che la fanticella che il segno portava e ebbe informato maestro Simon del fatto" (IX:3, 19).

93. R. Howard Bloch argues that the wife's trick in this fabliau is "allied with jonglerie," *The Scandal of the Fabliaux*, 99.

94. Mazzotta, *The World at Play*, 208.

Conclusion

1. Mazzotta, *The World at Play*, 211.
2. Ibid., 77 and 247.
3. For levels of meaning and audience, see Marchesi, *Stratigrafie decameroniane*.
4. Mazzotta, *The World at Play*, 243.

BIBLIOGRAPHY

Editions and Translations

Abelard, Peter. *Sic et non: A Critical Edition.* Edited by Blanche B. Boyer and Richard McKeon. Chicago: University of Chicago Press, 1977.
Andreas Capellanus. *The Art of Courtly Love.* 1960. Translated by John Jay Perry. Reprint, New York: Columbia University Press, 1990.
Augustine. *De doctrina christiana.* Edited and translated by R.P.H. Green. Oxford; New York: Oxford University Press, 1997.
———. *De doctrina christiana: Liber quartus.* Translated by Sister Thérèse Sullivan. Washington, D.C.: Catholic University of America, 1930.
Barbazan, Étienne, and Dominique-Martin Méon, eds. *Fabliaux et contes des poètes françois des XI, XII, XIII, XIVe et XVe siècles, tirés des meilleurs auteurs.* 4 vols. Paris: B. Warée oncle, 1808.
Boccaccio, Giovanni. *Il Decameron.* Edited by Vittore Branca. 1980. Reprint, Turin: Einaudi, 1992.
———. *Decameron*, 2nd edition. Translated by George Henry McWilliam. Harmondsworth: Penguin, 1995.
Chaucer, Geoffrey. *The Riverside Chaucer.* 3rd ed. Edited by Larry D. Benson. Boston: Houghton Mifflin, 1987.
Chrétien de Troyes. *Arthurian Romances.* Translated by William W. Kibler. New York; London: Penguin, 1991.
———. *Le Chevalier au lion/Yvain.* Edited by David Hult. Paris: Livre de Poche, 1994.
———. *Le Chevalier de la Charrette/Lancelot.* Edited by Alfred Foulet and Karl D. Uitti. Paris: Bordas, 1989.
———. *Cligès.* Edited by Charles Méla and Olivier Collet. Paris: Livre de Poche, 1994.
———. *Le Conte du Graal/Perceval.* Edited by Charles Méla. Paris: Livre de Poche, 1990.
———. *Erec et Enide.* Edited by Jean-Marie Fritz. Paris: Livre de Poche, 1992.

Cicero, *Rhetorica ad Herennium*. Translated by Harry Caplan. Loeb Classical Library. London: William Heinemann; Cambridge, Mass.: Harvard University Press, 1954.
Dante Alighieri. *La "Commedia" di Dante Alighieri*. 3 vols. Notes by Robert Holland. Edited and translated by Simone Marchesi. Florence: Olschki, 2011.
———. *De Vulgari Eloquentia*. Edited and translated by Steven Botterill. Cambridge; New York: Cambridge University Press, 1996.
Eichmann, Raymond, and John Duval, eds. and trans. *The French Fabliaux: B.N. MS. 837*. New York; London: Garland, 1984.
Fiero, Gloria K., Wendy Pfeffer, and Mathé Allain, eds. and trans. *Three Medieval Views of Women*. New Haven, Conn.: Yale University Press, 1989.
Gautier de Coinci. *Les Miracles de la Sainte Vierge*. Edited by Abbé Poquet. 1857. Reprint, Geneva: Slatkine, 1972.
———. *Les Miracles de Nostre Dame*. 4 vols. Edited by V. Frédéric Koenig. Geneva: Droz, 1955.
Herbert. *Le Roman de Dolopathos*. Edited by Jean-Luc Leclanche. Paris: Champion, 1997.
Jacobus de Voragine. *The Golden Legend*. Translated by William Granger Ryan. Princeton, N.J.: Princeton University Press, 1993.
Johannes de Alta Silva. *Dolopathos, or, The King and the Seven Wise Men*. Translated by Brady B. Gilleland. Binghamton, N.Y.: Center for Medieval and Early Renaissance Studies, 1981.
———. *Historia Septem Sapientum II. Johannis de Alta Silva Dolopathos*. Edited by Alfons Hilka. Heidelberg: C. Winter, 1913.
John of Salisbury. *Metalogicon*. Edited by J. B. Hall and K.S.B. Keats-Rohan. Turnhout, Belgium: Brepols, 1991.
———. *The Metalogicon of John of Salisbury*. Translated by Daniel D. McGarry. 1955. Reprint, Gloucester, Mass.: Peter Smith, 1971.
Johnston, Ronald Carlyle, and Douglas David Roy Owen, eds. *Fabliaux*. Oxford: Blackwell, 1965.
Lee, Charmaine, ed. *Prospettive sui fabliaux*. Padua: Liviana, 1976.
Marie de France. *Die Fabeln der Marie de France*. Edited by Karl Warnke. Halle: M. Niemeyer, 1898.
———. *Les Fables*. Edited by Charles Brucker. Leuven, Belgium: Peeters, 1991.
———. *The Fables of Marie de France*. Translated by Mary Lou Martin. Birmingham, Ala.: Summa Publications, 1984.
———. *Lais*. Edited by Karl Warnke and translated by Laurence Harf-Lancner. Paris: Librairie Générale Française, 1990.
Méon, Dominique-Martin, ed. *Nouveau recueil de fabliaux et contes inédits des poètes français des XIIe, XIIIe, XIVe et XVe siècles*. 2 vols. Paris: Chasseriau, 1823.
Mills, Leonard R., ed. *L'Histoire de Barlaam et Josaphat. Version champenoise*

d'après le ms. Reg. lat. 660 de la Bibliothèque apostolique vaticane. Geneva: Droz, 1973.
Misrahi, Jean, ed. Le Roman des Sept Sages. Paris: Droz, 1933.
Montaiglon, Anatole de and Gaston Raynaud, eds. Recueil général et complet des fabliaux des XIIIe et XIVe siècles imprimés ou inédits, publiés d'après les manuscrits. 6 vols. Paris: Librairie des Bibliophiles, 1872–90.
Montgomery, Edward D., Jr., ed. Le Chastoiement d'un père à son fils. Chapel Hill: University of North Carolina Press, 1972.
Noomen, Willem, and Nico van den Boogaard, eds. Nouveau recueil complet des fabliaux (NRCF). 10 vols. Assen, Netherlands: Van Gorcum, 1983–98.
O'Gorman, Richard, ed. Les Braies au cordelier: Anonymous Fabliau of the Thirteenth Century. Birmingham, Ala.: Summa Publications, 1983.
Pearcy, Roy, and Ian Short, eds. Eighteen Anglo-Norman Fabliaux. London: Anglo-Norman Text Society, Birkbeck College, 2000.
Petrus Alfonsi. Disciplina Clericalis. Edited by Cristiano Leone. Rome: Salerno, 2010.
———. Etude et édition des traductions françaises médiévales de la "Disciplina Clericalis" de Pierre Alphonse. http://www.unige.ch/lettres/mela/recherche/disciplina.html.
———. Petri Alfonsi Disciplina clericalis I. Edited by Alfons Hilka and Werner Söderhjelm. Acta Societatis scientiarum fennicae t. 38, 49. Lateinischer Text. Helsinki: Druckerei der Finnischen Literaturgesellschaft, 1911.
Le Roman de Renart. Edited by Naoyuki Fukumoto, Noboru Harano, and Satoru Suzuki. Translated by Gabriel Bianciotto. Paris: Librairie Générale Française, 2005.
Le Roman de Renart. Edited by Armand Strubel. Bibliothèque de la Pléiade, 445. Paris: Gallimard, 1998.
Rossi, Luciano, ed. Fabliaux érotiques. Paris: Livre de Poche, 1992.
Speer, Mary B., ed. Le Roman de Sept Sages de Rome. Lexington, Ky.: French Forum, 1989.
Vernay, Philippe, ed. Richeut: Edition critique. Bern: A. Francke, 1988.

Studies

Adams, Tracy. "The Cunningly Intelligent Characters of BNffr 19152." MLN 120 (2005): 896–924.
———. "Making 'Sens' in BNF fr. 19152." New Zealand Journal of French Studies 22.2 (2002): 22–33.
Adrado, Francisco Rodriguez. History of the Græco-Latin Fable. 3 vols. Translated by Leslie A. Ray. Boston: Brill, 1999–2003.
Alfie, Fabian, and Andrea Dini, eds. "Accessus ad auctores": Studies in Honor of

Christopher Kleinhenz. Tempe, Ariz.: Arizona Center for Medieval and Renaissance Studies, 2011.

Allen, Graham. *Intertextuality*. New York; London: Routledge, 2000.

Almansi, Guido. "Lettura della quarta novella del *Decameron*." *Strumenti Critici* 13 (1970): 308–17. Reprinted as "Il Monaco e l'abate," *L'Estetica dell'osceno*. Turin: Einaudi, 1974: 131–42.

———. *The Writer as Liar*. Boston: Routledge, 1975.

Avril, François, and Marie-Thérèse Gousset. *Manuscrits enluminés d'origine italienne*. 2 vols. Paris: Bibliothèque Nationale, Département des Manuscrits, 1984.

Azzam, Wagih, and Olivier Collet. "Le Manuscrit 3142 de la Bibliothèque de l'Arsenal: Mise en recueil et conscience littéraire au XIIIe siècle." *Cahiers de Civilisation Médiévale* 44 (2001): 207–45.

Badel, Pierre-Yves. *Introduction à la vie littéraire du moyen âge*. 1969. Paris: Bordas, 1984.

———. *Le Sauvage et le sot: Le fabliau de "Trubert" et la tradition orale*. Paris: Champion, 1979.

Baratto, Mario. *Realtà e stile nel "Decameron."* Vicenza: N. Pozza, 1970.

Barsella, Susanna. "Boccaccio and Humanism. A New Patristic Source of *Proemio 14* and the Pestilence: Basil the Great's *Homily on Psalm 1*." *Studi sul Boccaccio* 32 (2004): 59–79.

Bartoli, Adolfo. *Precursori del Boccaccio e alcune delle sue fonti*. Florence: Sansoni, 1876.

Bédier, Joseph. *Les Fabliaux*. 1894. Paris: Champion, 1982.

Bell, Susan Groag. "Medieval Women Book Owners: Arbiters of Lay Piety and Ambassadors of Culture." *Signs* 7 (1982): 742–68.

Bertolucci Pizzorusso, Valeria. "La réception de la littérature courtoise du XIIe au XIVe siècle en Italie: Nouvelles propositions." In *The Court Reconvenes: Courtly Literature across the Disciplines*. Edited by Barbara K. Altmann and Carleton W. Carroll. Cambridge, UK; Rochester, N.Y.: D. S. Brewer, 2003: 3–13.

Beyer, Jürgen. "The Morality of the Amoral." In *The Humor of the Fabliaux*. Edited by Thomas D. Cooke and Benjamin L. Honeycutt. Columbia: University of Missouri Press, 1974: 15–42.

Billy, Dominique. "Un genre fantôme: Le lai narratif: Examen d'une des thèses de Foulet." *Revue des Langues Romanes* 94 (1990): 121–28.

Blackham, Harold John. *The Fable as Literature*. London; Dover: Athlone Press, 1985.

Bloch, R. Howard. *The Scandal of the Fabliaux*. Chicago: University of Chicago Press, 1986.

Borghi Cedrini, Luciana. *Une branche d'armes: Preliminari a un'edizione dell'837 (ms. f. fr. B.N. di Parigi)*. Turin: G. Giappichelli, 1982.

Bornäs, Göran. *Trois contes français du XIIIe siècle tirés du recueil des Vies des pères*. Lund, Sweden: Gleerup, 1968.

Boutet, Dominique. *Les Fabliaux*. Paris: Presses Universitaires de France, 1985.
Bradley-Cromey, Nancy. "Dialectic and Chrétien de Troyes: Exploration of Interrelationships between Romance Literature and the Schools." In *1983 NEH Institute Resource Book for the Teaching of Medieval Civilization*. Edited by Howell Chickering. Amherst, Mass.: Five Colleges, 1984: 44–54.
Bramanti, Vanni. "Il 'Purgatorio' di Ferondo (*Decameron*, III, 8)." *Studi sul Boccaccio* 7 (1973): 178–87.
Branca, Vittore. *Boccaccio medievale*. Florence: Sansoni, 1956.
———. *Boccaccio: The Man and His Works*. Translated by Richard Monges. New York: New York University Press, 1976.
———. "Coerenza dell'introduzione del *Decameron*. Rispondenze strutturali e stilistiche." *Romance Philology* 13.4 (1960): 351–60.
Brown, Catherine. *Contrary Things: Exegesis, Dialectic, and the Poetics of Didacticism*. Stanford, Calif.: Stanford University Press, 1998.
Brown, Katherine A. "*Bérengier au lonc cul* and the *Pastourelle*." *Romance Notes* 47 (2007): 323–31.
———. "Boccaccio Reading Old French: *Decameron* IX:2 and *La Nonete*." *MLN* 125.1 (2010): 54–71.
———. "Inversion and Parody: Generic Implications of the Digitization of Old French *Fabliaux*." In *Dame Philology's Charrette: Approaching Medieval Textuality through Chrétien's "Lancelot."* Edited by Gina L. Greco and Ellen M. Thorington. Tempe, Ariz.: Arizona Center for Medieval and Renaissance Studies, 2012: 215–29.
Brownlee, Kevin, and Marina Scordilis Brownlee. *Romance: Generic Transformation from Chrétien de Troyes to Cervantes*. Hanover, N.H.: University Press of New England, 1985.
Brownlee, Marina Scordilis. "Wolves and Sheep: Symmetrical Undermining in Day III of the *Decameron*." *Romance Notes* 24.3 (1984): 262–66.
Bryan, William Frank, and Germaine Dempster, eds. *Sources and Analogues of Chaucer's "Canterbury Tales."* Chicago: University of Chicago Press, 1941.
Burbridge, Roger T. "Chaucer's *Reeve's Tale* and the Fabliau 'Le meunier et les .II. clers.'" *Annuale Mediaevale* 12 (1971): 30–36.
Burgess, Glyn S. *Marie de France: An Analytical Bibliography*. Supplement no. 3. Woolbridge, Suffolk: Tamesis, 2007.
Burr, Kristin L., John F. Moran, and Norris J. Lacy, eds. *The Old French Fabliaux: Essays on Comedy and Context*. Jefferson, N.C.; London: McFarland and Company, 2007.
Busby, Keith. *Codex and Context*. 2 vols. Amsterdam; New York: Rodopi, 2002.
———. "Courtly Literature and the Fabliaux: Some Instances of Parody." *Zeitschrift für Romanische Philologie* 102 (1986): 67–87.
———. "Courtly Literature and the Old French *Isopet*." *Reinardus* 6 (1993): 31–45.
———. "*Esprit gaulois* for the English: The Humour of the Anglo-Norman Fa-

bliau." In *The Old French Fabliaux: Essays on Comedy and Context*. Edited by Kristen L. Burr, John F. Moran, and Norris J. Lacy. Jefferson, N.C.; London: McFarland and Company, 2007: 160–73.

Butterfield, Ardis. "Medieval Genres and Modern Genre Theory." *Paragraph* 13.2 (1990): 184–201.

Caporello-Szykman, Corradina. *Boccaccian Novella: Creation and Waning of a Genre*. New York: P. Lang, 1990.

Cecere, Amalia. "Usi retorici boccacciani nel *Proemio* del *Decameron*." *Annali-Sezione Romanza* 31.1 (1989): 147–59.

Cerquiglini-Toulet, Jacqueline. "Le Clerc et l'écriture: *Le Voir Dit* de Guillaume de Machaut et la définition du *dit*." *Literatur in der Gesellschaft des Spätmittelalters* (GRLMA) 1 (1980): 151–68.

Cigni, Fabrizio. "La ricezione medievale della letteratura francese nella Toscana nord-occidentale." In *Fra toscanità e italianità: Lingua e letteratura dagli inizi al Novecento*. Edited by Edeltraud Werner and Sabine Schwarze. Tübingen: Francke, 2000.

Collet, Olivier. "Les collections vernaculaires entre diversité et unité: À propos d'une nouvelle recherche sur la mise en recueil des œuvres littéraires au moyen âge." In *L'Écrit et le manuscrit à la fin du Moyen Âge*. Edited by Tania Van Hemelryck and Céline Van Hoorebeeck. Turnhout, Belgium: Brepols, 2006: 57–66.

Connochie-Bourgne, Chantal. "*L'Image du monde*, une encyclopédie du XIIIe siècle: Édition critique et commentaire de la première version." Ph.D. diss., Université de Paris IV-Sorbonne, 1999.

Cooke, Thomas D., and Benjamin L. Honeycutt, eds. *The Humor of the Fabliaux*. Columbia: University of Missouri Press, 1974.

Cottino-Jones, Marga. "Comic Modalities in the *Decameron*." *Genre* 9.4 (1977): 429–49.

——. "Desire and the Fantastic in the *Decameron*: The Third Day." *Italica* 70.1 (1993): 1–18.

——. "Observations on the Structure of the *Decameron* Novella." *Romance Notes* 15 (1973): 378–87.

——. *Order from Chaos: Social and Aesthetic Harmonies in Boccaccio's "Decameron."* Washington, D.C.: University Press of America, 1982.

Crocker, Holly A., ed. *Comic Provocations: Exposing the Corpus of the Old French Fabliaux*. New York: Palgrave Macmillan, 2006.

Curtius, Ernst Robert. *European Literature and the Latin Middle Ages*. Translated by Willard R. Trask. New York: Bollingen, 1953.

Degani, Chiara, and Vittore Branca. "Studi sugli *exempla* e il *Decameron*." *Studi sul Boccaccio* 14 (1984): 178–208.

Delcorno, Carlo. "Studi sugli *exempla* e il *Decameron*, II: Modelli esemplari in tre novelle (I:1, III:8, II:2)." *Studi sul Boccaccio* 15 (1985–86): 189–214.

Delcorno Branca, Daniela. *Tristano e Lancillotto in Italia. Studia di letteratura arturiana*. Ravenna: Longo, 1998.
De Negri, Enrico. "The Legendary Style of the *Decameron*." *Romanic Review* 43 (1952): 165–89.
Derolez, Albert. *The Paleography of Gothic Manuscript Books*. Cambridge; New York: Cambridge University Press, 2003.
Dronke, Peter. "The Rise of the Medieval Fabliau: Latin and Vernacular Evidence." *Romanische Forschungen* 85 (1973): 275–97.
Dunbabin, Jean. *The French in the Kingdom of Sicily, 1266–1305*. Cambridge: Cambridge University Press, 2011.
Eichmann, Raymond. "In Search for Originals in the Fabliaux and the Validity of Textual Dependency." *Romance Notes* 19 (1978): 90–97.
Eusebi, Mario. "*Il Pelerinage Renart* del ms 1598 della Biblioteca Casanatense." *Etudes de langue et de littérature du moyen âge, offertes à Félix Lecoy*. Paris: Champion, 1973: 95–114.
Faral, Edmond. "Le Fabliau latin au moyen âge." *Romania* 50 (1924): 321–85.
———. *Les Jongleurs en France au moyen âge*. 1910. Paris: Champion, 1987.
Foehr-Janssens, Yamina, Olivier Collet, and Wagih Azzam, "Les Manuscrits littéraires français: Pour une sémiotique du recueil médiéval." *Revue Belge de Philologie et d'Histoire* 83 (2005): 639–69.
Feola-Baladier, Antonella. *Le Merveilleux dans le cycle des "Sept Sages de Rome."* Lille: Atelier National de Reproduction des Thèses, 2008.
Foulon, Charles. *L'Œuvre de Jehan Bodel*. Paris: Presses Universitaires de France, 1958.
Fowler, Alastair. "Transformations of Genre." In *Modern Genre Theory*. Edited by David Duff. Harlow, UK; New York: Longman, 2000: 232–49.
Frappier, Jean. "Remarques sur la structure du lai: Essai de définition et de classement." *La Littérature narrative d'imagination*. Paris: PUF, 1961: 23–37.
Freeman, Michelle. "Chrétien's *Cligès*: A Close Reading of the Prologue." *Romanic Review* 67 (1976): 89–101.
Gaunt, Simon. *Gender and Genre in Medieval French Literature*. Cambridge: Cambridge University Press, 1995.
Genette, Gérard. *Introduction à l'architexte*. Paris: Éditions du Seuil, 1979.
Getto, Giovanni. *Vita di forme e forme di vita nel "Decameron."* 1958. Turin: Petrini, 1986.
Gibaldi, Joseph. "The *Decameron* Cornice and the Responses to the Disintegration of Civilization." *Kentucky Romance Quarterly* 24 (1977): 349–57.
Godzich, Wlad, and Jeffrey Kittay. *The Emergence of Prose*. Minneapolis: University of Minnesota Press, 1987.
Grand, E.-D. "*L'Image du monde*: Poème didactique du XIIIe siècle." *Revue des langues romanes* 37 (1893): 5–58.
Gravdal, Kathryn. "*Vilain*" and "*Courtois*": Transgressive Parody in French Litera-

ture of the Twelfth and Thirteenth Centuries. Lincoln: University of Nebraska Press, 1989.

Grigsby, John L. The "Gab" as a Latent Genre in Medieval French Literature. Cambridge, Mass.: Medieval Academy of America, 2000.

Grimaldi, Emma. Il Privilegio di Dioneo. Naples: Edizioni Scientifiche Italiane, 1987.

Guggenbühl, Claudia. Recherches sur la composition et la structure du ms. Arsenal 3516. Romanica Helvetica 118. Basel: A. Francke, 1998.

Hillers, Delbert R. "Two Notes on the Decameron (III vii 42–43 and VIII vii 64, IX v 48)." MLN 113.1 (1998): 186–91.

Hollander, Robert. Boccaccio's Dante and the Shaping Force of Satire. Ann Arbor: University of Michigan Press, 1997.

Hollander, Robert, and Courtney Cahill. "Day Ten of the Decameron: The Myth of Order." In Boccaccio's Dante and the shaping force of satire. Ann Arbor: University of Michigan Press, 1997: 109–68.

Honeycutt, Benjamin L. "An Example of Comic Cliché in the Old French Fabliaux." Romania 96 (1975): 245–55.

Huizinga, Johan. Homo ludens. Translated by R.F.C. Hull. London: Routledge, 1949.

Hunt, Tony. "Aristotle, Dialectic, and Courtly Literature." Viator 10 (1979): 95–129.

———. "The Dialectic of Yvain." Modern Language Review 72 (1977): 285–99.

———. Miraculous Rhymes: The Writing of Gautier de Coinci. Cambridge: D. S. Brewster, 2007.

Huot, Sylvia. From Song to Book. Ithaca, N.Y.: Cornell University Press, 1987.

Hutton, Gabrielle. "La Stratégie dans les fabliaux." Reinardus 4 (1991): 111–17.

Jauss, Hans-Robert. "Une approche médiévale." In La Notion de genre à la Renaissance. Edited by Guy Demerson. Geneva: Slatkine, 1984: 35–57.

———. "Cinq modèles d'identification esthétique." In XIV congresso internazionale di linguistica e filologia romanza, Napoli, 1974: Atti. Vol. 1. Naples: Macchiaroli; Amsterdam: Benjamins, 1976: 145–64.

———. "Littérature médiévale et théorie des genres." Poétique 1 (1970): 79–101.

Jodogne, Omer. "Le Fabliau." In Typologie des sources du moyen âge occidental. Turnhout, Belgium: Brepols, 1975: 7–29.

———. "La Naissance de la prose française." Bulletin de la Classe des lettres et des sciences morales et politiques 49 (1963): 296–308.

Jolles, André. Formes simples. Translated by Antoine Marie Buguet. Paris: Éditions du Seuil, 1972.

Karnein, Alfred. "De amore" in volkssprachlicher Literatur: Untersuchungen zur Andreas-Capellanus-Rezeption in Mittelalter und Renaissance. Heidelberg: C. Winter, 1985.

Kay, Sarah. Courtly Contradictions: The Emergence of the Literary Object in the Twelfth Century. Stanford, Calif.: Stanford University Press, 2001.

Kelly, Samantha. *The New Solomon: Robert of Naples (1309-1343) and Fourteenth-Century Kingship*. Leiden, Netherlands: Brill, 2003.
Kern, Edith. "The Gardens in the *Decameron Cornice*." *PMLA* 66 (1951): 505-23.
Kiesow, Reinhard. *Fabliaux: Zur Genese und Typologie einer Gattung der altfranzösischen Kurzerzählungen*. Berlin: Schäuble, 1976.
Kircher, Timothy. "The Modality of Moral Communication in the *Decameron*'s First Day in Contrast to the Mirror of the *Exemplum*." *Renaissance Quarterly* 54.4 (2001): 1035-73.
Kirkham, Victoria. "Love's Labors Rewarded and Paradise Lost (*Decameron* III.10)." *Romanic Review* 72.1 (1981): 79-93.
Kittredge, G. L. "Chaucer's Discussion of Marriage." *Modern Philology* 9.4 (1912): 435-67.
Koelb, Clayton. "Some Problems of Literary Taxonomy." *Canadian Review of Comparative Literature* 4 (1977): 233-44.
Kohler, Michelle. "Vision, Logic, and the Comic Production of Reality in the *Merchant's Tale* and Two French *Fabliaux*." *Chaucer Review* 39.2 (2004): 137-50.
Kunstmann, Pierre. "*L'Annominatio* chez Gautier: Vocabulaire et syntaxe." In *Gautier de Coinci: Miracles, Music and Manuscripts*. Edited by Kathy M. Krause and Alison Stones. Turnhout, Belgium: Brepols, 2006.
Lacy, Norris J. "Courtliness and Townspeople: The Fabliaux as a Courtly Burlesque." *The Humor of the Fabliaux*. Edited by Thomas D. Cooke and Benjamin L. Honeycutt. Columbia: University of Missouri Press, 1974: 59-73.
———. "Fabliau Women." *Romance Notes* 25.3 (1985): 318-27.
———. *Reading Fabliaux*. New York; London: Garland, 1993.
———. "Subject to Object: Performance and Observation in the Fabliaux." *Symposium* 56.1 (2002): 17-24.
Landau, Marcus. *Die Quellen des "Dekameron."* Stuttgart: J. Scheible, 1884.
Lange, Marius. *Vom Fabliaux zu Boccaccio und Chaucer*. Hamburg: Friederichsen und de Gruyter, 1934.
Langlois, Ernest. *Notices et extraits des manuscrits français et provençaux de Rome*. Vol. 33, part 2. Paris: Institut National de France, 1889.
Lausberg, Heinrich. *Handbook of Literary Rhetoric*. Edited by David E. Orton and R. Dean Anderson. Translated by Matthew T. Bliss, Annemiek Jansen, and David E. Orton. Leiden; New York: Brill, 1998.
———. *Handbuch der literarischen Rhetorik*. Munich: M. Hüber, 1960.
Lee, A. Collingwood. *The "Decameron": Its Sources and Analogues*. New York: Haskell House, 1972.
Lefèvre, Sylvie. "Le Recueil et l'œuvre unique: Mobilité et figement." *Mouvance et jointures: Du manuscrit au texte médiéval*. Edited by Milena Mikhailova. Orléans: Paradigme, 2005: 203-28.
Legros, Huguette. "Un auteur en quête de son public: Les *fabliaux* de Jean Bodel." *Romania* 104 (1983): 102-13.

Leiner, Wolfgang, ed. *Chrétien de Troyes: "Le Chevalier de la Charette (Lancelot)"*: *Le 'Projet Charrette' et le renouvellement de la critique philologique des textes.* Special issue of *Œuvres et critiques* 27.1 (2002): 5–251.

Léonard, Émile G. *Boccace et Naples: Un poète à la recherche d'une place et d'un ami.* Paris: Droz, 1944.

Léonard, Monique. *Le "Dit" et sa technique littéraire, des origines à 1340.* Paris: Champion, 1996.

Leupin, Alexandre. *Barbarolexis: Medieval Writing and Sexuality.* Translated by Kate M. Cooper. Cambridge, Mass.; Harvard University Press, 1989.

Levy, Brian J. *The Comic Text: Patterns and Images in the Old French Fabliaux.* Amsterdam; Atlanta: Rodopi, 2000.

Lindgren, Lauri. "Analyse de la langue de l'*Image du monde* de Gossouin de Metz." *Neuphilologische Mitteilungen* 73 (1972): 499–544.

Livingston, Charles Harold. *Le Jongleur Gautier le Leu: Étude sur les fabliaux.* Cambridge, Mass.: Harvard University Press, 1951.

Lynde-Recchia, Molly. *Prose, Verse, and Truth-Telling in the Thirteenth Century.* Lexington, Ky.: French Forum, 2000.

Maddox, Donald, and Sara Sturm-Maddox. "*Genre* and *Intergenre* in Medieval French Literature." *L'Esprit Créateur* 33.4 (1993): 3–9.

Marchesi, Simone. "Boccaccio's Vernacular Classicism: Intertextuality and Interdiscursivity in the *Decameron*." *Heliotropia* 7.1–2 (2010): 31–50.

———. "'Sic me formabat puerum': Horace's *Satire I, 4* and Boccaccio's Defense of the *Decameron*." *MLN* 116.1 (2001): 1–29.

———. *Stratigrafie decameroniane.* Florence: L. S. Olschki, 2004.

Marcus, Millicent Joy. *An Allegory of Form.* Saratoga, Calif.: Anma Libri, 1979.

———. "Seduction by Silence: A Gloss on the Tales of Masetto (*Decameron* III, 1) and Alatiel (*Decameron* II, 7)." *Philological Quarterly* 58.1 (1979): 1–15.

Marino, Lucia. *"Decameron" "Cornice": Allusion Allegory, and Iconology.* Ravenna: Longo, 1979.

Mathieu-Castellani, Gisèle. "La Notion de genre." In *La Notion de genre à la Renaissance.* Edited by Guy Demerson. Geneva: Slatkine, 1984: 17–34.

Mazzacurati, Giancarlo. "Rappresentazione." In *Lessico critico decameroniano.* Edited by Renzo Bragantini and Pier Massimo Forni. Turin: Bollati Boringhieri, 1995: 269–99.

Mazzoni Peruzzi, Simonetta. *I manoscritti d'Italia: Jean de Condé.* 2 vols. Florence: Olschki, 1990.

Mazzotta, Giuseppe. *The World at Play in Boccaccio's "Decameron".* Princeton, N.J.: Princeton University Press, 1986.

McCash, June Hall, ed. *The Cultural Patronage of Medieval Women.* Athens: University of Georgia Press, 1996.

Ménard, Philippe. *Les Fabliaux: Contes à rire du moyen âge.* Paris: Presses Universitaires de France, 1983.

———. "Les Sources françaises d'un conte de Boccace: *Décameron* (IX:6)." In *Boccaccio e le letterature romanze tra medioevo e rinascimento*. Edited by Simonetta Mazzoni Peruzzi. Florence: Alinea, 2006: 113–33.
Meyer, Paul. "De l'expansion de la langue française en Italie pendant le Moyen-Âge." In *Atti del Congresso Internazionale di Scienze Storiche*. Rome: R. Accademia dei Lincei, 1904–7.
———. "Le Fableau du *Héron* ou la fille mal gardée." *Romania* 26 (1897): 85–91.
———. "Fragment d'*Aspremont* conservé aux archives du Puy-de-Dome." *Romania* 19 (1890): 201–36.
Migiel, Marilyn. "Beyond Seduction: A Reading of the Tale of *Alibech* and Rustico (*Decameron* III, 10)." *Italica* 75.2 (1998): 161–77.
———. *A Rhetoric of the Decameron*. Toronto; Buffalo, N.Y.: University of Toronto Press, 2003.
———. "Some Restrictions Apply: Testing the Reader in *Decameron* III:8." *Boccaccio in America*. Edited by Elsa Filosa and Michael Papio. Ravenna: Longo, 2012: 191–208.
Mikhailov, André D. "Les Genres narratifs dans la littérature française médiévale." In *XIV congresso internazionale di linguistica e filologia romanza, Napoli, 1974: Atti*. Vol. 5. Naples: Macchiaroli; Amsterdam: Benjamins, 1981: 343–52.
Minnis, Alastair J. "Late-Medieval Discussions of *Compilatio* and the Rôle of the Compilator." *Beiträge zur Geschichte der deutschen Sprache und Literatur* 101.3 (1979): 391–92.
Monson, Don Alfred. *Andreas Capellanus, Scholasticism, and the Courtly Tradition*. Washington, D.C.: Catholic University of America Press, 2005.
Morier, Henri. *Dictionnaire de poétique et de rhétorique*, 2nd edition. Paris: Presses Universitaires de France, 1975.
Muscatine, Charles. *The Old French Fabliaux*. New Haven, Conn.: Yale University Press, 1986.
———. "The Social Background of the Old French Fabliaux." *Genre* 9.1 (1976): 1–19.
Neuschäfer, Hans-Jörg. *Boccaccio und der Beginn der Novelle*. Munich: W. Fink, 1969.
Nichols, Stephen G. "'Art' and 'Nature': Looking for (Medieval) Principles of Order in Occitan *Chansonnier* N (Morgan 819)." In *The Whole Book: Cultural Perspectives on the Medieval Miscellany*. Edited by Stephen G. Nichols and Siegfried Wenzel. Ann Arbor: University of Michigan Press, 1996: 83–121.
Nolan, Barbara. "Turning over the Leaves of Medieval Fabliau-Anthologies: The Case of Bibliothèque Nationale MS. Français 2173." *Medieval Perspectives* 13 (1998): 1–31.
Noomen, Willem. "Auteur, narrateur, récitant de fabliaux: Le Témoignage des prologues et des épilogues." *Cahiers de Civilisation Médiévale* 35 (1992): 313–50.
———. "Le 'Lai de l'Esprevier': Une mise au point." In *Mélanges de linguistique, de*

littérature et de philologie médiévales, offertes à J. R. Smeets. Edited by Q.I.M. Mok, I. Spiele; P.E.R. Verhuyck. Leiden, Netherlands: 1982: 207–25.

———. "Qu'est-ce qu'un fabliau?" *XIV congresso internazionale di linguistica e filologia romanza, Napoli, 1974: Atti.* Vol. 5. Naples: Macchiaroli; Amsterdam: Benjamins, 1981: 421–32.

Nykrog, Per. *Les Fabliaux.* 1957. Geneva: Droz, 1973.

Ocaña, Antonio Ortijo. "A Morphological Study on the Prologues and Epilogues of the Fabliaux: A Rhetorical Approach." *Romanische Forschungen* 110 (1998): 185–201.

Olson, Glending. "The *Reeve's Tale* as a Fabliau." *Modern Language Quarterly* 35 (1974): 219–30.

Omont, Henri, ed. *Catalogue général des manuscrits français.* 25 vols. Bibliothèque Nationale de France: Département des manuscrits. Paris: Bibliothèque Nationale de France, 1868–.

Osgood, Charles G. *Boccaccio on Poetry.* Princeton, N.J.: Princeton University Press, 1930.

Padoan, Giorgio. "Mondo aristocratico e comunale nel Boccaccio." *Studi sul Boccaccio* 2 (1964): 81–216.

Paolella, Alfonso. "I Livelli narrativi nella novella di Rustico ed Alibech "romita" del *Decameron*." *Revue Romane* 13 (1978): 189–205.

Paris, Gaston. "Le Lai de l'Epervier." *Romania* 7 (1878): 1–21.

———. *Les Contes orientaux dans la littérature française du moyen âge.* Paris: A. Franck, 1875.

Parkes, Malcolm B. "The Influence of the Concepts of *Ordinatio* and *Compilatio* on the Development of the Book." In *Medieval Learning and Literature: Essays Presented to Richard William Hunt.* Edited by J.J.G. Alexander and M. T. Gibson. Oxford: Oxford University Press, 1976.

Payen, Jean-Charles. "Fabliaux et Cocagne: Abondance et fête charnelle dans les contes plaisants du XIIe et XIIIe siècles." In *Epopée animale, fable, fabliau: Actes du IVe Colloque de la Société internationale renardienne, Evreux, 7–11 septembre 1981.* Edited by Gabriel Bianciotto and Michel Salvat. Paris: Presses Universitaires de France, 1984: 435–48.

Pearcy, Roy J. "An Instance of Heroic Parody in the *Fabliaux*." *Romania* 98 (1977): 105–8.

———. "Intertextuality and *La Damoiselle qui n'ot parler de foutre qu'i n'aust mal au cuer*." *Zeitschrift für Romanische Philologie* 109 (1993): 526–38.

———. *Logic and Humour in the Fabliaux: An Essay in Applied Narratology.* Cambridge: D. S. Brewer; Rochester, N.Y.: Boydell and Brewer, 2007.

———. "*Le Prestre qui menga les meures* and Ovid's *Fasti*, III, 745–60." *Romance Notes* 15 (1973): 159–63.

———. "Relations Between the *D* and *A* Versions of *Bérenger au lonc cul*." *Romance Notes* 14 (1972): 173–78.

Picchio Simonelli, Maria. "Il 'grande canto cortese' dai provenzali ai siciliani." *Cultura Neolatina* 42 (1982): 201–38.
Picone, Michelangelo. "Il *Decamerone* come macrotesto: Il problema della cornice." In *Introduzione al "Decameron."* Edited by Michelangelo Picone and Margherita Mesirca. Florence: Franco Cesati, 2004: 9–31.
———. "Preistoria della cornice del *Decameron*." In *Studi di Italianistica*. Edited by Paolo Cherchi and Michelangelo Picone. Ravenna: Longo, 1988: 91–104.
———. "Il Principio del novellare: La Prima Giornata." In *Introduzione al "Decameron."* Edited by Michelangelo Picone and Margherita Mesirca. Florence: Franco Cesati, 2004: 57–78.
———. "Tre tipi di cornice novellistica." *Filologia e Critica* 13 (1988): 3–26.
———. "La Vergine e l'eremita: Una lettura intertestuale della novella di Alibech (*Decameron* III:10)." *Vox Romanica* 57 (1998): 85–100.
Pinet, Christopher. "From *Fabliau* to Farce: A Case Study." In *Essays in Early French Literature*. Edited by Norris J. Lacy and Jerry C. Nash. York, S.C.: French Literature Publications Company, 1982: 92–108.
Pitts, Brent A. "*Merveilleux*, Mirage, and Comic Ambiguity in the Old French Fabliaux." *Assays* 4 (1987): 39–50.
———. "Unfinished Business: Character Conflict, Judgment Scenes, and Narrator-Audience Dialogue in the Old French Fabliaux." *Medioevo Romanzo* 11 (1986): 379–400.
Potter, Joy Hambuechen. *Five Frames for the "Decameron."* Princeton, N.J.: Princeton University Press, 1982.
Preminger, Alex, ed. *Princeton Encyclopedia of Poetry and Poetics*. Princeton, N.J.: Princeton University Press, 1974.
Press, Alan Robert. "Death and Lamentation in Chrétien de Troyes's Romances: The Dialectic of Rhetoric and Reason." *Forum for Modern Language Studies* 23.1 (1987): 11–20.
Prior, Oliver H. "*L'Image du monde*" de Maître Gossouin: Rédaction en prose. Paris: Librairie Payot, 1913.
Propp, Vladimir. *Morphologie du conte*. Translated by Marguerite Derrida. Paris: Éditions du Seuil, 1970.
Raynaud, Gaston. "Trois dits tirés d'un nouveau manuscrit de fableaux: *Des Avocas, De la jument au deable, De Luque la maudit.*" *Romania* 12 (1883): 209–29.
Revard, Carter. "From French 'Fabliau Manuscripts' and MS Harley 2253 to the *Decameron* and the *Canterbury Tales*," *Medium Ævum* 69 (2000): 261–78.
———. "*Giolte et Johane*: An Interlude in B. L. MS Harley 2253." *Studies in Philology* 79 (1982): 122–46.
Rey-Flaud, Bernadette. *La Farce, ou la machine à rire: Théorie d'un genre dramatique 1450–1550*. Geneva: Droz, 1984.
Ribard, Jacques. *Un Ménestrel du XIVe siècle: Jean de Condé*. Geneva: Droz, 1969.

Riffaterre, Michael. *The Semiotics of Poetry*. Bloomington: Indiana University Press, 1978.

Rossi, Luciano. "A propos de quelques recueils de fabliaux." *Moyen Français* 13 (1983): 58–94.

———. "In luogo di sollazzo: I fabliaux del *Decameron*." In *'Leggiadre donne...': Novella e racconto breve in Italia*. Edited by Francesco Bruni. Venice: Marsilio, 2000: 13–27.

———. "Jean Bodel et l'origine du fabliau." In *La Nouvelle: Formation, codification et rayonnement d'un genre médiéval*. Edited by Michelangelo Picone, Giuseppe Di Stefano, and Pamela D. Stewart. Montreal: Plato, 1983: 45–63.

———. "Observations sur l'origine et la signification du mot *flabel*." *Romania* 117 (1999): 342–62.

Runte, Hans. R. "Marie de France dans ses fables." In *In Quest of Marie de France: A Twelfth-Century Poet*. Edited by Chantal A. Maréchal. Lewiston; Queenston; Lampeter: Edwin Mellen Press, 1992: 28–44.

Runte, Hans. R., J. Keith Wikeley, and Anthony J. Farrell, eds. *The "Seven Sages of Rome" and the "Book of Sindbad."* New York: Garland, 1984.

Rychner, Jean. *Contribution à l'étude des fabliaux: Variantes, remaniements, dégradations*. Neuchâtel: Faculté des Lettres, 1960.

———. "Deux copistes au travail." In *Medieval French Textual Studies in Memory of T.B.W. Reid*. Edited by Ian Short. London: Anglo-Norman Text Society, 1984: 187–218.

Schenck, Mary Jane Stearns. *The Fabliaux: Tales of Wit and Deception*. Amsterdam: Benjamins, 1987.

Segre, Cesare. "Funzioni, opposizioni e simmetrie nella giornata VII del *Decameron*." *Studi sul Boccaccio* 6 (1971): 81–108.

———. "La Letteratura franco-veneta." *Storia della letteratura italiana*, vol. 1, *Dalle origine a Dante*. Edited by Enrico Malato. Rome: Salerno, 1995: 631–47.

———. *Semiotica filologica*. Turin: Einaudi, 1979.

Singleton, Charles. "On *Meaning* in the *Decameron*." *Italica* 21 (1944): 117–24.

Smarr, Janet Levarie. "Symmetry and Balance in the *Decameron*." *Mediaevalia* 2 (1976): 159–87.

Spencer, Richard. "Le *Courtois-Vilain* Nexus in *La Male Honte*." *Medium Ævum* 37.3 (1968): 272–92.

Spiegel, Gabrielle M. *Romancing the Past: The Rise of Vernacular Prose Historiography in Thirteenth-century France*. Berkeley: University of California Press, 1993.

Stemmler, Theo. "Miscellany or Anthology? The Structure of Medieval Manuscripts: MS Harley 2253, for Example." In *Studies in the Harley Manuscript: The Scribes, Contents, and Social Contexts of British Library MS Harley 2253*. Edited by Susanna Fein. Kalamazoo, Mich.: Medieval Institute Publications, 2000: 111–21.

Stewart, Pamela D. *Retorica e mimica nel "Decameron" e nella commedia del cinquecento*. Florence: Olschki, 1986.
Storey, Harry Wayne. "Parodic Structure in 'Alibech and Rustico': Antecedents and Tradition." *Canadian Journal of Italian Studies* 5 (1982): 163–76.
Suomela-Härmä, Elina. "Le *Roman de Renart* et les fabliaux." In *Et c'est la fin pour quoy sommes ensemble: Hommage à Jean Dufournet*. Edited by Jean-Claude Aubailly, Emmanuèle Baumgartner, François Dubost, Liliane Dulac, and Marcel Faure. Paris: Champion, 1993: 1319–31.
Taylor, Andrew. *Textual Situations: Three Medieval Manuscripts and Their Readers*. Philadelphia: University of Pennsylvania Press, 2002.
Tobler, Adolf. "'Le Dit du Magnificat' von Jean de Condé." *Jahrbuch für romanische und englische Literatur* 2 (1860): 82–104.
Todorov, Tzvetan, ed. and trans. *Théorie de la littérature: Textes des formalistes russes*. Paris: Éditions du Seuil, 1965.
Togeby, Knud. "The Nature of the Fabliaux." *The Humor of the Fabliaux*. Edited by Thomas D. Cooke and Benjamin L. Honeycutt. Columbia: University of Missouri Press, 1974: 7–13.
Tona Kaercher, Françoise. *Ruse féminine dans ses aspects sociologiques, idéologiques et narratifs dans les fabliaux et les nouvelles du Moyen Age*. Villeneuve d'Ascq.: Presses Universitaires du Septentrion, 1999.
Trachsler, Richard. "Le Recueil Paris, BN fr. 12603." *Cultura Neolatina* 54 (1994): 189–211.
Tronci, Francesco. *Novella tra letteratura, ideologia e metaletteratura: Studi sul "Decameron"*. Cagliari: C.U.E.C., 2001.
Tudor, Adrian. "Les Fabliaux: Encore le problème de la typologie." *Studi Francesi* 141 (2003): 599–603.
Uitti, Karl D. "Chrétien de Troyes's *Cligés*: Romance *Translatio* and History." In *Conjunctures: Medieval Studies in Honor of Douglas Kelly*. Edited by Keith Busby and Norris J. Lacy. Amsterdam; Atlanta: Rodopi, 1994: 545–57.
———. "Foi littéraire et création poétique: Le Problème des genres littéraires en ancien français," *XIV congresso internazionale di linguistica e filologia romanza, Napoli, 1974: Atti*. Vol. 1. Naples: Macchiaroli; Amsterdam: Benjamins, 1976: 165–76.
———. *Linguistics and Literary Theory*. Englewood Cliffs, N.J.: Prentice-Hall, 1969.
———. *Story, Myth, and Celebration in Old French Narrative Poetry, 1050–1200*. Princeton, N.J.: Princeton University Press, 1973.
Vacca, Diane Duyos. "Converting Alibech: 'Nunc spiritu copuleris.'" *Journal of Medieval and Renaissance Studies* 25 (1995): 207–27.
van den Boogaard, Nico. "Le *Nouveau recueil complet des fabliaux*." *Neophilologus* 61 (1977): 333–46.
van Os, Jaap. "Autour de Guillaume: A propos d'un recueil de fables et de fabliaux

(Paris, BNF fr. 2173)." In *Non Nova, Sed Nove*. Edited by Martin Gosman and Jaap van Os. Groningen, Netherlands: Bouma's Boekhuis, 1984: 183–93.

———. *Les Fabliaux du manuscrit Cologny Bodmer 113: (XVe siècle)*. Groningen, Netherlands: Rijksuniversiteit Groningen, 1989.

Vàrvaro, Alberto. "Elaboration des textes et modalités du récit dans la littérature française médiévale." *Romania* 119 (2001): 1–75.

Velli, Giuseppe. *Petrarca e Boccaccio: Tradizione, memoria, scrittura*. Padua: Antenore, 1995.

Virgulti, Ernesto. "Lies My Father Told Me: Boccaccio's *Novelletta* of Filippo Balducci and His Son." In *The Italian Novella: A Book of Essays*. Edited by Gloria Allaire. New York; London: Routledge, 2003: 15–32.

Voisenet, Jacques. *Bêtes et hommes dans le monde médiéval*. Turnhout, Belgium: Brepols, 2000.

Weaver, Elissa B., ed. *The "Decameron" First Day in Perspective*. Toronto: University of Toronto Press, 2004.

Welter, Jean-Thiébaut. *L'Exemplum dans la littérature religieuse et didactique du moyen âge*. 1927. Reprint, New York: AMS Press, 1973.

Wetherbee, Winthrop. *Platonism and Poetry in the Twelfth Century*. Princeton, N.J.: Princeton University Press, 1972.

Williams, Harry F. "French Fabliaux Scholarship." *South Atlantic Review* 46.1 (1981): 76–82.

Witt, Catherine. "Le Chiasme et la poésie courtoise." *Œuvres et Critiques* 27.1 (2002): 155–220.

Zumthor, Paul. "La Brièveté comme forme." In *La Nouvelle: Formation, codification, et rayonnement d'un genre médiéval*. Edited by Michelangelo Picone, Giuseppe Di Stefano, and Pamela D. Stewart. Montreal: Plato, 1983: 3–8.

———. *Essai de poétique médiévale*. Paris: Éditions du Seuil, 1972.

INDEX

Abelard, Peter, 3.
Adams, Tracy, 36–37, 43, 180n54. See also *Metis*
Aesop, 49, 69, 85, 101. See also Fable
Almansi, Guido, 103–4, 115–16, 143, 148, 196n99, 201n53
Andreas Capellanus: *De Amore*, 105, 132, 194n76
Anecdote, 72, 86–87, 93, 97, 128–29
Angevins, 47, 126, 139, 140–42
Anthology, 45, 85; compared to *Decameron*, 102, 117, 119–20, 123–24, 165; compilers of, 39, 43, 50, 81, 88, 95, 114; definition of, 4; *exempla* in, 85, 96, 99, 188n3; intertextuality and, 45, 82; organization of, 35–44, 60, 77, 83, 99, 101; Eastern collections and, 86, 93–4, 98, 102, 124, 164; role of fabliaux in, 2, 5–8, 38, 42, 46, 102, 165. See also Miscellany
Anticlericalism, 36, 44, 82, 159
Antifeminism: in *Decameron*, 109–10, 123; in *Dit de la femme*, 77; in Eastern works, 87, 90–94, 164, 191n30; in fables, 69, 82, 146; in fabliaux, 21, 42, 185n48
Arabia, 85, 86, 89
Avril, François, 48

Baratto, Mario, 145
Barlaam et Josaphat, 85, 86, 91, 94, 101, 113; *Decameron* IV: Intro. and, 93, 108–10, 114, 191n40; *exempla* and, 96–97, 120, 191n41; *La Grue* and, 30
Bédier, Joseph, 92, 176n25, 183n18, 189n14, 191n41

Bell, Susan Groag, 140
Boccaccio, Giovanni: *Ars combinatoria*, 114, 124 (*see also* Combination); *Ars narrandi*, 103–4, 113; *Genealogia Deorum Gentilium*, 140
—*Decameron*
—*Proemio*, 103–7, 110, 113, 121, 146, 166, 194nn77–8, 195n80
—Day I, 116–18, 120–21; I:*Introduction*, 103–4, 196n103; I:1, 119, 121, 159, 160, 188n3, 194n70; I:3, 120, 121; I:4, 8, 17, 116, 120–21, 143–46, 166, 171, 201nn51,53; I:5, 120; I:7, 121; I:9, 122
—Day II, 115–17; II:5, 171; II:7, 194n70; II:9, 188n5; II:*Conclusion*, 146
—Day III, 102, 115–18, 122–24, 143, 146, 157, 160, 165; III:*Introduction*, 123; III:1, 122; III:2, 171; III:3, 157; III:4, 157, 171; III:6, 157, 171; III:7, 157; III:8, 8, 122, 157–60, 162, 171, 202nn87,89,90; III:9, 157; III:10, 8, 24, 110, 122, 146–49, 151–58, 167, 171
—Day IV, 102, 115, 117, 118; IV:*Introduction*, 93, 103–4, 107–11, 178n39; IV:1, 117; IV:10, 210n58; IV: *Conclusion*, 117
—Day V, 115, 117–18; V:4, 117; V:9, 171; V:10, 171
—Day VI: 116, 118, 122, 139
—Day VII, 116, 118, 122–24; VII:1, 123, 146, 157, 171, 201n57; VII:2, 123, 171; VII:3, 157; VII:4, 114, 123, 157, 171, 190n17; VII:5, 17, 123, 157, 171; VII:6, 123, 138, 171, 190n17; VII:7, 123, 157, 171; VII:8, 123, 157, 171; VII:9, 22, 171; VII:10, 157; VII: *Conclusion*, 119

—Day VIII, 116, 118–19, 122, 124; VIII:1, 160, 171; VIII:2, 171; VIII:3, 191n44, 202n88; VIII:4, 171; VIII:5, 171; VIII:6, 171, 191n44, 202n88; VIII:8, 171; VIII:9, 202n88; VIII:10, 190n17
—Day IX, 118–19, 124; IX:2, 8, 17, 124, 127–37, 142–47, 166–67, 171, 198n19, 199n23; IX:3, 8, 124, 157–58, 160–62, 172, 191n44, 203n92; IX:4, 124; IX:5, 124, 191n44, 202n88; IX:6, 22, 124, 172; IX:8, 124; IX:10, 124, 172
—Day X, 116, 118–19; X:5, 138; X:8, 114, 190n17; X:10, 119, 121
—*Conclusione dell'Autore*, 103–4, 107, 110, 142, 196n95;
Braccini, Gaetano, 114
Branca, Vittore: on *exempla*, 85, 188n3; on fabliaux; 106, 127–28, 138, 143, 157, 202n87; on sources of *Decameron*, 92, 114, 148; on Boccaccio's language, 110, 153, 196n95
Brigata (*Decameron*): as audience, 112–17, 120, 122–23, 155, 165–68; as narrators, 8, 93–94, 103–4, 106, 136, 139; Dioneo, 118–19, 121, 146–53, 155, 201n58; Elissa, 122, 130, 132, 136, 139; Emilia, (See *Decameron* IX:2); Fiammetta, 117–18; Filomena, 116, 146; Filostrato, 117, 201n58; Lauretta, 118–19, 158; Neifile, 121; Pampinea, 116, 120; Panfilo, 121, 159
Brownlee, Marina, 122
Busby, Keith, 38, 44, 88, 179nn50,53, 181n67, 193n64

Calandrino (*Decameron*), 119, 122, 124, 158, 160–62, 191n44
Chaucer, Geoffrey, 37, 101, 138, 177n28; *Canterbury Tales*, 36, 38, 43, 96, 113, 168, 180n54
Chrétien de Troyes, 3, 29–30, 38, 72, 200n37; *Le Chevalier au lion/Yvain*, 3, 72, 73, 74, 186n54; *Le Chevalier de la Charrette*, 3, 29, 178n43, 200n37; *Cligès*, 3, 30; *Le Conte du Graal/Perceval*, 38, 186nn54,55
Christianization of texts, 30, 85–86, 91–93, 109, 147, 152
Cicero. See *Rhetorica ad Herrenium*

Collection: definition, 2–6. See also Anthology; Miscellany
Combination, 58, 162–63, 167, 178n45, 196n101; in *Decameron*, 8, 121, 127–29, 143, 146–52, 154–57; of East and West, 7, 92, 101–2, 111–14, 119, 124; in *fabliaux*, 7, 18, 29, 33–34, 74, 84

Dante Alighieri, 105, 107, 125, 177n30, 194n78, 195n94, 202n90
Degani, Chiara, 85, 157, 188n3
Dialectic. See Abelard, Peter; Logic
Didacticism, 4, 9, 163–68; *Decameron* and, 149–51, 157; Eastern texts and, 9, 87, 93–94; *exempla* and, 74, 87–88, 95, 97, 110; fables and, 7, 72, 80, 163; fabliaux and, 19, 29, 35, 71, 78, 136, 183n18; Western texts and, 34, 50–51, 82, 86, 90–92, 98–99, 189n12
Diegesis, 104, 122, 124; extradiegesis, 103–4, 108, 112, 114, 123, 165; intradiegesis, 103–4, 118, 123–24; metadiegesis, 103–4
Dit: definition of, 39–40, 84, 100, 180nn58,59, 187n1; in MS K, 48, 51, 74, 77, 81
Dit de la femme, 48, 77, 100
Du Noble lion, 41

Encyclopedism, 72, 77, 80, 85, 95–96, 140
England, 41, 75, 87, 88; and Anglo-Norman French, 24, 87, 185n31
Étienne de Bourbon, 96
Exemplum: collections of, 84–88, 95–100, 188n3, 192nn53,55; definition of, 5–7, 106, 146–47, 156–57, 189n11. See also Negative exemplarity

Fable: collections of, 6–7, 84–85, 95, 98, 101, 120, 188n6; morals and, 183n17, 184n27; taxonomy and, 13, 70, 106–7, 158, 176n17, 183n18. See also Marie de France
Fableor, 88, 138, 185n45. See also *Trouvère*
Fables Pierre Aufors, 87, 88, 189nn15,16. See also Petrus Alfonsi
Fabliaux: *Barat et Haimet*, 171; *Bérengier au lonc cul*, 17–18, 175n14, 176n22; *Boivin de Provins*, 171, 193n59; *La Borgoise d'Orliens*,

157, 171, 202n87; *Le Bouchier d'Abeville*, 171; *Les Braies au cordelier*, 128–29, 171; *Les Braies le priestre*, 128, 171; *Cele qui se fist foutre sur la fosse de son mari*, 48, 51, 65–74, 77–79, 184n29, 185n45; *Celui qui bota la pierre*, 19, 48, 52, 55–58; *Le Chevalier qui fist parler les cons*, 14–15, 42, 178n44, 187n67; *Le Chevalier qui fist sa femme confesse*, 17, 171; *Le Chevalier qui recovra l'amor de sa dame*, 17, 88, 171; *Le Clerc qui fu repus derriere l'escrin*, 138, 171; *La Coille noire*, 48, 51, 61–65, 78–9; *Constant du Hamel*, 171; *Le Cuvier*, 88, 171, 190n16; *La Dame escoillee*, 17, 171; *La Dame qui fist trois tors entor le moustier*, 90, 171; *La Damoisele qui ne pooit oïr parler de foutre*, 18, 147, 150–52, 155, 171; *L'Esquiriel*, 38; *L'Evesque qui beneï le con*, 17, 143, 171, 201n52; *Frere Denise*, 17, 19, 28, 147, 151, 153, 171; *La Gageure*, 42; *Gombert et les deus clers*, 22, 172; *La Grue*, 7, 11, 68, 92, 120, 147, 163, 177n29; *Guillaume au faucon*, 171; *Le Héron* (See *La Grue*); *La Housse partie*, 92; *Jouglet*, 15, 16, 101; *La Male Honte*, 41, 48, 75–77, 79, 82, 186nn57,61; *Le Meunier d'Arleux*, 171; *Le Meunier et les deus clers*, 22, 172; *La Nonete*, 8, 17, 127–36, 137–43, 150, 171; *Les Perdrix*, 12, 16, 92; *Le Pet au vilain*, 120–21, 180n58, (see also Rutebeuf); *Le Pliçon*, 138–39; *Le Povre mercier*, 40; *Le Prestre crucifié*, 48, 74, 78; *Le Prestre et Alison*, 171; *Le Prestre et la dame*, 171; *Le Prestre qui abevete*, 22–24, 171, 201n53; *Le Prestre qui menga mores*, 36–37; *Le Prestre qui ot mere a force*, 36–37; *La Pucele qui voloit voler*, 18, 38–39, 172; *Les Putains et les lecheors*, 38–39, 180n58; *Les Quatre souhais St. Martin*, 20–22, 34–35, 42, 178n44; *Le Segretain moine*, 171; *Le Sentier batu*, 139; *St. Pierre et le jongleur*, 17, 180n58; *Les Trois aveugles de Compiegne*, 101; *Les Trois dames*, 42; *Les Trois dames qui troverent l'anel*, 92, 157, 171, 202nn87,90; *Trubert*, 17, 100, 171; *Un chevalier et sa dame et un clerk*, 171; *Le Vallet aus douze fames*, 18–19; *La Vielle qui oint la paume au chevalier*, 48, 74, 78–80, 82; *Le Vilain de Bailleul*, 8, 17, 157–62, 171, 172; *Le Vilain de Farbu*, 17; *Le Vilain qui conquist paradis par plait*, 17, 175n13

Filippo Balducci. See Boccaccio, Giovanni: *Decameron*, Day IV:*Introduction*
Florence, 94, 103, 107–8, 112–14, 139
Fortune (personification), 5, 116, 122, 132–36, 145
Framing devices, 83, 86–87, 94, 99, 112–13, 166, 180n54; *Cornice* (*Decameron*), 121, 123, 163; definition of, 2, 89, 188n6, 196n99; sources 94, 98, 119; summary of, 112–14, 115; Mise an abyme and, 61, 81, 97, 103–4, 106, 121, 186n61

Gafsa, 147–48, 152, 154
Garin, 15, 36, 37, 179n53
Gaunt, Simon, 18–22, 176n24
Gautier de Coinci: *Miracles Nostre Dame*, 95, 98, 175n8
Gautier le Leu, 36, 185n45
Genre: 168, 181n71, 192n55; intergeneric comparisons in collections, 4, 8, 34, 42–7, 51, 72, 80–83, 100; mixing in *Decameron*, 2, 74, 105–6, 121, 155–56, 162; single-genre collections; 95–98, 102; taxonomy, 51, 99, 101, 185n49; variety in fabliaux: 5, 7–9, 11, 19, 35, 183n18
Getto, Giovanni, 114, 121
Gibaldi, Joseph, 114
Gossuin de Metz. See
Gousset, Marie-Thérèse. See Avril, François
La Grue: chiasmus and, 24–29; manuscripts and, 34–41, 44; overview of, 7, 11, 68, 92, 120, 147, 163, 177n29; tower motif and, 29–33
Guillaume de Lorris: *Le Roman de la Rose*, 137–38, 141

Hainaut, 126, 137, 140, 142
Heaven, 17, 122–23
Hell, 122, 147–48, 151, 153–54, 156
Herbert. See Johannes de Alta Silva
Hilka, Alfons, 88
Hollander, Robert, 105, 116, 118–19

224 Index

Humor: *Decameron* and, 160; fables and, 52, 63; fabliaux and; 1–2, 17–18, 24, 39, 55, 128, 175n11; wordplay as, 27, 41, 79, 184n28. *See also* Parody

Huot, Sylvia, 100

Hypocrisy, 128, 130–32, 134, 136, 142–45, 201n51

Image du monde (Gossuin de Metz), 46, 72, 74, 98, 186n61; description of, 48–51, 182n12; microcosm and macrocosm in, 80–82, 187n68

Imagination, 5–6, 157, 163–68, 174n20

India, 85–86, 93

Intertextuality: *Decameron* and, 118, 120–27, 129, 137, 157, 196n99; definition of, 5, 166–68, 174n18; manuscripts and, 42, 44, 46–47, 72–74; *La Nonete* and, 143, 146

Intratextuality: and *Decameron*, 124, 142–43, 146, 166; definition, 5, 8, 174n18; and fabliaux, 60, 65–72

Inversion: *Decameron* and, 84, 122–24, 131, 136, 143–46, 153, 194n78; definition of, 2, 7, 9, 11, 14, 20–24, 163; in fables and fabliaux, 51–52, 55, 58, 61, 63, 74–82; *La Grue* and, 26–28, 33

Jacobus de Voragine. See *Legenda Aurea*

Jacques de Vitry, 87, 96, 191n41

Jean de Condé, 128–29, 131, 136–43, 200n46. *See also* Fabliaux: *La Nonete*; Hainaut

Jean de Meun. *See* Guillaume de Lorris

Johannes de Alta Silva, 11, 15, 91
—*Dolpathos:* and chiasmus, 3, 11, 13, 15–16; Latin, 30, 105, 107, 175n7, 191nn31–32; Old French, 89, 91–94, 101, 178n45, 193n65

John of Salisbury, 3, 4, 176n27, 185n45

Jongleur (giullari), 16, 39, 47, 126, 183n18. *See also* Gautier le Leu

Judgment, 4, 9, 51, 175n13; *Cele qui se fist* and, 70–72, 77, 80, 82; *La Coille noire* and, 64; *Decameron* and, 159, 167; *exempla* and, 88, 91

Kay, Sarah, 3, 175n9, 178n41, 185n31

Kelly, Samantha, 139, 182n5

Kircher, Timothy, 121

Kirkham, Victoria, 117–18

Kunstmann, Pierre, 14, 175n8. *See also* Rhetorical devices: *Adnominatio*

Lais (anonymous), 99, 101, 200n28. *See also* Marie de France

Landau, Marcus, 88, 138, 157, 191n44, 202n87; Boccaccio, 97, 126–28, 197n6; Eastern works, 92, 189n9

Langlois, Ernest, 137

Lausberg, Heinrich, 10, 174n2

Le Bien des fames, 77

Le Blasme des fames, 40, 77

Le Chastoiement d'un père à son fils, 35–37, 87–88, 101, 189nn9,12

Le Roman de Renart, 90–91, 93, 124, 137, 189n15, 191n44

Le Roman des sept sages de Rome. *See* Seven Sages of Rome

Lefèvre, Sylvie, 34–35, 43, 117, 124

Legenda Aurea (Jacobus de Voragine), 93, 97, 128, 191n44

Leone, Cristiano, 88, 188n6, 189nn10–12,15, 190nn18,24

Les Cent Nouvelles nouvelles, 38, 168, 180n54

Les Fables. *See* Marie de France

Les Sept vices et sept vertus, 34–35, 120

Logic: contradiction, 3–5, 10; fables and, 53, 58–59, 64; fabliaux and, 28, 70, 79, 130–31; chiasmus and, 68, 82, 96–98, 185n34, 186n58; dialectic, 3, 4, 6, 174n10; fallacy and, 39, 65, 66, 82, 175n11,13; opposition in, 2–5, 9, 12, 16–17, 54

Love (personification): in *Decameron*, 149–50; in Old French, 130–36, 198n20

Manuscript layout: *Explicit*, 48, 51, 75; *Incipit*, 99; *Mise-en-page*, 34, 51, 192n46,51

Manuscripts of fabliaux, 169–70; (By abbreviation): MS A, 16, 34–35, 42–44, 100, 120, 179n47,50; MS B, 36, 38–39, 43–44, 55, 101, 118, 143; MS C, 19, 44; MS D, 18, 35–38, 42–44, 88, 101, 180n54; MS E, 39–41, 120–21; MS F, 29, 41, 43–44, 101, 177n31; MS H, 44, 101, 193n59; MS I, 19, 101; MS J, 91, 98–101, 193n64; MS K, 46–51, 80–83, 100, 146, 184n26, 185n31;

Index   225

MS M, 15, 42–43, 88, 137–41 (*as MS R*);
MS O, 101; MS P, 193n59; MS X, 88, 101;
MS Y, 16, 88, 101, 193n65; MS Z, 42–43,
88, 101, 194n66; MS a, 43; MS i, 25, 29, 41,
177n31, 178n42; MS j, 44, 100; MS l, 49,
77, 182n14; MS q, 101; MS Chartres, B. M.
no. 620, 91; MS London, British Library,
Harley 527, 88, 190n16. *See also* Jean de
Condé
Marchesi, Simone, 114, 129, 195nn87,94
Marcus, Millicent, 103, 108–9, 116–18, 188n3,
194n78, 201nn54,57
Marguerite de Navarre: *L'Heptaméron*, 168,
180n54
Marie de France, 47, 66
—Fable titles : "Le Chat mitré," 61–64;
"La Contrarieuse," 52, 58–61, 63, 78; "La
Femme et la poule," 61, 64; "La Femme
qui fit pendre son mari," 51, 65, 69, 74;
"L'Home qui avoit feme tencheresse," 52,
57–61
—*Isopet: La Grue* and, 35, 39, 41, 176n25;
mixed with fabliaux, 52, 60–61, 65, 69,
74–75, 80–82, 194n67; MS K and, 48–51,
184n26; Western collections and, 95, 101,
181n2, 186n61, 191n44, 194n67
—*Lais*: as collection, 6, 93, 95, 98, 178n45,
193n59; "Guigemar," 29, 178n45; "Yonec,"
29–33, 193n59
Mazzotta, Giuseppe, 165–67, 173n4, 195n90
McCash, June Hall, 140–41
Metis, 36, 37, 179n52. *See also* Adams, Tracy
Migiel, Marilyn, 151–56
Minnis, Alastair, 96
Miscellany, 4, 43, 95, 98–99, 174n16, 192n51.
See also Anthology.
Montgomery, Edward, 87, 189n12
Morals: in *Decameron*, 145–49; in *exempla*,
86–87, 97–98, 101, 162; in fables, 58–65, 81,
184n27; in fabliaux, 18–19, 55, 57–58, 78,
176n17. *See also* Proverbs

Naples, 126, 127, 139–42, 188n5, 197n6, 200n41
Negative exemplarity, 60, 120; of fabliaux,
4–5, 35, 44, 72, 82, 100, 164, 179n50; and
Decameron, 118, 152, 162
Nolan, Barbara, 50, 57, 72

Noomen, Willem, 24, 179n53
Il Novellino, 97, 107, 188n3, 189n9, 193n58,
195n86, 201n53
Nykrog, Per: *contes à triangle*, 18, 77, 78, 159;
definition of fabliaux, 176n16, 180nn58,59,
183n18, 186nn53,56, 194n66

1001 Nights, 113, 189n9
Ovid, 105, 107, 153, 191n44, 194n76

Padoan, Giorgio, 116, 126, 141
Panchatantra, 85, 188n3
Paolella, Alfonso, 148, 153–4, 156
Paris, 63, 120, 137, 171, 192n55, 197n6
Paris, Gaston, 90, 183n18
Parkes, Malcolm B., 96, 192n46
Parody: in fabliaux, 2, 11, 18, 73, 76, 147,
176nn16–17; in *Decameron*, 110, 148
Patronage, 137–38, 140–42, 186n61
Pearcy, Roy J., 18, 52–5, 78, 184nn28,29,
185n39; definition of fabliaux, 175nn11,13,
180n58; logical fallacies, 3, 54–55, 59, 76,
175nn11,13, 185n34; on *aequivocatio*, 70,
75, 186n58; on fables as fabliaux, 52, 60,
66, 191n30. *See also* Rhetorical devices:
aequivocatio
Persia, 85–86, 89
Petrus Alfonsi, 86–9, 188n6; *Disciplina
Clericalis*, 93, 96, 123, 189n11; in Old
French, 7, 86–87, 188n8, 189nn12,15;
source for Boccaccio, 88–90, 94, 113–14,
123, 189n9
Picardy, 137, 139, 183n18, 198n22
Picone, Michelangelo, 103–4, 112–13, 120–21,
148, 152, 196n103, 197n123
Plague, 94, 103–4, 112–14, 118
Potter, Joy, 103–5, 107, 110, 194n77,78, 195n85
Proverbs, 16, 86–89, 176n17, 177n.31; ambiguous interpretation of, 11, 20, 28–29, 55,
57–58; in *Decameron*, 135–36, 148; irony,
18–19, 79, 176n22
Purgatory, 122, 159–60, 202n90

Revard, Carter, 42–43, 173n1
Reversal: definition, 2–9. *See also* Inversion;
Rhetorical devices: chiasmus
Rhetoric ad Herrenium, 10

Rhetorical devices, 2, 7–9, 105, 195n80; *adnominatio*, 14, 53, 56, 60, 61, 175n8; *aequivocatio*, 60, 70, 75, 79, 186n58; antithesis, 10, 105, 174n2; antonym, 54, 56; chiasmus, 7, 10–16; *commutatio*, 10, 174n2, 175n3; paronomasia, 13, 67, 175n8

Riffaterre, Michael, 2

Rossi, Luciano, 127–29, 142–43, 183n18, 198n19, 199n23, 201n51

Rutebeuf, 35–36, 39, 90, 120, 153

Saint Mary of Egypt, 153–56; *Vie de Sainte Marie l'Egyptienne*, 148 (*see also* Rutebeuf); *Vita S. Mariae Aegyptiacae*, 153–54

Saints' lives: as genre, 147–49, 152–54, 156, 167, 202n90; in collections, 35, 81, 93, 95, 97–98

Scholasticism, 99, 101–2, 192n51; *collectio*, 96, 100; *compilatio*, 87, 96, 100; *ordinatio*, 96, 97, 99, 100, 112, 192n46

Seven Sages of Rome, 100, 164, 178n43,45, 190n24, 196n101; in the East, 30, 89, 94, 96–97, 113; *Le Roman des Sept Sages* (Old French), 38, 90–92, 101, 190n23,24; *Septem Sapientu* (Latin), 113, 189n9; *Sindbad* (Middle Eastern), 89, 189n9, 190n24, 191n32; in the West, 7, 21, 90–92, 114–15, 120, 191n29

—Titles: *Aper*, 89; *Avis*, 89, 91; *Canis*, 89, 91, 191n32; *Gaza*, 91; *Inclusa*, 91–92, 178n45; *Puteus*, 90–92, 114, 178n45; *Senescalcus*, 89; *Tentamina*, 91.

Sicily, 11, 47

Smarr, Janet Levarie, 118, 123, 157

Spain, 87

Speer, Mary B., 89, 190n23, 191n32. *See* Seven Sages of Rome

Spencer, Richard, 75, 76

Stemmler, Theo, 4, 174n16

Stewart, Pamela, 106, 195n80

Storey, H. Wayne, 148, 154

Swiss School, 42, 181m65

Symmetry, 5, 8, 11, 22, 71; in *Decameron*, 105, 118–19, 122, 156–57, 165–66, 196n95

Syracuse, 114

Tobler, Adolf, 137

Topos, 18, 112, 127; *adynaton*, 54, 57, 184n25; affected modesty, 107; *beffa*, 8, 116, 118–19; *brache del prete*, 128–29, 133–34, 136, 143, 198n13; *in flagrante delicto*, 135, 144, 160

—Exchange: and chiasmus, 7, 10, 23–29, 31–33, 67–68; misunderstanding, 37–38, 40, 76, 156

— "Matron of Ephesus," 74, 91, 191n30; as fable and fabliau, 47, 51, 65–72, 77, 81, 146, 184n29; in *Yvain*, 72–74; *ruses d'une femme*, 52, 65, 77; tower, 24–26, 28–34, 178n43; *translatio studii*, 50; trickster-tricked, 4, 11, 16, 90, 156, 195n87; woman as devil, 154; "world upside-down," 184n25

Transmission of fabliaux: oral, 1, 75, 87, 126, 129, 152, 177n29; written, 87, 100, 129, 130, 137–43

Troubadours, 3, 198n7

Trouvère, 37, 47, 129, 137–39

Umbria, 47

Vacca, Diane Duyos, 148, 154–55

van den Boogaard, Nico, 24, 177n29

van Os, Jaap, 47, 49, 182n4

Vàrvaro, Alberto, 43, 181n71, 192n51

Venice, 47

Vergil, 50, 184n25

Vie de Sainte Marie l'Egyptienne. See Saint Mary of Egypt

Vincent de Beauvais, 87, 96, 192n46

Vitae Patrum, 152, 154

Vita S. Mariae Aegyptiacae. See Saint Mary of Egypt

Welter, Jean-Thiébaut, 96, 189n11, 192nn53,55. *See also Exemplum*

Katherine A. Brown is a specialist in French and Italian literature of the Middle Ages. She has published articles in *Viator*, *Romance Notes*, and *MLN*.

www.ingramcontent.com/pod-product-compliance
Lightning Source LLC
Chambersburg PA
CBHW020836160426
43192CB00007B/680